KV-575-837

The Privatization of State Education

Public partners, private dealings

Christopher Green

Routledge
Taylor & Francis Group

LONDON AND NEW YORK

First published 2005
by Routledge
2 Park Square, Milton Park, Abingdon, Oxon OX14 4RN

Simultaneously published in the USA and Canada
by Routledge
270 Madison Ave, New York, NY 10016

Routledge is an imprint of the Taylor & Francis Group

© 2005 Christopher Green

Typeset in Sabon by
Newgen Imaging Systems (P) Ltd, Chennai, India
Printed and bound in Great Britain by
MPG Books Ltd, Bodmin

British Library Cataloguing in Publication Data
A catalogue record for this book is available
from the British Library

Library of Congress Cataloging in Publication Data
A catalog record for this book has been requested

ISBN 0–415–35473–0 (hbk)
ISBN 0–415–35474–9 (pbk)

Contents

Illustrations

Preface and acknowledgements

The world is a free market economy. It is perfectly logical therefore to consider the advantages of using free market forces and private sector companies to provide schooling and educational services. Nevertheless, there is often a sense of indignation, felt especially by those from less than privileged circumstances, when there is any suggestion of an undermining of an equitable and just system of education for all, a system in fact built upon the ethics, values and traditions of state education within a welfare state. Those who have enjoyed privilege are sometimes slow to recognize the successes of state-provided education. Even though there is a history of independent and state schools working together and some recent, if limited, government schemes to encourage such collaboration, ideas about the nature and purposes of education can be very different.

Globally, the post-welfare 'state we are in' has become universally accepted as capitalist forces have overtaken socialist influences. Expectations have changed. Power and innovation reside in private sector companies working in collaborative arrangements with each other and with governments at national, state and local levels. Private and public sector networks and partnerships drive improvement. The networked system in which an institution finds itself, or in which an individual is placed, is often rather more significant than the system of government prevailing. Indeed, the policies to promote the privatization of state education by both leading political parties in the UK (with regard to English schools) and those in the USA, many Australian states and New Zealand, at the beginning of 2005, have little to separate them; private involvement in the provision of state education is seen as the popular technique to raise standards and bring improvement.

In reality, schools (and the education services which provide and support schools) owe their success to the efforts of the individuals who work within and live around them. Whether leading or governing a school, teaching, learning or studying within it, or supporting it in a role as a parent, employer, citizen or local taxpayer, it tends to be these groups of people (rather than the system in which they find themselves), who actually make schools and education services the decent and principled organizations that they most often are. It is the quality of the people involved and their commitment to facing challenges and securing the schools' or services' successes that give education its soul and make it work. The emphasis in England in 2005 on the notion of 'personalized learning' reinforces this point. High standards are achieved with high equity, and by being concerned with the individual first and foremost. But systems, whether private or public, can both help and hinder.

The intellectual, moral and social aims of education exist not only for the growth and development of individuals but also for the benefit of local and global society. Economic implications are huge both for the individual and for the creation and regeneration of successful and prosperous communities. It is not surprising therefore that tensions arise about the nature and character of education systems and what they should be like. Argument and debate is around what system or collection of systems best fit the intellectual, social and economic purposes of education and can bring much needed improvement in a changing world, whilst protecting principles of morality, equality and justice. Claims and counter claims abound about the interpretation of educational results and the data which is gathered to rank success.

Who can we trust to understand how to shape systems which will bring together the skills of highly professional staff in schools with caring efforts to raise and educate young people in their homes and across their communities? This book explores how the privatization of state education is occurring. It commentates on the range of influences driving the different networks and on the nature of the public partners and the private dealings now shaping the provision of state education.

I wish to acknowledge the contribution of those many biddable pupils and students in classrooms across the world who, being the close observers of real education that they are and having a strong sense of what is good and what is ridiculous, have kept me on my toes and realistically informed over four decades. My thanks also go to the many head teachers, teachers, parents, consultants and LEA colleagues who have shared ideas about effective ways to raise standards and move education forward, particularly in England in Northamptonshire, Bromley and Walsall and in the many schools I have visited and inspected elsewhere.

It is the aggregation of these observations that help separate hollow political rhetoric about creating so-called 'excellent schools' from what might be regarded as the more tangible ambition of providing 'decent schools' for all. Success for every child depends upon a place being available in a decent school. In this regard I thank the 13 profile exhibitors for their honest appraisals of the situations they each present.

Links made (through the University of Miami and the University of Oxford's Norham Centre for Leadership Studies) with educators in universities and schools in the USA, principally in New Mexico, Pennsylvania, Long Island, New York and Georgia have been invaluable. Similarly, schools visited in New Zealand and Dubai, courtesy of the Education Review

Office and Sunny Varkey respectively, have provided first-hand perceptions of global diversity.

The commentary is about the market forces which have led to a significant increase in the privatization of state education; a drive which began gathering momentum in the early 1980s and has continued through the 1990s and on into 2005. Drawing, as I do, on first-hand experience and on an extensive network of professional colleagues, I wish to acknowledge the help and support of my close colleagues in Northamptonshire's Inspection and Advisory Services (NIAS) during this period, and particularly those who helped shape traded services in this developing 'market' so successfully. These and many other colleagues world-wide continue to press for the best for all pupils in schools, whether in a privatized sector of education or not. From these associations I also thank Trevor Scholey and David Hill for their help in proof reading the manuscript for this book and Nadine Blackmore and Jackie Watson for their support with research and word processing. Responsibility for any errors or omissions lie with me and the views expressed, outside those within the profile exhibits, are my own and do not necessarily reflect the views held by the many groups of people who have helped to shape the story.

Chris Green

Acronyms

AC	Audit Commission
AST	Advanced Skills Teacher
ATL	Association of Teachers and Lecturers
BAFO	Best and Final Offer
BCSIP	Black Country School Improvement Partnership
BS	British Standard
BSF	Building Schools for the Future
BSP	Behaviour support plan
BSQM	Basic Skills Quality Mark
BVP	Best Value Plan
CCT	Compulsory Competitive Tendering
CEO	Chief Education Officer
CERI	Centre for Educational Research and Innovation
CfBT	Centre for British Teachers
CPA	Comprehensive performance assessment
CSCo	Church Schools Company
CSE	Certificate of Secondary Education
CTC	City Technology College
CYPP	Children and Young People's Plan
DCMS	Department for Culture, Media and Sport
DES	Department of Education and Science
DfE	Department for Education
DfEE	Department for Education and Employment
DfES	Department for Education and Skills
DSSE	Director of Strategy and School Effectiveness
DTLR	Department for Transport, Local Government and the Regions
EAZ	Education Action Zone
EDP	Education development plan
EiC	Excellence in Cities (and Clusters)
ERA	Education Reform Act (1988)
EYDCP	Early Years Development and Childcare Partnership
GCE	General Certificate of Education

GCSE	General Certificate of Secondary Education
GEMS	Global Education Management Systems
GM	Grant maintained (school) (status)
HLTA	Higher-level teaching assistant
HMCI	Her Majesty's Chief Inspector (Ofsted chief)
HMI	Her Majesty's Inspectorate (or Inspector)
HNC	Higher National Certificate
ICT	Information and communication technology
IDeA	Improvement and Development Agency
IEP	Individual education plan
IIP	Investors in People
ISC	Independent Schools Council
ISI	Independent Schools Inspectorate
ISO	International Standard Organisation (Series)
ITN	Invitation to Negotiate
KS	Key Stage
LEA	Local education authority
LEP	Local education partnership
LES	Local education strategy
LGA	Local Government Association
LMS	Local Management of Schools
LSA	Learning support assistant
LSC	Learning and Skills Council
LSP	Local Strategic Partnership
MBC	Metropolitan Borough Council
MCI	Management Charter Initiative
NAEIAC	National Association of Educational Inspectors and Advisers and Consultants
NAGM	National Association of Governors and Managers
NAHT	National Association of Head Teachers
NAS/UWT	National Association of Schoolmasters/Union of Women Teachers
NCC	Northamptonshire County Council
NCSL	National College for School Leadership
NPA	New Public Administration
NPM	New Public Management
NRWS	New Relationship with Schools
NSSIP	National Standards for School Improvement Professionals
NUT	National Union of Teachers
OECD	Organisation for Economic and Cultural Development
Ofsted	Office for Standards in Education
OPA	Old public administration
OU	Open University
PANDA	Performance and Assessment
PAT	Professional Association of Teachers

PFI	Private Finance Initiative
PfS	Partnership for Schools
PIC	Pre-inspection commentary
PPP	Public Private Partnership
PPS	Parent Partnership Service
PSA	Public service agreement
PSHE	Personal, social and health education
PUK	Partnership UK
PWC	PricewaterhouseCoopers
QAA	Quality Assurance Associates
QS	Quality Systems
QTS	Qualified teacher status
RAP	Raising Achievement Plan
RE	Religious education
RgIs	Registered inspectors
RISP	Regional Inspection Service Provider
SATs	Standard Assessment Tasks (and Tests)
SCITT	School-centered initial teacher training
SDP	School development plan
SEEVEAZ	South East of England Virtual Education Action Zone
SEN	Special educational needs
SEP	Single Education Plan
SHA	Secondary Heads Association
SIP	School improvement plan
SOC	School Organization Committee
SOP	School Organization Plan
SP	Strategic plan
SRB	Single Regeneration Budget
SSFA	School Standards and Framework Act (1998)
TA	Teacher Assessment; Teaching assistant (quoted as teachers' assistant by some groups)
TUPE	Transfer of Undertakings (Protection of Employment)
VA	Voluntary-Aided (School); Value-Added
VC	Voluntary-Controlled (School)

Introduction

Being good is good business.

(Anita Roddick b. 1943)

This book is for all, parents, teachers, head teachers, school principals and governors, student teachers, teaching assistants (TAs), researchers, administrators, private education company employees, government officials, politicians and taxpayers. It is for anyone, in fact, who is genuinely interested in improving the education provided by state schools. It is especially for those who are open-minded about the involvement of the public sector, the private sector, state and private schools in this endeavour and who wish to become better informed and more engaged in the process.

The aim is shared, noble and honest. It is to improve the quality of education available to, and received by, children, pupils and students. The consensus is that overcoming barriers to learning, coupled to the raising of standards of achievement, should be the central effort. In England the priority is 'education, education, education'. Similar emphasis is given to education in other countries and regions, though there are marked variations in how it is thought this should be tackled. This book is based on the assumption that access to a good school should be available to all and that the commitment to raising standards and to bringing improvements should not only be central but also continuous.

Major shifts in traditional political views are occurring and these are impinging heavily upon how state education is perceived. In his foreword to the Department for Education and Skills' (DfES) *Five Year Strategy for Children and Learners* (DfES 2004a), the Secretary of State for Education and Skills in England at that time, summarized three key ways in which the legislation of the 1940s for education, social welfare and children's services is now unhelpful for developments in public service. Whilst emphasizing the colossal reforms of the time, he cites:

1   the model of reform as monolithic because of the focus on a basic and standard product for all;

2   administrative divisions between health, schools and social services as
    sharp and therefore unhelpful;
3   the education settlement as based on 'an assumption that ability was
    confined to a limited group – it was fundamentally elitist' (ibid.: 3).

The original postwar moves towards entitlement for all, to secondary
schooling and to comprehensive education, were actually about challenging
elitism and giving everyone a better deal. As state education strategy shifts
in England and in other countries towards an increased role for the private
sector, questions arise as to whether this represents a shift back to the earlier
elitism but in a different form. The issues are charged with emotion because
they are important. They are also complex given the changes that have
occurred in society over the last half century and particularly in the last
decade.

We are engaged in a process. We have a situation where the gap between
the worst and the best schools should be narrowed, whilst trying to make
the best schools even better. Had the 'basic and standard product for all'
(ibid.) been achieved, then the gap would be less significant and all schools
could be at least adequate, but the fact is that it was not. 'It grieves me each
year to report . . . on the extent of the gap between the best schools in the
country and the least effective. The gap is still too great and if it is narrowing it is taking too long to narrow' (Bell 2004c: 15). Bringing rapid
improvement or closure to those schools which are the worst cases is now
an urgent priority. The question to be addressed, however, is whether
privatizing state education will help in this process of improvement, and if
so, to what extent and at what cost.

Finding answers is tangled by a host of politically based ideologies, not
least the issues surrounding privilege and class which prevail in school
choice and access to the private school sector. Old arguments about comprehensive schools versus selective schools linger and new ideas about
independent specialist schools within the state sector of education have
been introduced. Whether there is genuine benefit for all in bringing private
and public sectors closer together in education is at the heart of it all. The
arguments extend beyond schools to the services which support them,
traditionally to the local education authorities (LEAs).

Education markets – what do we know already?

Markets in education have been seen as healthy ways to provide education
since the early 1980s. There is an assumption, almost a consensus, that
education provided through the bureaucracy of the welfare state induces
a population dependent upon that state, whereas a competitive market
encourages enterprise and ideas, self-reliance and independence, initiative
and entrepreneurship, the very qualities in fact required for individuals and
nations to be successful. Competition is a natural phenomenon. It relates to

the 'survival of the fittest', the state of affairs that organizes our biological and economic worlds.

The education market is based on the premise of giving parents the freedom to choose schools and allowing schools the freedom to compete amongst themselves for the custom of those parents. In this situation, it is thought that the best schools flourish and grow, the weak schools either improve rapidly or fail to survive. The premise becomes even more attractive if it is thought that standards in state schools are declining and, therefore, these schools can raise their achievement to be more in line with the higher levels perceived and reported in private schools. If people can also express their individuality in the kind of school they choose then so much the better. Politically, the education market had huge appeal; it offered a simple, free trade system for education that appeared to be able to improve school performance at little cost to the taxpayer by giving parents more freedom to choose from a range of competing schools.

When the literature is reviewed about this in England, the USA, Canada, Australia and New Zealand, there appears to be little evidence to substantiate that markets have achieved either higher standards or more choice. What persists is a belief that they *should* rather more than a fact that they *do*. The movement towards the idea of the education market being a good thing is based on ideological faith not rational evidence. 'Critics see no magic in the market but an attempt to shift the nature of the educational competition in favour of the middle class...The reality is that across social groups, there are significant numbers of parents who cannot get their children into the school that they prefer...this experience of "disappointment" is systematically structured according to class and ethnicity' (Lauder *et al.* 1999: 20, 61, 62).

But things have moved on since the 1980s and 1990s. The use of raw competition in the education market place is no longer the central theme, certainly not in England. Collaboration has emerged. Using the private sector with the public sector in collaborative mode is the successor to marketization.

Privatizing state education is not the same as marketizing education, although many of the measures and indicators to inform so-called choice and the environmental factors that prevail, are the same. The features that distinguish the move to privatization are that:

- schools, be they state schools or private schools, should attempt to work collaboratively and provide choice and diversity through offering a distinct ethos and specialisms;
- education authorities and schools should use private companies to improve the efficiency, effectiveness and economy of education provision, and that the role of the LEAs in turn become the democratic champions of parents and pupils;
- taxpayers' resources are used to balance national and individual interests by investing heavily in improving provision in areas of greatest poverty and social need, whilst utilizing private investment and expertise to help tackle intractable problems and break recurring cycles of underachievement.

Due to the continuity of the issues around choice and the use of performance measures such as test and examination results, league tables and inspection reports to judge education, the arguments about the education markets of the 1980s and 1990s merge into the debate about privatization of state education in 2005. The two ideas, whilst different, are not mutually exclusive.

The Privatization of State Education: Public Partners, Private Dealings is about examining the responses so far to the challenge of improving education by using the private sector. It is about helping to clarify what is happening in state education and finding ways to accelerate improvements in education by considering the use of public and private resources and privatized means. The matter is still one of faith rather than of evidence. The faithful are quick to resort to evidence when it is convenient but are slow to admit the principal lack of it in the validity of the concept. The book explores the scene in detail in England whilst taking account of what is happening across the world and provides a commentary on what is actually happening under the banner of 'privatizing education'. It is worth noting that in Wales, the Welsh Assembly Government has used its powers of devolution to limit the degree to which private sector initiatives have been used in delivering education services, quite a different policy direction to its statutory neighbour in England and to other English-speaking countries such as the USA, Canada, Australia, New Zealand, the United Arab Emirates and many European countries.

Whether privatization is part of a large-scale system change or of more local small-scale partnership arrangements, the purpose is similar. The objective is about getting decent schools for everyone. A 'decent' school is different to an 'excellent' school. 'Decent' may not seem a strong enough term to use in a climate of high aspiration, but it avoids the over-used, political and hackneyed superlative tones of 'excellent'.

Claims that schools are excellent, or are aiming to be so, have become predictable, tiresome and trite. Such claims and the expectation that such aspirations are required from those who work in education are a contributory cause to the sense of state education being ground down, a feeling that the school system never works with the perfection that their advocates expect. How can schools have the perfection of excellence if they are to face the real challenges of society and make genuine improvement? Those who preach, for example, that excellent education will be achieved by giving state secondary schools a quasi-independence, minimal private sponsorship or a new specialist status are usually people who do not use state schools or work in them. Their motives are more often drawn from political or professional ambition. We have seen similar motives drive the excessive systems of accountability and testing which occur from nursery schools through to universities. There is a difference between keeping a check on what is going on in schools from the monster of tests and inspection which we have created, just as there is a difference between running a decent, successful and honest school and having to claim a state of approaching perfection. It is time for more honesty in education and less hype. Most people would be happy to see a range of good schools; schools in fact that they would describe as decent places for children and young people to attend for the 13 or 14 years which make up most people's school life.

Decent schools are those where pupils learn a lot about real things, generally enjoy school, do reasonably well in their tests and examinations, behave well, feel safe and are properly guided and cared for by the teachers and adults around them. Decent schools are more than adequate; they are good and respectable places in which to spend time. They strive to improve and challenge complacency. They do not make unrealistic claims, tend not to be at the top of the league tables but do not cause concern and stay well clear of having 'serious weaknesses' and being in need of 'special measures'.

Views differ over how more decent schools might be achieved. Issues about private involvement are contentious and prod at the heart of what education is about, especially where education has been an entitlement through the provision of a welfare state financed by direct taxation. Despite education's long-standing traditions, significant investment by the taxpayer and direct intervention in schools by government, there continues to be wide variation and lack of equity in the quality of school provision. The questions are simple enough. How do we get better schools for everyone? How do we get more decent schools which consistently satisfy parents, students and the needs of the wider community in the twenty-first century?

But simple questions beg complex definition. What is satisfaction in schooling? What constitutes the wider community? What needs to be done to bring about the improvements called for? What are education partnerships? What is privatization in education? Definitions are one thing; answers to how improvements are to be achieved are another!

The breadth of the privatization canvas

A 'free' place at a state school is only one of the entitlements supposedly enjoyed by citizens of many Western democracies and indeed, other political regimes. The privatization of state education sits within a much broader canvas of social policy and public services. There has been an international trend towards increasing the use of the private sector in the management and the delivery of public services. This has been motivated by the desire to restrain public expenditure and increase the perceived benefits offered by private sector expertise in a competitive environment. All along, change in the balance from public to private sector delivery of services is being forced.

In England for example, since 1997, the government has made improvement of public services one of its key objectives. It has made a commitment to intervene in 'failing' services at a local level. The rhetoric from the government has been about taking 'decisive and tough action'. Indeed it had intervened in a quarter of local government councils by 2002, of which 20 were in education departments.

The government also made education its leading domestic priority. As with the health service, it has consistently looked to private contractors and the internal market to bring in a change. The introduction of market competition to aspects of secondary schooling is a theme throughout the government's *Five Year Strategy for Children and Learners* (DfES 2004a). It has placed the idea of independent state education at the centre of its drive to improve public services by encouraging the private sector to bring about improvements in overall performance and to break the status quo.

Moves to privatize are often presented within partnership arrangements. 'Partnership' as a term has appealing connotations. Politicians like it. Public Private Partnerships (PPPs) abound and they exist in a variety of initiatives and forms and include in no particular order:

- Private Finance Initiatives (PFIs);
- PPP's faces of the Office for Standards in Education (Ofsted);
- academies;
- independent specialist schools;
- former Education Action Zones (EAZs) and Excellence in Cities and Clusters (EiCs) programmes;
- private schools in partnership with state schools;
- state schools run by private firms;
- historical links between schools and charities and the church;
- local education partnerships (LEPs);
- interventions by the DfES into the work of LEAs forcing a range of 'partnerships'.

The relationships within and across these partnerships are often laced with controversy. This book describes these privatizing partnerships and commentates upon some of their early contributions. The active roles played by inspection agencies and management consultancy firms are also explored, as these are very influential privatized forces on schools and LEAs, as they provide the 'scientific/technical/professional evidence' that is 'used' by government in deciding on the particular actions to take and the interventions to make.

Whilst education policy in England has used internal markets and private partnerships as major paths to reform, similar concepts are clearly identifiable in many other countries, notably the USA, Canada, Australia, New Zealand and in parts of the Middle East, Europe, Asia, Africa and South America. The trend is global. However, there is often a lack of clarity over how different initiatives fit into any overall strategy or national framework.

Therefore, public participation in the debate about education policy and its subsequent implementation is difficult. It is nevertheless vital that citizens are engaged in such a public issue, otherwise education is reduced to that of mere private consumption rather than social good. Measures of educational achievement are often reduced to oversimplifications, which thwart true responsibility and accountability. There is difficulty in honest interpretation of the plethora of generalized numerical gradings which appear in the sets of international, national and local targets, audit and inspection reports and the wide array of league table rankings. Yet, it is the publication of such performance data which supposedly informs public opinion and parental choice.

The aim on these pages is to further an understanding of what is actually happening in education. This book does not purport to be an in-depth study of all the forms of education privatization, or a quantitative analysis of the relative performance of private and state provisions. That is the business of the research agencies and the university education policy departments. These chapters provide some perceptions of what is happening in the world of schooling and educational leadership which is being touched, in varying degrees, by privatizing initiatives (Profile exhibit 0.1). The perceptions are of those who have experience of being at the sharp end of shaping strategy and ensuring the delivery of education at school and classroom levels. Throughout the chapters, 'Profile exhibits' give a series of personal views from people who belong in this group and who share valid, insightful, but often differing, opinions on the role the private sector and state can play in improving standards, leadership and participation.

Profile exhibit 0.1 Privatizing education: the creation of a 'learning establishment' to meet the needs of children

The development and evolution of education in England has produced a unique, innovative and diverse range of schools to coexist. Although this has not been without controversy, politically and educationally, it has meant that education in England has been dynamic and revolutionary. Evolution is challenging in itself and the controversy has led to high-level dialogue between theorists and practitioners. It is a fact, however, that English educationalists are innovative: they create their own ideas as well as using the best practice from around the globe. In many cases, they throw them into a melting pot to produce variations that become the envy of the world.

We should therefore be seen to encourage existing strengths and further innovation. The private sector is a vehicle to be used to develop and to build on the present mixed system we have and to extend the concept of 'school' into the idea of the 'learning establishment'.

In creating a private education company in the early 1990s, we gained a great deal of experience weighing up the attitudes to 'privatization' amongst schools, LEAs, Her Majesty's Inspectors (HMI) and other educational groups. There is certainly a mixed view in the market place. In many instances, it was, and still is, very evident that there is mistrust amongst practitioners, government departments and local authorities. There are doubters: the ones who believe that your only desire to conduct business is for personal gain and that there is no way you can have the interests of pupils at heart. It is these very people that find it difficult, if not impossible, to look 'outside the box' and actually hold back the development of education to the detriment of the pupils they are trying to serve. It is not coincidental that some of our best schools develop away from the constraints of the code of ethics held by some local authorities and government officials.

It is important to allow enterprise and thinking 'outside the box' to meet the needs of children and adults. For too long, state schools have been disconnected from other forms of care provision. However, private schools have, for generations, cared for their pupils in a way that is alien to the majority of society. As a result, many private school parents are chastised for their belief that schools can provide a mixture of the two, caring for their children from eight in the morning to six o'clock in the evening, not to mention the 24-hour care service provided by the boarding school.

Having taught in both the state and the private sector, we are able to compare the advantages of both systems from first-hand experiences. For anyone to belittle the other without seeing the virtues of an education system they have not had the privilege to see at first-hand, produces ideas and concepts that do a disservice to education as a whole. Also, it is to turn a blind eye to reality to think that state schools do not already provide a crucial support service for children and their parents. Teachers are at the forefront of our social service system and, often, the only point of contact a worried parent has between the complexities of home life and the outside world.

Traditional 'state' concepts that constrain development need to be challenged. Why should children only have access to the classroom during the daytime period? Why should they have to change schools at the age of 7 or 11? Why should they only be able to attend just one school even if that school doesn't offer the types of courses they want to do? Why shouldn't they take total ownership over their own learning with the support of a learning mentor? Why should they stop attending school when they reach a particular age? Why shouldn't teachers have the ability to refuse to teach those that do not show them respect? Why should pupils have to put up with teachers who are just not up to the job?

We believe that we can achieve a respectful society where all individuals achieve their potential if enterprise and open-thinking operate within a system that has no restrictions on how a learning establishment should operate and to whom it should appeal. The most effective way to achieve this success is through funds following the individual pupil. Those establishments that are creative and innovative and meet the needs of the society we serve will be the ones that flourish.

From our own time in education, teaching in a wide range of private and state schools it is clear to see that we have much to learn from both. The concept of the boarding school, for example, is not one that has been explored fully. We are not advocates of the 'leaving home' principle, but believe that there is much to consider, in modern society, of the idea that schools need to offer much more than just the 9 a.m. to 3.30 p.m. ritual. Many schools are beginning to explore the benefits of the 'breakfast club' and the after-school care schemes, and, with the constraints of the workforce reform, are looking at more creative ways of developing after-school provision. Certainly, if we see schools as learning establishments that have a social function, the 'all-day' facility does not move itself too far away from the reasons why boarding schools are used. Busy parents, unable to find sufficient time to care for their children outside the traditional school time, need additional support. They should not feel guilty about the fact that they cannot be home to meet their children from school because they have to work until five or are on night shifts. The private school function of running 'prep' time and having the common room available for relaxation can be seen as a real bonus for the child/parent relationship, such as the eradication of the stress created between parent and child to ensure homework is completed. This idea, this wider spectrum of social care should be promoted for those parents and children who would gain greatest benefit from it.

Let us accept that society has a mix of individuals with different kinds of learning potential and different kinds of intelligence, and whose social circumstances are unique to them. Surely it is the responsibility of the learning establishment to meet these needs and to devise the best ways this can be achieved without stereotyping and ridiculing people because they are different. Let us all open our eyes to what the future can hold by meeting the needs of a changing society.

Source: Malcolm Greenhalgh, Former Chairman, Bench Marque Ltd, Maggie Greenhalgh, Former Senior Manager, Inspection and Training, Bench Marque Ltd.

The chapters that follow are intended to encourage greater participation from all levels of the community in raising standards and improving ethical leadership and participation in education. The question of how to engage contributors effectively, whether professional or lay, voluntary or paid, individual or collective, as citizens or consumers, in a reforming global system is critical. Though answers to this question may be elusive, the question needs to be examined from the standpoints of those involved and from the opportunities which appear to be presenting if real progress is to be made.

Introduction to chapters

Chapter 1   *Forcing educational change in the public sector*

Schools, whether state or private, are costly places to set up and maintain. The sheer scale of the human and the capital investment in schools, and the fundamental importance of their purpose, mean that it is important to everyone that schools and the education systems which exist to help schools to be successful, achieve their purpose. This chapter looks at some key issues that recur and cause dissatisfaction with schools and education services and the ideas that lie behind the reforms to bring improvement by the involvement of the private sector. It draws upon the wide canvas of education in the local government and the strategic community leadership responsibilities invested in them. Approaches to change using commercial models, as recommended by the Audit Commission (AC), are examined in terms of aspiration for a modern educational system within the culture of universal 'managerialism' characterized by system-driven compliance and accountability rather than 'professionalism' with its features of judgement based on expertise, trust and integrity.

Chapter 2   *Ancient and modern: aims, history and private and public education systems*

The historical backdrop to education and the development of present day schooling in Western cultures are important in framing the issues around moves to increase private provision. This chapter explores something of the ethics and the traditions around the notions of what education is actually about.

In dealing with the history of private and state education it explains the origins of public access to education through private means, and then the development of state entitlement to free education. There is a reminder of the idea of education being a service in a welfare state; the notion of it helping to achieve a just and prosperous society based on the values and ideals of good citizenship. It explores and links some of the aims and purposes of education in historical and contemporary contexts and identifies the nature of democratic participation in a global education economy, participation that could be seen to be threatened by the advancement of privatizing strategies. In England, links between modern state education and the ancient foundations which have run private schools since the Middle Ages are being encouraged. Does the key to the future of state education lie in this private school past?

There is a double harness in education. This double harness, of increasing social inclusion whilst raising standards, is the challenge that so far has not been met, although it has been recognized throughout time. Many of the ancient, charitable and privately endowed or sponsored schools have earned reputations for high academic achievement whilst addressing, in many cases, the education of the poor and the excluded. To what extent are these ancient and private educational traditions relevant to solving contemporary issues about inclusion in state education?

Chapter 3 *Privatization, partnerships, democracy and citizenship*

Contemporary moves to use private companies in partnership with schools and public bodies in order to bring improvements in state education call into question the established influences and controls of local democratic processes. This chapter follows the hypothesis that social and political participation in education is desirable and that two conditions greatly assist in achieving this; first, that democratic governments should earn and receive the critical support of their professional communities; and second, that standards are raised most effectively by leaders who are close to their constituents, staff, pupils and communities.

Recognizing that 'partnership' is a popular word with politicians, the chapter clarifies the detail in the plethora of private initiatives and PPPs that are found in education. It draws distinctions between those partnerships that have significant private funding from those that do not. Tensions between local democratic controls and contracted services are described including the anomalies of privatizing education services which are rooted in statute as citizenship entitlements. It explains that using private business, in a field where true market forces do not actually exist, changes the very nature of those services.

Whilst explaining that using the top English 'public schools' as a typical model of private education is not centrally relevant to the strategic moves towards the privatization of education, the operation of small to medium-sized private companies in running private schools and the effect of the market economy on the running of large-scale contracted-out education services is covered. It argues that the entitlements and rights of citizens may be weakened by moves to privatize, but private firms are able to cross-subsidize from their market products and pursue a socially adjusted goal in the allocation of their resources and through reinvestment of profit. A broad evaluation of private initiatives and of PPPs is made in order to begin an assessment of comparative standards achieved, leadership and management quality, and levels of citizenship participation.

Chapter 4   Sources of evidence, audit and inspection of education

This chapter examines the main sources of evidence used to drive the agenda for the privatization of education in England, these being the various regimes of inspection and audit. The work of the privatized function of Ofsted in inspecting state schools is described and compared with the non-privatized Ofsted functions. Comparisons are made between the processes of inspecting state schools and private schools.

A dramatic increase was achieved in the scope of Ofsted's capacity for the national inspection of schools by using a privatized system of contractors following legislation in 1992. However by 2005 and faced with making efficiency reductions across the civil service, the flexibility within the expanded privatized parts of the Ofsted system was used to adjust procedures to match economies. From that large-scale privatization of the school inspection system, the trend in 2005 is swinging back to a greater dependency on a public and a central operation.

Tensions have existed between different agencies that have seen themselves as responsible for finding the evidence upon which to base ideas for future policy. The range of inspection regimes operating in schools and public services, their frequency and the aspects of moderation used are key elements to consider when judgements about standards in education are being made. Whether private services actually provide better quality and value than those provided by the public sector is highly questionable. These judgements are in turn central in determining whether government interventions should occur which may lead to the legal enforcement of private contracting for local education services.

The nature and quality of the processes used and the validity and the reliability of inspection evidence and the conclusions drawn from it are vital if these are to be used in informing schools, LEAs, corporate firms of management consultants and government about the indicators for potential privatization. With the extensive Ofsted database so comprehensively driving the publication of information that forms advice on education policy, whether on privatization or otherwise, the validity and reliability should not only be secure, but it also should be generally felt to be so.

Chapter 5   Local education partnerships (LEPs), government intervention and participation

This chapter examines partnership working in education systems, particularly in LEAs. It deals with the contentious subject of intervention by government to force change in low performing LEAs and the use of private companies in the negotiated action to bring improvement.

The chapter also examines some of the partnerships with the private sector known as the New Model Projects and the initial work of the agency, Partnership for Schools (PfS), set up to facilitate the Government initiative of Building Schools for the Future (BSF) in 2004.

At the heart of this chapter are those issues dealing with private sector tendering in an education market generally unfamiliar with government intervention and with leadership of the education service within a system that is set within a locally organized democracy. The way targets are determined for contract delivery by private firms and the conditions upon which these might be changed relative to earning bonus or penalty are clearly contentious.

Aspects of political and public participation in relation to aspirations for state education and contract specification with the private sector are brought into consideration alongside the gathering of inspection evidence and reporting described in Chapter 4. The process of both intervention and creating a private sector partnership with an LEA is extended in the case study in Chapter 6. The intensity of audit from the various competing inspection regimes and the additional management load caused by over-inspection is compared to other models where more effective approaches are employed.

Chapter 6 Government intervention: a case study

Using Walsall LEA as a case study of privatization following government intervention, the author draws on personal experiences of the process from the position as the Chief Education Officer (CEO). Employed to bring about the statutory outsourcing of some LEA functions to a private company within a Strategic Partnership, the conflicting issues arising from different viewpoints and the impact on the education service from the different inspection regimes working across the Council over the intervention period are exposed. Contract procurement and the identification of a preferred bidder, by employing management consultancy firms, Pricewaterhouse-Coopers (PWC) in this example, are described. How an appropriate private company was selected to undertake the contract work and the subsequent action leading to a second inspection, is traced chronologically. Although such contracts, once procured, are held by the LEAs, the private sector providers had to satisfy the government as to their worthiness to be on the central list of potential providers, hence questions about the extent to which accountability was compromised between the two are raised. An inside view is offered about the hands dealt by the inspection agencies and by government officials in this situation.

Chapter 7 Parents, choice and information

How far is parent choice assisted by information such as that drawn from league tables and inspection reports? Given the centrality of these forms of accountability and the types of targets that underpin private contractors' performance measures, how important will they be in the future scenario of education?

This chapter deals with the parents' influence on educational direction and policy. What influence do parents actually have in state and private schools? What options are available to overcome the scarcity of adequate school places? The role of parents goes beyond that which is expected of them as electors and as consumers who exercise choice. It considers parents as direct participants in the formal education of their children at school as well as at home.

Information available to parents in England and Wales is viewed alongside partnerships that have been set up by LEAs with parents. Since 2002, all LEAs have been required to maintain a Parent Partnership Service (PPS), which must meet defined minimum standards. Origins of the PPS are rooted in DfES grant funding established in 1994 and aimed to ensure parents of children with special educational needs (SEN) have access to information, advice and guidance, so that they can make appropriate and informed decisions about their children's education. *The Special Educational Needs and Disability Act* (DfES 2001b) has brought disability rights and inclusion to the very heart of schooling. This type of service for parents has a potentially wide clientele, but to what extent do parents actually utilize and participate in these partnerships? The chapter suggests how these partnerships might contribute to being part of the voice that champions the interests of parents and pupils across the educational system.

Chapter 8   *State schools in a changing culture of privatization*

The well-publicized innovations of new school categories in England, and their sources of funding from public and private means are examined. Many of the privately funded innovations in education, described as successful, are actually only receiving minimal private contributions. Case studies chosen include academies and specialist schools. The historical demise of grant maintained (GM) schools and the phoenix-type rise of foundation status schools, promoted by the influential Specialist Schools Trust, is considered in this new privatization and independent state school context. Is choice between schools real or merely the illusion that is often claimed?

School innovation and effective leadership are important factors in the success of new strategies, be they public or private. There is a high degree of correlation between the behaviour of the head teacher and the progress and achievement of the people inside the school. How far is private sector engagement influencing the thinking and the actions of these leaders? One concern is that educational improvement is being driven by marginal attempts to select particular cohorts of students based on past achievement, aptitude or parental aspiration, a trend of 'privileging the academic'.

The chapter looks at how privatizing initiatives might find selective options attractive to making apparent success more easily achievable.

Chapter 9   *Future standards: leadership and partnership, compliance and participation*

This concluding chapter draws the scenario together, linking ideas about leadership, participation and the improvement of standards beyond solely the academic. Definitions of democracy are given and the expectation that schools should be centres of entrepreneurship and enterprise are explained. The chapter falls in favour of the privatization of state education; alternative routes are presented as not pragmatic and going private is almost the 'only show in town'. The option of LEAs collaborating to provide support for other LEAs in difficulty has merit, but there is little central political will for this option. Confidence, especially in academies, appears well placed (though not in Wales). However, the evidence of success so early in the life of academies and specialist schools is sparse. Academies are established in the most difficult areas of educational provision and, providing that they admit local pupils, deserve the support of their communities even though they receive preferential terms of establishment. Early faith of this kind in these schools is based on trust, a commodity which education policy and practice needs more. But given the dangers and the inequalities described throughout the book, the conclusion calls for checks and balances that are different to those of the previous two decades. Local authorities should have a key role in ensuring equality of access through the control of fair and equitable pupil admissions processes.

It tackles the shape that answers might take to the questions raised. It projects the characteristics of a greater role for privatized education set within the powerful economic forces which prevail. The shift towards a future for more private influences on education is inevitable because it satisfies such a broad political constituency seeking modernization in a global economy. The world is becoming one; whilst recognizing that people are all different, global education empowers people not only to see how they vary but also to see how they are the same.

The core business of education will need redefinition with a new and different base to provision. Entitlement for inclusive education and better indicators of inclusion are needed alongside comparative performance of attainment. Keeping and building new levels of trust across the educational landscape is a real issue for the future.

The chapter projects more flexible resourcing of education with curriculum requirements being met increasingly by the vehicle of technology. It concludes that meeting wide-ranging needs in diverse communities is more likely to be successful using market solutions which in turn utilize modern technologies effectively. But the key, it argues, will be to achieve economically viable services that have visible characteristics of personal local service, opportunities for real participation, democratic accountability and a citizenship basis.

Warnings are raised. Is privatization simply the back door to choice for some and an illusion for others? The common good is a bigger aspiration. For pupils to do well, markets, charitable contributions and professional effort require a political climate which regards people as neighbours and citizens first, and consumers and competitors second.

Outcomes and efficiency in education require more than compliance and the application of best value practices. Remodelling the school workforce with trained teaching assistants (TAs) is acknowledged but with safeguards about respecting the professionalism of qualified teacher status (QTS). 'Value for money' in a particular sector is not enough. There are wider social measures to be applied. Education includes attaining high standards, having training for productive development and regeneration, generating the capacity to meet local, national and global challenges with effective solutions and mutually beneficial activity with improved levels of social justice.

The conclusion finally points to leadership in strategic partnerships needing to build trust and to generate fresh ideas. The way forward is to create openly negotiated public–private relationships set on shaping long-term vision and planning. Close scrutiny by local groups concerned with both the community and the global educational outcomes, with more participation by families is projected. Mutual commitment is the emphasis, rather than imposed intervention, superficial cooperation and falsely named partnership.

1 Forcing educational change in the public sector

> He who would do good to others must do it in minute particulars; general good is the plea of the scoundrel, the hypocritical flatterer. For Art and Science cannot exist but in minutely organised particulars.
>
> (William Blake 1757–1827)

Most people go to school. Schools, whether state or private, are costly places to set up and maintain. The sheer scale of the human and the capital investment in schools and the fundamental importance of their purpose in a modern economy mean they have come under close political scrutiny. Also, the education systems which are there to provide and maintain schools and help them to succeed, are placed under similar analysis. If education is the road to economic competitiveness and prosperity then the systems around schools must reflect good business practice. Education and training in its formal sense rest within strategic systems which are based upon philosophical, social, cultural and economic values. It is the set of economic values that have come to the fore over the last quarter of a century. The state has not been seen as delivering education that is orientated sufficiently towards a competitive economic culture.

However, the business of learning and going to school is a very personal matter. Education in practice is fundamentally based upon the interactions of individuals who find themselves within this global system of schooling. Changes can be made within the system, at the school and by the individuals.

The law of education in England reflects these levels with a constitutional distribution of functions across national, local, school and personal levels. Increasingly, duties and responsibilities sit within an international context and this also needs to be taken into account. Such a constitutional approach allows for diversity within the democratic majority, with the minorities and the individuals able to take initiatives themselves. Success depends upon an appropriate balance of participation being achieved at each of these levels and this requires dialogue between the various participants to achieve an understanding of what is being sought. Ideas need to be drawn from the constituent members. Proper participation is difficult to achieve when people feel excluded from the process or feel that they are being told what to do and are then forced to do it.

Most people want to have some degree of involvement in those things in life that matter to them. For too many people in the world, ensuring survival and satisfying their very basic needs for security, shelter, food and clean water dominate their lives. For others, amongst the daily trivia of life in times of comfort, important things matter a lot. They are keenly interested in where they live, in having a job and in where their children go to school. Most parents are keen to participate and help their children with their learning, especially if good opportunities exist for them to do this.

However, the more 'technical' education seems to become, the more 'managerial' the modernizing processes are then the greater is the danger of education becoming even further removed from the lives of the very people for which state education was created. It is these people who need to be increasingly involved if education is to be successful. Telling people what they need and forcing change into systems (whilst perhaps not untypical of the historical actions in conservative societies) is not actually consistent with the nature of real education and true democracy.

The privatizing process in education is seen to have two objectives:

1   to improve the whole culture of economic competitiveness across the education system and subsequently across society so as to achieve greater economic success;
2   to engage parents directly in a process of active choice about schools and schooling and by so doing heighten the sense of their role as consumers.

Reforming education as a global priority

In many parts of the world, reforming education by increasing the involvement of the private sector is now the central political imperative. It is seen to achieve both these objectives. On the one hand, it puts the private sector market rigours straight into the heart of the operation of education; and on the other, it introduces to the individual parent or pupil (and teacher) different options within the private sector range. Opportunities to realize individual aspirations seem more available. Personal involvement through being able to make choices about schools appears more likely in a privatized environment. All this is quite different to the perception that state education is monolithic and without choice. Yet, it has been the blatant centralizing of education strategy in many countries since the 1980s that has brought about the monolithic condition.

Since 1997, the government in the UK has made education its leading domestic priority. In England, the high profile given to those strategies to raise academic standards in reading, writing and maths and to improve education leadership is well known internationally. Important initiatives to improve social and educational inclusion are generally lower key. Many of the initiatives in England have been taken from, or informed by, practices in different parts of the USA, Europe, Canada, New Zealand and Australia. The work in England has caused reciprocal responses. Influences from parts of the Middle East and Asia are also recognized as worthy, particularly when considering the commercial dynamics of education-for-profit.

There is now an open-mindedness within the political views expressed in England, as 'what works is what matters'. This simple pragmatism has popular appeal. Since 2000, a number of professors of education involved in school improvement and leadership from the UK, Canada, the USA and Australia have interchanged their working locations. The messages emanating from the leading universities across the world on school improvement and leadership are usually about serious change. They are much more about 'reform' than 'development'.

England as an explicit model of reform

Although something of a transformation is claimed for primary education in England over the eight years leading up to 2005, dubiously some might say, the transformation in secondary education is still being sought. It is to the private business sector that the challenge of this transformation of secondary education is mainly pitched. The issues, though, are still across primary and secondary schools. The international educational community watches these English experiences in educational reform and transformation with some interest, just as it has watched, utilized and adapted other features of the English educational system throughout history, although it has to be said that the days of the world sending its children primarily to England for their schooling rather than other countries have largely passed.

A political consensus was broadly achieved during the 1980s and 1990s that market forces would raise the attainment levels in schools and the performance of educational systems. The literature, however, suggests that this revitalization did not occur. Businesses were reluctant to invest in education and dependency on the state prevailed. The competitive culture of creating 'the autonomous school' where the system produced a climate of 'school versus school' broke down because it dismantled the social imperatives and purposes of having schools across communities.

Education is just part of the drive to improve public services by using the private sector to bring about improvements in performance and to break the status quo. In order to hinge education within the folds of these shifting changes and to illustrate this culture of economic competitiveness with more consumer choice in action, it is necessary to find a common starting point for the discussion. The starting point chosen here is 2001 and the theme is at the local level.

Changing local services

In a letter to all CEOs in England and Wales, the then Controller of the AC, Sir Andrew Foster, announced the publication of a small booklet,

Change Here! Managing Change to Improve Local Services (Audit Commission 2001). His letter explained that this guide was intended to help top managers in local government and the National Health Service. The guide emphasized that change should begin and end with users' experiences and expectations. For anyone actively involved in developments in education and who has maintained a commitment to the importance of improving the quality of what pupils and students actually receive through school, this message strikes immediate accord.

Change Here! is a simple and useful device to set the scene as to why privatization is the perceived way forward. It describes a world where, it is argued, a gap has opened up between what commercial services can deliver and what can be expected from public services. The examples offered of these improved commercial services are:

- the huge increase in the availability of mobile telephone calls and associated communications;
- supermarkets that are open 24 hours a day, 7 days a week (or available for shopping via phone or personal computers) with cheap fresh food from around the world;
- easy access to over 40 TV channels.

Against these are placed only two examples of public service that fall rather short and so create this perceived gap. The two examples given are:

- the difficulties in finding a public library open before or after work and at any time on Sunday;
- doctors' surgeries that are similarly limited in their opening hours.

Although not dismissing the good efforts of public service workers, the claim by the AC is that the widening gulf between what we can buy as customers and what we get as public service users has created this credibility gap which has resulted in many people becoming alienated from the political process and disaffected with public services in general. The evidence for such a credibility gap is highly debatable. Much opinion raises greater dissatisfaction about some private sector efficiencies (so-called), especially about trying to find meaningful information which falls outside the routine script learnt by those in globalized call centres, than about the opening hours of libraries and doctors' surgeries. Nevertheless, *Change Here!* is useful in the illustrations it brings.

Case studies: a baseline for change

Change Here! covers the fundamental aspects of:

- leading, managing and owning change;
- sustaining a focus on key priorities and on users;

- drawing on best practice;
- building capacity for continuous improvement;
- maintaining effective strategic and operational leadership and management at all levels.

It draws on 21 examples, case studies, from different public services in England and Wales and uses these to generalize key points for learning about managing change effectively. The examples are wide ranging, they emphasize that services should fit together well and be complementary. 'Joined-up' strategic planning is a recurring theme within the leadership and management of services, with references to making good use of 'outsiders' in their various guises. In this, top teams need a shared high-level picture of the change journey required and a view of the end results.

In *Change Here!* less than a fifth of the case studies are about education, four in fact, and it is these that are of particular interest here because they each signal a key area that continues to drive change in education through privatization routes.

Case study 1.1 Empowering localities to improve: reducing surplus places at 'unpopular' schools to create more places at 'decent' schools

This is supposed to be about empowering localities, but the example does not illustrate such empowerment. The case study is actually about the planning of school places and pupil admissions. It draws on *Trading Places* (Audit Commission 1996), which contributed to the move to make LEAs accountable for the supply and allocation of school places. Quite correctly, it describes the LEAs' powers of school closure and a resulting reduction in surplus places (64,000 between 1997 and 2001) with a corresponding efficiency saving. However, the claim by the AC that this report suggested 'a clear way out of "policy gridlock" and became a powerful lever for change...empowering localities to plan and manage their own resources' (Audit Commission 2002: para. 21), is a considerable management simplification of its impact on the actual issue. It is more about AC's self-congratulation and advertising. Given the perpetual problems surrounding pupil admissions and each 'autonomous school' being its own pupil admission's authority, empowering localities to improve access to schools so that processes are seen as open and transparent is not what has been achieved. It is difficult to see why private sector interests would have motives to improve on this anyway and therefore why it should be included as an example in *Change Here!*

  Whatever the claims about the impact by the AC in 2001, the government's *Five Year Strategy for Children and Learners* (DfES 2004a) now removes the surplus places rule anyway. All successful and popular schools may propose to expand. The issues have moved beyond those of surplus places to those of admission policies. The Ofsted report *School Place Planning* (Ofsted 2003a) was hard hitting in urging LEAs to challenge restrictive admissions practices. Fairness over access is now the issue. Pupils are often selected, both overtly and covertly, when schools manage the rules of their own admissions and when there is little accountability to a higher authority. These issues are explored further in Chapter 8.

Case study 1.2 Targeting key audiences to build support for change: failing schools and school inspection

This second case study is the account of the turnaround following the failure and well-publicized notoriety of The Ridings School in Halifax. At this school discipline had broken down badly. Ofsted had placed the school in the failing category of in need of 'special measures'. The case study describes the central role of Ofsted in judging comparative standards in schools and the development of shared vision and a managed approach to engaging key stakeholders in setting the course to improvement. It is the engagement of key stakeholders following inspection that is the relevant point in the privatization and citizenship contexts.

An examination in Chapter 4 is made of the inspection regimes and the processes used by Ofsted particularly and other agencies such as the AC. It is the findings of these inspection regimes that are used as the basis for judgements about the standard and quality of education in schools and LEAs. Where failure is reported, the government then use these findings to decide whether interventions should occur and whether the private sector should be used in the recovery process. Accountability through Ofsted inspection has been a huge factor in the direction and development of change in state education in England and Wales since 1993. Therefore, having trust and confidence in inspection findings are essential ingredients. Although confidence has largely been gained, issues about uncertain moderation and ambiguity still exist. These come about largely because of changes in the inspection criteria. There are also concerns about the tone of reporting of inspectors' judgements, almost as scientific fact, rather than the human judgements that they actually are. Quite different sets of accountabilities exist for private schools from those applied in state schools and state systems. The environments are different and so are the inspection criteria; like is not compared with like. Despite this, the private sector is seen as a support for improvement and change in the state sector.

Case study 1.3 Sustained focus on a clear objective: education targets and national strategies

This is based on the highly directive DfES Literacy Strategy in primary schools. It describes the impact this has had on raising standards in literacy for 11-year-old pupils against previously low levels of performance in national tests. It projects that the programme was likely to meet its target set for 2002, which did not prove to be the case (*Change Here!* was published prior to the failure of the education system to reach the Government's targets for literacy and the subsequent furore that followed when David Bell, Ofsted's chief inspector (known as Her Majesty's Chief Inspector (HMCI)), 'suggested' that this might be due to a lack in primary teachers' subject knowledge). The case study also makes reference to England's low position in the European league table in standards of adult literacy. The imperative, it explains, is to drive up standards through national strategies and achieving quantifiable targets.

Two questions arise here which are relevant to privatization and they recur throughout this book:

1   Do strategies such as these provide a means of directly linking educational outcomes to contractual obligation? Is this a basis upon which to construct the contract specification and performance measures when private companies are used to deliver such functions?
2   Are the conclusions that are drawn reliable and is the information presented, for example in league tables, actually helpful?

Case study 1.4 Focusing on core priorities: improving pupils' attendance at school

This case study explains how an education welfare service had been criticized by Ofsted for being too broad based rather than concentrating on the areas that mattered most; improving attendance and reducing school exclusions. By focusing on core priorities in partnership with schools over a two-year period, the service showed improvement in attendance rates without any increase in cost. The AC did not comment on the progress or otherwise in relation to reducing exclusions within this case study.

Focusing on core priorities is clearly an effective management strategy. However, what is often passed over is the conflicting nature of priorities and the inverse proportional impact when targets and measures are applied. For example, by excluding a pupil who reads poorly or is frequently absent from school (either at the time of admission to school or later) has the effect of raising overall results for the school as a whole towards achieving targets set for English and attendance. The compartmentalized approach of focusing on core priorities in privatized contractual terms carries similar difficulties; by excluding negative influences at source then performance on other priorities is improved. If the local political desire is to have excellent reading across the schools and perfect attendance, then the contractual temptation to manoeuvre weak readers and pupils with poor school attendance somewhere else is obvious.

Identified concerns and emerging questions

Each of these case studies illustrates a significant area of concern about levels of understanding when seeking improvements to publicly provided state education by using private sector solutions:

- How will moves towards the privatization of state education improve the match of supply and demand and actually give better access to a place at a decent local school?
- Are the current regimes of regulation and school improvement through rigorous external inspection by agencies like Ofsted and the AC giving a reliable and balanced picture of what can be realistically expected of schools and teachers and LEAs and LEPs?
- How will the performance of private schools measure up against the criteria in these inspection frameworks?
- Are national initiatives, national strategies and national tests and examinations driving up standards?
- Do the measures of performance and the public presentation of results help parents and students to make properly informed choices?
- Given that the national targets for 2002 were still not met by 2004, are national strategies and national test results a sound basis upon which to specify performance measures for private companies?
- Does choice improve for the majority by involving private schools and the private sector in state education, or is there merely an illusion of choice?
- Will steps to privatize education reduce the pressures on schools to exclude disaffected pupils?
- Will privatization lead to more inclusive education with greater participation and democracy?

Education within the reform of Public Services

The Office of Public Services Reform was established soon after the publication of *Change Here!* In its publication *Reforming Public Services,*

Principles into Practice (Office of Public Services Reform 2002) following a foreword by Prime Minister Tony Blair (ibid.: 2), the main themes recur though set in a national rather than local context:

- putting the customer first;
- maintaining high standards through accountability;
- extending devolution and delegation;
- expanding flexibility and choice.

The themes are not taken far in turning 'principles into practice', despite the promise of the title. The appeal from the Prime Minister is that a genuine partnership between government and providers is required. The partnership he sees is one where government provides the overall vision and investment, listens and learns and supports those providers in delivering improvements. With this level of commitment from government and with traditional constraints eased, the way seems clear to working within such a partnership and getting on with what needs to be done to make state education better. Political rhetoric can obscure educational realities. Step change is called for but national targets, raised year on year, are clearly incremental. Incremental change is often more realistic, but what is it that the Office of Public Service Reform actually wants?

With step change, what are fair, realistic and aspirational expectations on schools? Private sector practices may well be able to strike this balance more effectively than traditional public service. Each sector has its merits and faults. Where commitment is often high in the public services, the risks involved in aiming high are not supported. The more easily achieved differential pay and conditions in the private sector may produce different and, perhaps, better conditions to accept risk for higher aspiration. Moves within the 'remodelling of the school workforce' provide opportunities for high-level TAs to teach groups of pupils directly and for TAs and teachers to negotiate contractual conditions which do not necessarily conform to national pay agreements for either groups.

The provision of education is often equated to the delivery of other public services of a wholly different order. Running a school or organizing an education provision are not equivalent to operating many other kinds of businesses, yet generalizations about management efficiencies are readily drawn across, often appropriately, sometimes less so.

The proper openness of educators has invited a landslide of interest from the public and private executive managers who enjoy high levels of international approval for their collective wisdom on 'managerialism' or 'New Public Management (NPM)'. But how relevant are these management methods for teaching and learning? Short-term, goal-orientated activity, efficient as it may be in achieving set targets, is seen as not contributing to the establishment of long-term trust and to the commitment required to raise children properly and to develop their understanding of what their contribution should look like in building communities. The nature of the task in education is different to building a road or to running a light railway. It is also different from other service industries. With these differences come the need to evaluate the reliability of the acceptance and approval of this 'managerial' approach when applied either comprehensively or to particular aspects and priorities in education.

Traditions and values in state education

Avoiding sentimentality, what are the main distinctions between the traditions and values in state education from those of the commercial world? The fundamental distinction is probably that of ethos.

Writing about 'the public sector ethos under attack', George Jones (2001) sets out a succinct comparison of the shifts in values which characterize British central and local government, in three periods starting prior to 1970 through to 2001.

Jones describes the traditional values of government as integrity, objectivity, impartiality, appointment and promotion on merit, accountability through democracy, treating like cases alike, not promoting personal or sectional interests and a concern with the long-term public interest. State education in England is traditionally a national system administered through local government, and therefore those involved in education, be they national or local politicians, school governors, head teachers, teachers, other members of staff in schools, parents or pupils, have largely shared these values. Jones describes these values as characterizing public administration from the 1920s to the 1970s and contrasts them with the characteristics of the rival doctrine of the 1980s. The main features are presented in Table 1.1.

Jones suggests that the 1980's characteristics have been retained into the new millennium with some distinctive twists. The overriding goal is now modernization. It has moved on from political accountability in the 1970s and marketization in the 1980s to a new set of features in 2001, the main characteristics of which are shown in Table 1.2.

Jones describes this approach to the public sector in 2001 as having three major worrying features all of which apply directly to education. First, 'It is inherently centralising, undermining local government' (Jones 2001: 68). State schools in England, whilst a function of local government since 1902, have accepted huge central government influences since the Education Reform Act of 1988 (ERA) and continue to do so in 2005. 'Central government is seen as the repository of all wisdom, with other parts of the public services regarded as instruments to achieve central policy objectives' (ibid.).

Second, 'By increasing external controls over local officials, demanding conformity to external standards, it stifles local initiatives, innovation and experimentation. It damages learning about how to tackle the problems facing society' (ibid.).

Third, 'By entangling the public sector with the business sector, and insisting that the public sector behave like the private sector, it is undermining the

Table 1.1 Features of old public administration (OPA) between 1920s and 1970s compared to the New Public Administration (NPA) of the 1980s

1920s–1970s	1980s
• Governing is different from running a business because it is rooted in and driven by the political processes of representative democracy	• Governing is like running a business
• Officials serve their duly elected governments, implementing and advising on policy	• Public functions should ideally be privatized – handed over to businesses
• Officials are organized hierarchically to facilitate accountability	• If functions have to remain in the public sector, they should be the responsibility of bodies acting like businesses, testing their activities against competitors and operating as if subject to market disciplines
• The methods of the public sector are different from those of the private sector	• Officials should copy the methods, style organization language and culture of business
• There is an emphasis on coordination between officials	• Fragmentation to facilitate competition rather than coordination is preferred
• The public and private sectors keep at arm's length to avoid distorting the public interest with private and sectional interests	• The public and private sectors should be closely intertwined in collaborative activities
• Officials are trusted and do not need regulation by external codes other than the law	• Officials are not to be trusted and require regulation and inspection to keep them up to pre-stated standards

Source: Adapted from Jones (2001).

positive values of the old public administration. A culture change involving being entrepreneurial, cutting corners and taking risks raises the potential of corruption, unfair practices, promotion of sectional interests, and self seeking' (ibid.). Let us avoid the tiresome polarization of over simplified 'for and against' arguments. The contests about 'one political party versus another', 'old versus new', 'private schools versus state education', 'grammar versus comprehensive schools', 'modern versus traditional teaching methods' or 'single-sex versus co-educational arrangements' go round in circles and advance education little. It is the facets and subtleties of the environmental conditions for change and improvement that matter considerably more than these stark polarizations. The classification by Jones is therefore much more helpful in clarifying the shifts in the ethos of public service in which state education sits and where improvements are sought than in pursuing the traditional and polarized education stances.

Table 1.2 Features of public administration in 2001

• Business is to be involved, consulted, used and should contribute finance, because business creates profit and jobs, which are preferable to welfare benefits as a way to tackle poverty	• A major concern is for joined up government, to break down the silo mentality which inhibits taking cross-cutting issues that require integrated policy making and implementation
• The focus is on the consumer and user of services, not the producer and the provider, the professional association or public sector union	• Information technology should be deployed to make decision making and delivery more speedy and flexible, with customers wired up to enable them to express their views directly to government, thus avoiding intermediaries
• The views of individuals should be sought through surveys, referendums, panels, focus groups and citizens' juries, at all stages from policy formation to implementation, since market signals alone are inadequate	
• There is an emphasis on outcomes, not inputs or even outputs; hence a concern with targets, since results are what people care about, not who delivers or how it is delivered, and ends are more important that the means	• Control over officials should be achieved by inspection through regulators auditing, checking and supervising to ensure national standards; and codes of conduct are required because officials themselves
• The need is form continuous improvement, ever rising standards and better quality	• Government is so joined-up in a seamless web that all public sector officials should see themselves as part of a public service and collaborating
• Openness and transparency are praised	
• Policy should be evidence-based, so research is needed into domestic and foreign experiences by consultants, think tanks and academics, not by officials alone	• Within this public service there should be an emphasis on personal, not collective responsibility

Source: Adapted from Jones (2001).

Privatization proposals for state schools and school systems are about forming new and multifaceted relationships between families, schools, political systems and private companies. Priority must be given to the wishes of the users and the consumers of education, but the users and the consumers are also themselves key providers. They are citizens and neighbours and as such are vital educators. Parents, children and students are the providers of their own life-long learning, set within a partnership with external providers. The practical arrangements for schooling are more about working relationships than a discrete service or a set of treatments.

These relationships must be developed responsibly and in ways that address educational inequalities. There is no doubt that inequalities are ongoing. The problems of inequality are persistent and need to be resolved. Challenges are big; there is no single solution, no last word on how things should be done. The opportunity is for new conversations and action befitting education in the twenty-first century.

State education must be for the benefit of those who receive it. However, the consumer of education has a greater responsibility to contribute than the customer in other market activity. Paying the bill is not enough; there are attitudinal and behavioural dimensions that need to be engendered in order to secure trust, integrity and commitment to the educational process as an ongoing endeavour throughout school and life. Whilst the use of the private sector to deliver education is probably inevitable, urgent consideration is needed to ensure there is minimal loss of effective practice from the public sector and that the consequent fragmentation of the public service does not bring disincentive to those striving to achieve valid and traditional personal and social goals.

Personal and professional influences on change

Education systems run on like an unstoppable train on its track. To envisage how an individual might have any influence in actually changing anything of significance within such enormous ideological, political and social machinery, is overwhelming. Yet, individuals are indeed quick to blame 'the system' for frustrations and inadequacies over which they feel they have little or no control.

The quotation from William Blake at the beginning of this chapter was used in a lecture *Teaching Today – for Tomorrow* by Len Marsh (1986). He used this quotation to emphasize the greater importance of the aggregation of each individual's contribution in education over the system itself. He went on to suggest that the Department of Education and Science (DES) in England at that time was too busy pushing out one publication after another (a charge still made about the DfES and Ofsted today who produce over 20 sheets a day for head teachers to read), and that the truly great ideas about education were rarely followed through because they were too quickly lost in the haste for more documents with their associated political cache about wholesale system change. He argued that we should get close to children and to people and use our hunches about their learning first of all, and then move forward from these.

Although parents, teachers and politicians follow their hunches all the time, this suggestion as a serious approach to improving education now seems quite cranky! Since the mid-1980s, the world has moved on into implementing a set of approaches and accountabilities that were actually devised in the very early part of the twentieth century, by the scientific management movement. Efficient accountability procedures have been systematically developed. Many countries have some form of state or national curriculum and national testing. National inspection and audit in England and New Zealand have a system of 'locally' managed schools and use national inspection criteria. In the USA, Canada and Australia, site-based management schemes hold schools to account against a range of state-level competency indicators. The context for education is very different to that of the mid-1980s. To follow a hunch openly, one needs to have it framed as a carefully worded hypothesis with a battery of statistical evidence carefully analysed, interpreted and reviewed.

But following hunches is how most people operate. Parents choose schools by following a 'feeling about the place'. We shop on intuition and it is by following hunches that new research ground is sometimes broken or discoveries made. The point to be taken from Marsh's use of the quote is about how ordinary and professional people can make their impact on the wider educational system. These are people who usually care about the healthy growth and development of children and young people and know a lot about the particulars of learning and teaching in families and in schools.

How do policy makers encourage local people to make things better for everybody within the ever more tightly prescribed national systems in which they find themselves? In other words, how do ordinary everyday educators contribute to social and educational inclusion and to the raising of academic and vocational standards? How can the policy strategists make room for teachers and parents to contribute fully within a public or private system? Will the privatization of state education bring solutions?

The answer is not an easy one. Easy or not, it clearly must include ideas about proper participation, about moral leadership at a variety of levels and it must be about identifying proper and honest benchmarks from which we set values and measure success. Has the time come around for an emphasis on the use of more professional approaches to the management of education, where accountabilities are held more locally through communities than through national and international league table measures?

The two Profile exhibits 1.1 and 1.2 are from practising senior staff in schools, which both provide British education in parts of the world other than Britain. Given the differences between their schools and in their writing, it is interesting that both choose to emphasize the aggregation of contributions from individuals at the institution level as critical factors in the successes they describe. Features of the system in which they are placed are important, but in both profiles, these are subordinate to the importance of the quality of collective local individual contributions.

Profile exhibit 1.1 Privatized services for primary schools: the jury is out

The contrast is marked between the service that was available to primary schools from LEAs in the mid-1990s and that which is currently available from LEAs and from private sectors providers. Unfortunately the government's *Five Year Strategy for Children and Learners* (DfES 2004a), holds little promise for reducing the gap. As LEA services move to champion the cause of parents and pupils, this represents significant deterioration in the breadth of access and in the quality of the support available to leadership teams in primary schools.

Private sector services for primary schools are underdeveloped, partly because the single-customer unit is small. School budgets are too tight for a primary school to employ a private consultant for any substantial amount of work. Cluster or centrally organized inputs are the only feasible and economic options. This takes the analysis of need, planned action and delivery, administration and organization beyond individual school control. Relevance and accountability then become diluted. This was not the case a decade or so ago.

LEA advisers knew their schools and the context in which they operated. They 'clustered' them rationally and ensured that head teachers were in the driving seat on analysis and management. Support, training and development is invariably better when it is targeted, responsive to identified need and refined in light of close knowledge of the school and its circumstance. LEAs, I always found, did this well.

Empowered and empowering LEAs have become history. Sadly, the root cause of their demise seemed to be a blinkered belief by successive governments that LEAs should not provide, or even trade, services directly with schools, but should instead have a minimal role in helping schools commission or procure 'value-for-money services' from the private sector.

The private sector market for primary work though, has never really developed. LEAs have increasingly become reduced to working only in schools that were causing concern. The developmental role that LEAs had provided for most schools is squeezed to an absolute minimum. Even where LEAs were successful in selling their services to schools through 'buy-back' arrangements, the demand on schools to do the 'required' government training limited the schools' capacity to follow their own priorities.

The work of national literacy and numeracy consultants and others who encourage from the pages of the DfES prepared programmes, along with the swathes of privately contracted inspectors and performance management assessors, advisers and consultants is fine, at a level. However, this is not the educational support that is needed by most primary schools. Nor sadly, is it of the range and quality that was available prior to the straightjacket of national strategies and accountability regimes. National polices have systematically dismantled valuable LEA advisory services leaving leadership teams to barter in an overpriced market place offering limited expertise in pedagogy, curriculum delivery and leadership and management of primary schools.

Will availability improve should the 'best serving primary head teachers' be chosen to become school improvement partners, as is happening with secondary head teacher colleagues? It is difficult to see how. If you are an effective primary head teacher maintaining high standards in your school, it is not easy to envisage becoming a part-time 'school improvement partner' to another head teacher who might be having difficulty. Where difficulties exist, the task is generally bigger than playing 'partner'. As an experienced primary head teacher the popular idea, for example, of head teachers of formerly GM schools, travelling the country as 'executive principals' offering 'their opinions to schools' does little to counter the reality for me of a reduction in the quality and the quantity of real support services.

The idea of head teachers planning an exit and a succession strategy as they enter their first headship, portfolio heads as they are described (Flintham 2004), is an approach which identifies a new breed of head teacher. The portfolio head teacher may consider a headship as one peak in a leadership career before moving on; seemingly bringing only short-term commitment to the school but more availability for recruitment to private sector education services. Flintham describes portfolio heads, practising a model of distributed leadership which empowers middle and senior leaders, as having the potential to provide a robust environment for teaching and learning. May be this will be so but primary schooling is hugely diverse and one primary headship can be slender experience, even given excellent distributed leadership, from which to build a robust environment.

Currently in my fifth primary headship in a school within Service Children's Education in Cyprus, the prospect of getting access to service via 'a privatized system' in this environment is slim. My fourth headship was in a temporary role in England, where I was drafted in full-time to turn around a school that was 'causing concern'. Prior to that, over the years, I had three headships of primary schools with quite different characteristics. All have been reasonably successful, the children got a consistently good deal; the schools produced a number of head teachers and, for what it is worth, Ofsted inspections reported favourably on them all. Much of that success is due to LEA services.

The prospect of being deemed a 'best head teacher' or having one so deemed as my 'school improvement partner' to work on developments, is a poor alternative to what used to be in place and fraught with organizational difficulty. So it is proposed, within the discussions about the New Relationship with Schools (NRWS), that LEAs continue to serve this function for primary schools, though not for secondary schools. An LEA link advisor, connected to a network of local and regional advisory groups is invaluable. However, as these teams are already heavily depleted, and as they lose their connections with team colleagues in secondary schools, I doubt that the role of LEA adviser or school improvement partner will be seen as attractive in the future.

Primary head teachers in my experience are good at sharing their expertise, although some government initiatives such as the introduction of GM schools and foundation status schools tempted some off to middens of arrogance. To make a political initiative out of the 'partnering' of two secondary head teachers but not for primary, surely indicates that the government is bereft of genuine strategies to support the primary sector. Also, to pretend that private sector service options are realistic and affordable is similarly unhelpful.

Whilst initiatives such as building new schools and major curriculum and examination overhauls for 11–13-year olds and 14–19-year olds continue to draw in huge proportions of funding to secondary schools, private sector companies will see the market opportunity and will shape ways of turning this investment into lucrative services. Secondary schools should do well. Management consultancy firms, lawyers and accountants will, no doubt, do well too. Primary schools will benefit little, except with new buildings and by association with the secondary schools to which they contribute.

What is the government's vision for the next five years for primary schools? Integrated education and social care for pre-school children is a new and welcome opportunity for families and schools, and should attract private sector interest. Apart from that, for primary schools, there are four strands in the spectrum:

- continued emphasis on progress against targets in reading, writing and maths;
- new systematic opportunities for primary pupils to learn a foreign language with continued rhetoric about wider curriculum choice for music and competitive sports;
- more school profiling to satisfy the ritual of ever more public information;
- the best head teachers helping to improve the rest.

The vision is impaired; little is in sight to stimulate the movement most needed to take primary education from its mechanistic frame of accountability to something more appropriate, that is, to the educational needs of children and the professional needs of the staff. Even the National College for School Leadership (NCSL) will now be trading, and will be closed down should the government's opposition get in the 2005 UK election!

Successful primary education depends essentially on the quality of the detailed interactions between adults and children in the school and at home. The vision needs to be about rebuilding higher levels of trust and having a real commitment to primary school improvement services, privately contracted or otherwise.

Are there any private sector companies which specialize in primary school improvement services and can offer a package on teaching music, competitive sports, a foreign language and inclusion for the head teacher's role on the new Children's Trusts?

Source: Mary Murdoch, Head Teacher, Ayios Nikolaos Primary School, Cyprus.

Profile exhibit 1.2 Private schooling that focuses on teachers and pupils in classrooms

Since 2000, I have been a senior teacher at the British International School in Saudi Arabia and for the previous 30 years have taught in a variety of state schools in England. My contention is that this fee-paying (but non-profit making) school provides a far better education than all the previous ones of my experience.

This opinion is strongly shared by the teachers at the school, the majority of whom have previously taught in the UK. Parents, especially those whose children had been in schools in England and Wales, also speak most favourably. The pupils themselves state an overwhelming preference for this private school.

The school is for children from nursery to Year 11. The roll in 2003–2004 was 850, made up of a wide variety of nationalities but with 50 per cent British (it was closer to 1,200 before the school compound was bombed by terrorists in 2003). Class sizes are around 20 in number. There is no selection and pupils have a wide range of abilities. The school follows the National Curriculum of England and has a board of governors.

It is successful in terms of measured performance outcomes and client perception; academic attainment is high and pupils develop well and are happy at school.

Successful education depends on the teachers who are with the children daily. Simple assertions that there are good and bad teachers and that we should be weeding out the bad are unhelpful! The teachers who come to the British School are no different from those who teach in the UK: they are of all ages, all personalities, bring a variety of experiences and educational backgrounds, and levels of commitment. When they arrive they find a strong ethos within the school. At the heart of this is a positive relationship between the pupils and the staff, and between staff and management, and this leads to a uniformity of purpose.

Governors make provision for a pleasant working environment by providing ample resources (from small class sizes to easy access to computers and photocopiers); offering a remuneration package that is favourable and enlightened access to good quality professional development opportunities in the UK and elsewhere.

New teachers, be they good, bad or indifferent quickly adopt the tone of the school and become a part of it. In this way they help the ethos to become self-perpetuating. Pupils are fairly typical of those found in most schools. They are of different abilities, personalities, backgrounds and motivation. However, they too are quick to notice and to adopt the positive ethos (often an ethos that did not exist in their previous schools). Their work and study habits improve and they become happier, more sociable young people who respect their peers and their teachers. Behaviour and discipline are not problems. Parents recognize the importance of education at the classroom level.

In the absence of data on pupils' comparative prior attainment, it is difficult to argue that they perform better academically in examinations than if they had remained where they were. However, pupils do attain far higher-academic grades than those in the majority of schools in England and Wales. Although education is too often measured by examinations results, the 2004 results at our school are illustrative of exceptionally high-comparative attainment:

- General Certificate of Secondary Education (GCSE): 26 per cent of all subjects were 'A*' and a further 26 per cent were 'A'. Ninety-three per cent achieved A*–C.
- Standard Assessment Tasks (SATs) results were also very good:

  - At Key Stage (KS) 3, level 7 or 8 was achieved by 83 per cent in mathematics, 55 per cent in science and 37 per cent in English.
  - At KS 2, level 5 was achieved by 60 per cent in science, 42 per cent in mathematics and 32 per cent in English (and we have many pupils whose first language is not English).

Compare these results to the average in England!

What do pupils and parents think about the education received at any particular school? Too often, responses to this question in the UK are apathetic or, at best, lukewarm. Pupils and parents are too often not engaged in the system. At the British International School, they see relevance and think highly of the education provided. This nurtures a self-belief within the pupils that gives them a confidence to progress to higher levels of education and make the most of their potential. It creates a strong sense of pride in their school.

How many layers of people are needed in an educated democracy to make decisions about the detail of education above parents and teachers? Of course we need heads of department, head teachers, local advisers and national inspectors, but do we need the plethora of corporate officials at local and at national levels procuring the hugely expensive services of private management consultants to reshape the nature of the education system itself? I doubt it!

What is needed is a swift mobilization of those many decent teachers and parents, aware of their accountabilities to their client groups, to take initiative in doing their business well. Pre-occupation with system level change over the last 20 years has driven away the proper engagement of ordinary people. The future for successful education in England and Wales must be to create schools where there is this positive ethos and collective purpose.

Head teachers are heavily constrained in influencing education. They are dependent on the teachers in the classrooms and should focus attention on facilitating these professionals so they can best provide relevant education. Too often the heads' attention is taken off the central purpose. Certainly the head provides direction, but must also be prepared to follow the wisdom of Gandhi: 'There go my people and I must follow them for I am their leader'.

The school is a microcosm of the state. The government too must be prepared to listen rather than to tell, to provide and to facilitate so that schools can focus on the education of their charges in an atmosphere of positive and constructive encouragement. Small-scale privatization might well be the route to achieve this.

Source: Barry Hynes, Head of Curriculum, The British International School, Riyadh, Saudi Arabia.

Managerial and professional styles

The terms 'managerialism', (incorporating NPM) and 'professionalism' are often used to contrast fundamental differences in the approaches to the way organizations might be managed. Managerialism is often associated with privatized industrial and commercial practices, professionalism with 'the professions' such as teaching.

Under the heading 'Objections to industrial models of management in education' (West-Burnham 1994), comparisons are drawn of the differences between 'professional' and 'organic' approaches in managerial styles. 'Critics of management in education rarely cite specific texts or examples of managerial practice. Management theory is usually found to be derived from [Henri] Fayol or [Frederick] Taylor' (ibid.: 19).

Managerialism in education

The emphasis in these early twentieth century theories is on management by measurement, scientific analysis and objective definition, characterized by 'time and motion' and 'compliance'. West-Burnham suggests that when comparing management theory in education and in industry the 'profit motive' does not feature significantly. The emphasis in management is on the achievement of goals, which may of course include making a profit, but which may in turn be interpreted as just another function of customer satisfaction. He quotes Peter Drucker (1992) as questioning the extent to which the notion of profit drives the management model of business. 'They are however surely wrong in defining "performance" as nothing but immediate, short-term gains for shareholders. This subordinates all other constituencies . . . to the immediate gratification of people whose only interest in business is short-term pay-offs. No society will tolerate this for very long' (ibid.: 18).

The supremacy of 'management by objectives' in the 1950s and 1960s utilized many of the principles in Frederick Taylor's work. Management practices in contemporary education in much of the world reflects these features which are essentially authoritarian, concerned with establishing systems within which individuals become subordinated and where managers ensure compliance. This approach organizes work into specific, measurable and short outcomes, which dominate the individual's approach to the job. Throughout the 1990s, this approach could be identified within a range of globally sponsored 'total quality management' initiatives. Standards such as Quality Systems (QS) 9000, British Standards (BS) 5750, International Standard (ISO) 9000, Investors in People (IIP) and a host of other awards, badges and kite marks are commonplace in education, commerce and industry and serve as examples of this managerial model in action around the world.

Professionalism within managerialism

It is more difficult to identify examples of management through professionalism, although West-Burnham suggests that these are deemed appropriate in the management of education. He uses a quote about the importance of value and belonging in this: 'The school is seen as an organisation, a body, living, growing, flourishing, decaying. We are firmly in the land of culture, where value not structure, belonging not organisation, are paramount' (Shipman 1990: 143).

The differences here, between the relevance of managerialism and professionalism are essentially about degrees to which the outcomes, the product of the organization, are tangible and measurable. Managerialism is largely about accountability, whereas professionalism is more about trust and responsibility. Clearly, education has many very tangible targets but some of the outputs are considerably more measurable than others. The argument that emerges is about whether organizations, including schools, are driven to changing their purposes in order to achieve those outputs which are more easily measured. By so doing they can demonstrate their accountability more readily and so gain the advantages that this quality of managerialism can bring.

Whether managing education or other commercial organizations, realistically there has to be a mixture, a cocktail, of managerialism and professionalism. Performance on all fronts does need to be measured, yet, organizations are like organisms in that they do need the space to breathe, grow and flourish. On the one hand, by focusing on measurement, more constructive attention is paid to those areas chosen for measurement, on the other, measurement in itself does not bring growth and improvement; the pig is not fattened by constant weighing!

Historically, it has been the distinctive characteristics of 'professionalism' and 'managerialism' that have informed the arguments about the parallel and unparallel nature of education and commercialization. In practice, these characteristics occur in varying degrees of combinations. Given that privatization brings more contractual specification to education, it is helpful to separate out the essential qualities of the two approaches in order to consider appropriate balances of emphasis in different contexts and situations. Table 1.3 draws upon Bush and West-Burnham (1994) and Wilkins (2004).

In managerialism, neat cause and effect relationships are drawn from heavily compartmentalized sets of information. League tables, for example, present only partial data, with statistical caveats excluded and yet it is the position in league table rankings that are promoted as the reliable universal indicators of 'true knowledge' of performance. In professionalism, the place and significance of teacher integrity and trust in parents and adults as legitimate educators are emphasized. The balance in the use of the features of professionalism and managerialism throughout the process of the privatization of education are centrally critical factors.

The conflict between those who seek the balance between professionalism and managerialism in education is aptly put by the President of the Twenty-first Century Learning Initiative, UK, 'The Twentieth Century has seen a bitter struggle between those educationalists who see the ability to handle ambiguity, complexity and issues that by their very nature can't be quantified, as being the very essence of human creativity, as those who see such intangibles as ghastly distractions that have to be ruled out of the equation to enable economic efficiency to dominate. The final battle may now be about to begin, and it is most uncertain who will win' (Abbott 2002: 6).

Table 1.3 Features of professionalism and managerialism compared

Professionalism	Managerialism
• The aggregation of individuals' contributions in organizations serves the needs of other individuals most effectively in real terms	• The introduction of scientific methods into the design of working practices is necessary for efficient practices
• Professional reflection tends to see 'true knowledge' as a range of valid perceptions constructed through experience, culture and ongoing debate	• Scientific methods tend to see 'true knowledge' as objective facts
• Cooperation and collaboration brings best results in situations where real market forces do not exist	• Market forces, through competition, bring best results
• Management is fluid based upon working relationships with peers within a shallow 'flat-archy'	• Management is mechanistic – based on a hierarchy of command by experts
• Roles and responsibilities are set out with direct reference to the client (pupil, patient and customer)	• There is careful definition of roles and responsibilities set out in a line management relationship
• Continuous reflective practice as an essential and desirable feature of work, finds the best ways to improve	• Measuring and analyzing a process finds the best way to improve it
• Motivation is intrinsic to the individual worker, work is carried out through accumulated self-generated knowledge and experience and through independently accessed sources of information	• Selecting and training of workers to carry out work accordingly to 'the best way', is as told to them
• Owning and setting aspirational goals facilitated by freedom of choice	• Controlling and prescribing goals for others to achieve
• Symbols of reward are essentially personal levels of satisfaction over and above a fair working wage	• Symbols of reward are bonus packages, public accolades, medals, badges and plaques
• In discussions of this kind in education, assumptions are avoided	• In discussions of this kind in education, many assumptions are made

Source: Compiled from Bush and West-Burnham (1994) and Wilkins (2004).

Forcing in privatization to break the established mould

So, whatever the cocktail of professional and managerial ingredients, how can we participate from within our wealthy Western democracies and bring the transformation in education that is persistently requested from all sides and is so obviously needed in particular aspects and areas? Is it a matter of participation or simply submitting to a system-driven managerial will? The political belief held by many in different countries is that standards will be raised, leadership improved and participation enhanced by the privatization or partial privatization of education. This sentiment is caught in the typical words of Milton Friedman, 'Nothing else [other than private enterprises] will destroy or even greatly weaken the power of the current educational establishment – a necessary pre-condition for radical improvement in our educational system' (Friedman 1995).

Is it not generally believed that:

- the more you pay the better things are;
- private companies have better paid leaders than those in the public sector; and that
- they are better because of this;
- giving consumers choice from private sector competition is the best way to get real participation?

Each of these may be believed, but are they true? Although there must be a valid role for the private sector in education, can it be, whether alone or in partnership, the panacea that it is sometimes made out to be? The answer must surely be no! The strategic leadership of policy and system reform needs to give full consideration to the local public ideas and any bold plans for design and implementation need to take account of the 'minutiae' and of particular expectations.

2 Ancient and modern
Aims, history and private and public education systems

I left England when I was four because I found out I could never be King.
(Bob Hope 1903–2003)

Some traditions change very slowly. Indeed, who would want treasured historic practices to change at all? Despite all the rhetoric, a visitor to a classroom anywhere in the world, 100 years ago, would be likely to feel pretty much at home in many classrooms in 2005. Whether in England, the USA, Australia, New Zealand or in other parts of the world, there would be many familiar features because fundamentally things have not changed a lot! That same visitor would find dramatic changes in society during that same period. Expectation shapes what is done, but determining what is expected of schools and educational systems in times of such rapid change is not straightforward.

Whilst schools now have more luxurious buildings and sophisticated equipment, interactive whiteboards, computer-aided-learning, tighter security and perhaps have to deal with more overtly disaffected pupils and pupils from widely differing backgrounds, by and large, school systems and classrooms have been adapted rather than transformed. Attempts have been made to bring significant change in England and in the USA, as education has become higher on the political agenda. This is due, in part, to a perception that standards of literacy and numeracy are below those of other developed countries. As a result, governments and civil servants have taken a high profile in setting out different strategies for state education. Intervention has become an important element in the strategy for change in state schools.

There has been much less intervention, in practice, in private schools. Private schools are often known, confusingly, in the UK as public schools, and more accurately as independent schools, as mentioned later. Tradition and elitism are popular traits of the private sector which have consistently contributed to their own particular charm in the education market place. This sector, has wisely avoided much modern jargon and many of the acronyms associated with the state sector.

But a mere 100 years is nothing in the history of education!

Ancient times: the source of modern ideas

Most teachers can recant something about the teachings of Socrates, Plato and Aristotle. Much of civilization still bases its ideals of education on these Greek philosophers who had in turn adapted many of their ideas from earlier civilizations of Egypt and Asia. The Romans knew the importance of education. We know from them that paying for your education, or getting someone else to pay, is not a new idea. From these early times we learn and understand something of the value of a liberal education as a cornerstone of citizenship.

Taking the UK as the model for a brief survey into the history of schooling is relevant to many international systems. Although terminology has changed over the years and a plethora of sub-categories of schools has been invented by successive governments, broadly speaking, the following holds true.

Private fee-paying schools are independent schools. Some of these in England and across the UK, especially those with long standing foundations, are known as public schools. Public schools are therefore the oldest private schools, hence the confusion!

State schools are called maintained schools and include community, foundation, voluntary controlled, voluntary aided, community special and foundation special school categories. These schools are largely run on tax-payers' money. Many state and independent schools depend heavily on charitable donations and voluntary contributions. Through contemporary curious political turns, academies (formerly known as City Academies), City Technology Colleges (CTCs) and foundation schools, though almost entirely state funded, are not classified as maintained schools but as independent schools. They are 'state' independent schools! State secondary schools in England are being encouraged to take 'foundation status' by government as a part of their future plans for education beyond 2005.

The line between private and state education is becoming significantly blurred. Proposals in the government's *Five Year Strategy for Children and Learners* (DfES 2004a) include creating 'Independent Specialist Schools' (ibid.: 44) which will give all but failing secondary schools the freedom to own their own land and buildings, manage their assets, employ their staff, adjust the composition of their governing bodies and forge partnerships with outside sponsors and educational foundations. Threads running through many of the ideas in this five-year strategy can be found when researching the history of education. What is more, new partnerships are being encouraged between the traditions of ancient practices and the developments in modern schools and also between educators in the private and the state systems.

Commerce, charity and education

Many of the ancient public and grammar schools provided education for the poor, the orphans and the fatherless, receiving their funding from the church or from trade guilds and livery companies. Winchester College, Merchant Taylor's School and Christ's Hospital are famous examples. To this day the livery companies' support for schools continues, for example, Oundle School in Northamptonshire is supported by the Grocers' Company. The quality of such relationships is held in very high regard, as this extract from a letter by HRH Princess Anne demonstrates, 'The core of the Livery ethos is timeless: fellowship, welfare, education, supporting trade and at all times working in the best interests of the communities in which they operate' (HRH Princess Anne in The Livery Companies of the City of London 1997: 1).

With the government's drive for greater partnership between the private sector and the state-funded maintained sector, and as sponsorship by livery companies becomes closely linked to the government's education policies, (such as establishing increased numbers of academies) legitimate questions arise about the educational interests of these companies simply because the general public knows little about them and also for the reason that they have an air of exclusivity about them. Education in state schools has been the direct responsibility of locally elected council members in LEAs for the last 100 years or more. It is possible that those schools in disadvantaged areas and those which are underperforming could be improved by these ancient foundations. Such practice lies close to their original roots. The possibility of bringing to state sector education (and particularly to those schools in communities that are experiencing the most intractable difficulties) this timeless ethos described by HRH Princess Anne, can be seen as being very attractive.

The Mercers' Company in ancient and modern education

The Mercers' (Livery) Company has a long tradition of providing support for education dating back to at least 1518 when John Colet, the founder of St Paul's School, left his school to its care. Since that time, The Mercers' Company has given unswerving support as the trustee of John Colet's endowment. Relationships such as this and the environment in which they exist are steeped in tradition. In the words of the retiring head teacher (known as the High Master) of St Paul's School in 2004, 'Only for seven years of my life...has my daily life been spent other than as a full-time member of the school' (Baldock in *The Mercers' Company Review* 2003: 22). These words capture something of the essence of loyalty and continuity and of an independent school being a 'closed community'. According to Robert Boyd (2001), 'A closed community is a private, self-regulating community whose conduct is not specifically regulated by law and which to that extent is unaccountable and free to regulate its own affairs within the general framework of the law' (ibid.: 16). This definition accords with much of the contemporary ideal of greater autonomy for successful state schools.

Successful schools, decent schools even, are those with not only fair examination results but also where there is confidence in the leadership's vision and capacity for continuous improvement. Indeed, testimony to The Mercers' credentials can be found in a letter of 1519, 'And when Colet was asked the reason of so committing this trust to the Mercers' Company he answered to this effect: that there was no absolute certainty in human affairs, but for his part he found less corruption in such a body of citizens than in any order or degree of mankind' (from a letter by Erasmus in The Mercers' Company Review 2003: 19). Given the general decline of public confidence in politics and political judgement through 'spin' and 'misinformation' at the start of the twenty-first century, it may still be attractive to accept this historical view; that the private and charitable sectors provide more honourable leadership and trusteeship than democratic government!

The Mercers' Company has brought its tradition of supporting its 'Cluster' of schools directly to the twenty-first century and firmly includes state sector schools and the newly formed state-funded independent schools known as academies. In 2003, The Mercers' Company listed 94 grants to schools amounting to over £2 million. This list includes many schools with ancient foundations but also other new and contemporary state schools. For example, Thomas Telford School, a City Technology College in Shropshire which received £25,000; and the Walsall Academy, opened in 2003, received £60,000. The Walsall Academy is in fact featured as the case study of a successful academy in the government's *Five Year Strategy for Children and Learners* (DfES 2004a: 58). Another academy planned in nearby Sandwell is also supported by The Mercers' Company.

State finance with historic networks

Although the total financial investment by private sponsors in new academies is only small (around 10 per cent compared to the taxpayers' investment of around 90 per cent), their managerial networks and infrastructure are highly influential in the governance and administration of these schools. This brings many positive qualities such as the ethos described earlier, but it also brings tensions. For example, although academies are substantially state-funded schools and belong theoretically within the pattern of pupil admissions to state schools in the local area, they are actually classified as independent schools and are their own admissions authority. They operate as independent schools within the remit of their funding agreements which allow considerable freedom and release from the constraints which the government apply to other state schools. For example, they do not have to follow the statutory National Curriculum or use the national strategies, such as the KS 3 strategy for secondary schools.

Given the high capital investment and the ongoing running and maintenance costs met by the government for academies, compared to those for other new schools, and the greater freedom handed to their sponsors, it is hardly surprising that some controversy surrounds the academy strategy. Academies are seen as the solution in areas of disadvantage where inadequate secondary schools exist. The strategy for academies was considerably extended by the government in 2004 when a target was announced for 200 to be opened by 2010. The government's confidence in the sponsors of these new independent schools, many with long pedigrees and ancient traditions, is very evident.

Ancient traditions of the private sector and the modernizing reform of state education are working hand in hand in many examples, and seemingly successfully. Certainly, the track record of Thomas Telford School as an independent yet state-funded CTC is impressive as it sits high in, and sometimes tops, the league tables. The success is not just academic. The business activities of Thomas Telford School, for example, have enabled it to provide financial sponsorship to other less fortunate state schools so that they can qualify to apply for the Government's specialist school status and subsequently gain the financial rewards that such status brings (academies and specialist schools are discussed in Chapter 8). Knowing the right people in and around education is useful and ancient networks do help.

State entitlement and private power

It is necessary to unpick something of the story of education in the UK and its associations with class, privilege and power in order to understand something of the extent and depth of feelings that sit within society about entitlement to state education and what private education might offer with the benefits that sponsorships might bring. Buying education or buying into education and the privileges associated with such purchase have, throughout history, pointed to many contemporary attitudes, challenges and prejudices within and around PPP developments. Therefore, the remainder of this chapter is devoted to a commentary on how relationships in education have developed in the UK over the centuries and how perceptions about these relationships have been shaped in different ways from various social standpoints.

'Public' schools as class enclaves

It was around 600 CE that formal schools in the ecclesiastical centres of England can be traced and these, with others, developed into the system of 'public schools' we recognize today, many with their more permanently recorded origins in the fifteenth century. Building on established traditions and charging for this (whether payment is by a sponsor or the user) can be a successful thing to do.

'The term public school (publicae scolae) was used in the fifteenth century to denote schools in contrast to private establishments or private tuition' (Boyd 2001: 3). As time went on, it came to mean a school with certain characteristics. These included such things as having an ancient foundation which was often designed to support the poor who, unlike the nobility and later the rising class of merchants and traders, were unable to educate their children at home; a boarding facility where boys governed boys under a prefect system; its own system of rituals, custom, tradition, terminology and prejudices; and an ethos that favoured the strong and was designed to equip men for the highest offices in the church, military and state. Far less was available for girls; education for them was perceived as essentially domestic and included learning the importance of giving loving support to their husbands. Though it was provided in a different way, the education of the future wives of the educated classes included being taught to read and write. Schools were strictly male orientated. Order, continuity and the keen sense of loyalty which prevailed within these schools gave rise to 'the old boys' associations' and 'the old boys' network'.

The Renaissance in England through much of the sixteenth century was a revival which opened a climate for liberal education in the universities and public schools. Like never before, ideas and beliefs were questioned and critically examined. Artists and writers across Europe were commissioned by the nobility, the church and the prominent and the wealthy merchants and pushed ideas to new frontiers. This social and economic climate gave energy to the universities and the public schools of the time. There are parallels here with contemporary times. Although state education has been forced to focus on utilitarian objectives, the recognition for more attention for the arts, music and physical education, at least in primary schools, has firmly entered the debate and serious questions have been raised about the appropriateness of the secondary school curriculum.

However, other historic notions prevail in contemporary times. 'After the restoration in the mid-seventeenth century, the aristocracy and Anglican Church establishment saw education as partly responsible for the Puritan Revolution of Oliver Cromwell. Schools were seen as having been educating boys out of their proper social station' (Boyd 2001: 5). This perception of being in a 'proper social station' has doggedly persisted in the UK. It is part of the embedded class system. The idea of real opportunity emerging from achieving a better social class through private education, or by association with it, is still strong in the UK and in much of western psyche. 'Some parents are seeking firm and clear boundaries which cut their children off from "others" and provide exclusive access to institutions and routes of social advantage – class enclaves' (Ball 2003: 76). Whilst ideas and practices such as these continue to be nourished (however alluring they may be to some parents and to those politicians seeking their middle class votes) the achievement of contemporary aspirations for more inclusive communities will be stifled.

A class enclave is not a simple minority interest group, but it is close. This closeness creates a moral tension which in a democracy is difficult to resolve. On the one hand, there is a special freedom of choice and duty of care towards one's own child and a legitimate right to provide the 'best' education possible in whatever form the parents may perceive, on the other is the social injustice of buying into exclusive schools as 'class reproducing institutions' (Pakulski and Waters 1996: 90).

For some parents, rather like a period costume drama, there is an undeniably romantic appeal about the elite public schools and their historic associations. It is particularly apparent in those newer private schools which choose to emulate the somewhat eccentric uniforms and dress codes of the most ancient establishments. This affection (or affliction) lingers across large swathes of the population. Many people who can afford public school education would choose no other form of schooling for their children, many of those who cannot would if they could. In Britain for instance, more than 50 per cent of parents consistently tell pollsters that they would like to educate their children privately (*The Weekly Telegraph* 2004: 43), yet only 7 per cent do.

Despite the notoriety of the early public schools for flogging, cruelty and institutional bullying, the public schools grew in number through the nineteenth century. With reforms led by schools such as Rugby, Uppingham, Harrow and Oundle, they developed into what were and are often regarded as the best form of education for the potential leaders of the country. In terms of educating the country's leaders, little has changed in this respect in the UK over the centuries. Leaders in government, industry and commerce to this day are still drawn in disproportionately large numbers from the 7 per cent of the population who have attended independent schools of one sort or another, for example, both the prime minister and the home secretary of the UK (in January 2005) had each received education at the same private school.

State education with private support 1870–1944

This period brought state education within the reach of the mass of the population, for whom education became an entitlement. Following Forster's Education Act of 1870 up to 1902, elementary schools were run by school boards or by the church. In 1902, the school boards were replaced by the LEAs. The church had been a sponsor of many independent schools and the LEA continued to aid church schools. Now the church sponsors some of the new academies and other schools.

From 1902, elementary education was available for pupils up to 14 years of age. Secondary education for all emerged following the 1944 Education Act when it was structured and became compulsory for everyone up to 14 and subsequently up to 15 years of age. However, from 1902, direct grants were available for private schools which took pupils from elementary schools and some LEAs built new grammar schools to extend available places.

Apart from a few 'approved schools' for wrong doers and residential care education for children with particular SEN, boarding school education was almost entirely the preserve of private schools and generally remains so. Private schools therefore are not just for the elite and wealthy; they also serve the needs of others. Many children who need residential schooling for other reasons attend private boarding schools, for example, those whose parents' work take them overseas and the children of families in the Armed Services have access to such boarding schools. Private schools also have a tradition of being well supported by pupils and students from overseas.

The mix of state and private provision is set deeply within education's history. A series of reports were published between 1902 and 1944 with enlightened ideas about approaches to education, but the time was not ripe for implementation through legislation. Nevertheless, aspects of the these reports formed much of the basis for the later developments implemented after the 1944 Education Act, for example, the options for the organization of primary and secondary education. Later 'progressive' educational philosophies for the different age phases were presented in reports by Crowther (1959), Newsom (1963) and Plowden (1965). Throughout this period there was general support, consistently articulated in the Fleming Report and Committees (1944–1947), for the extension of the association existing between some of the private independent schools (especially those that were in receipt of direct grants) and the state sector.

Selective schools, comprehensive schools and centralization 1944–1997

The landmark 'Butler' Education Act of 1944 came into force at a time when school buildings were in a poor state, there was a severe teacher shortage and lack of resources. Shortages were experienced in both the private and the state sectors. Conservative Governments throughout the 1950s committed high levels of resourcing to new school buildings and educational equipment and to training more teachers. The preferred organizational model for state secondary schooling in most LEAs was the system of grammar and secondary modern schools.

Pupils were selected by the 11-plus exam and those who passed were allocated a place at the grammar school (more precisely, their parents were given the choice of the right kind of school for their child's attributes and abilities). A few LEAs had technical schools, which offered a more vocational curriculum, for those children who narrowly missed passing for the grammar schools. The pass rate depended on the places available and these varied from 10 per cent in some areas to 20 per cent in others. The process was clearly elitist, but it was elitism based on a measure, albeit a weak measure, of so-called ability. Drawing the line between those who got the chance of going to the grammar school and those who would not, was fraught with controversy.

Fairness and justice

One mark could make the difference between 'pass' or 'fail', the cut-off point being determined by the number of places available at the grammar schools. In some areas, second-chance tests were offered to border-line pupils or those who had made rapid 'late development' at 13 years of age. This was really a simple adjustment to changes that had occurred through mobility in the original numbers of pupils admitted at 11 years of age.

Comprehensive schools

Concerns about unfairness grew. Selecting pupils for secondary schooling in this way was seen as a major cause of social division. By the early 1960s, public support was moving away from selection at 11 years of age. With the Labour Government of 1964 under Harold Wilson came Circular 10/1965 which requested LEAs to submit plans for reorganization towards comprehensive education. Apart from a few authorities that were determined to keep selective schools, state secondary education generally became comprehensive. With this came a reduction in the commitment from the government to support private schools. Many direct-grant grammar schools moved to full independence although it was still possible for a few children to be sponsored via the assisted places scheme.

The ideological split between those preferring selective education (and in many cases selective private schools) and those seeing state-provided comprehensive education as the right and the just social option for all, became wider as views hardened. During this period, the private school relationship with state education and the collaboration between the state and the private sectors understandably fell away. It has taken 40 years for the collaboration between private and state schools to be reconsidered.

Curriculum freedom in schools

It was not only private schools that enjoyed independence in running their own affairs. State schools and the LEAs who maintained them enjoyed considerable freedom over how schools were organized and what was taught in them during this period from 1944 to 1988. Following the 1944 Education Act, the only statutory curriculum requirement on state schools was that religious education (RE) should be taught. The nature of the curriculum was determined as a local consensus. Ample conventional advice was available to head teachers and school managers and governors and in secondary schools, patterns of subject coverage were often chosen on the basis of particular examination syllabi. The choices made were usually quite conventional and rather academic with ample helpings of English and maths.

The Schools Council (1975) produced alternative and innovative ideas; some were taken up by the more forward-thinking schools and some were not. The successes in developing investigational science education are often accredited to the impetus created by the Schools Council 30 years ago. For state schools, decisions about these matters were taken at local and school levels just as they were for private schools. Traditional academic courses and qualifications were generally favoured in this regard in both sectors. The view that vocational and applied courses are of lower status is still deeply ingrained.

Opportunities to organize school systems differently

In some parts of the country, reorganization plans brought innovative solutions to old problems. Just as many private schools transferred their pupils across the preparatory, elementary and senior stages of schooling at ages other than 11 years, so LEAs opted for the three-tier system with transfer usually at 9 years to middle or junior high school and at 13 years to upper school. This organization was chosen for a range of reasons based on child development and maturation. A particular concern about transfer at 11 was that the interests and needs of the 11–13-year old pupils were often not well met in large secondary school institutions. The three-tier systems continue in 2005 in significant numbers across England. However, many LEAs have phased these out and have gone to the more conventional two-tier system with transfer at 11 years of age, mainly because the incentives and advantages of central education initiatives are easier to access when local systems fit into a single national pattern.

Once firmly in control, senior politicians in both national and local government tend to use 'system change' or 'regime change' as the markers of their political achievements. Shortly after the change occurred in Northampton as described in the Profile exhibit 2.1, the Leader of the Council announced that

Profile exhibit 2.1 Missed opportunity in Northamptonshire?

I have always been opposed to the principle of private money being used to provide state education, and to public funds being used to augment fees for private education. In recent years, I have seen and read little to cause me to change my mind.

During the 2004 round of creating 'Schools for the Future', Northamptonshire LEA missed a golden opportunity to build on the successes of earlier innovation. Instead of dismantling the Northampton three-tier school system which it did, the LEA should have recognized that, in an urban area with close proximity of schools, good systems of schooling need not necessarily conform to the status quo. The huge levels of new funding, boosted I am told by the private sector, could have been used to improve learning at all stages within the town's schools and achieve some of the objectives the government describes as necessary for the transformation of secondary schooling, particularly with regard to improved performance for 11–14-year olds and innovative 14–19 provision.

A little historical background is important. Aspirations reported in the first Hadow Report of 1926 were eventually taken into account in the Education Act of 1944 which made secondary education available, by right, for all 11–14-year olds. The Act was not before time. A difficult economy and the Second World War had delayed educational progress by 20 years. Although the impact of the 1944 Act was huge, it brought little change in teaching styles. Schools approached their postwar tasks much as they always had, with those pupils who passed the 'scholarship' progressing to grammar schools.

A further 20 years saw the Plowden and Newsom Reports on primary and secondary education, both innovatory. Lady Plowden pointed particularly to mismatches in the way schools operated in relation to the real needs of children. She pointed to the variables in child development not only as between boys and girls but also in their rates of maturation within the genders. The emotional needs and social interests of a 12-year old entering adolescence are very different from those of a 12-year old whose adolescence has yet to come. Her report recognized that the different development rates of children in class groups make difficult demands on teachers.

These findings reinforced the beliefs of educational leaders like Sir Alec Clegg, the CEO in the West Riding of Yorkshire up to 1974 (Darvill 2000), that the change from primary school organization, to the more inflexible and institutional practices of large secondary schools, should not be sudden at the age of 11, but rather a gradual transition depending on pupils' rates of development. It was not until the Government's White Paper of 10/1965 that flexibility was allowed and the age of transfer could be changed.

With a new town development bringing a huge growth in population to Northampton, the LEA decided that the three-tier system, with lower schools (5–9-year olds), middle schools (9–13-year olds) and upper schools (13–18-year olds), would overcome many of the problems in the two-tier system caused essentially by having 11 and 18-year olds in the same secondary school establishment.

In *21st Century Schools* (CABE and RIBA 2004) concern was still being expressed about the sudden change at 11 years of age. I quote, 'The contrast between the "caring" environment of the primary school and the large, autonomous secondary school can have a huge social impact. The secondary school experience can be a daunting one, and large unfamiliar environments (alongside peer pressure) can have a major influence on the life choices young people make' (ibid.: 7

quoting *Classrooms of the Future* DfES 2003a: 3). The paper goes on to say that overcoming this problem is the key challenge for designers, teachers and educationalists.

The three-tier system in Northampton had largely overcome these difficulties. Buildings provided 9–13-year olds with an attractive and a stimulating environment and were designed to facilitate appropriate learning styles. Lower schools, gave pupils understanding and confidence in basic skills and prepared them for entry into middle schools, which in turn provided flexible educational resources for both general class and specialist teaching. One only has to read the research by a past head teacher who traced the 30-year history of one middle school (Pearson 2004) to realize that pupils in the 11–13 age span were given opportunities and responsibilities that would not have been thought credible at the lower end of a comprehensive school.

It is difficult to find valid reasons to explain why Northamptonshire LEA should abandon so much of what was good. Standards in the three-tier system, though below rural primary and secondary schools in some aspects of their work, were generally comparable with similar groups of urban 11–18 schools. Most significantly, the social development (including behaviour) of the 11–13-year olds, and their attainment in sport and the arts, could not have been considered, for in these aspects parents consistently applauded the high levels of access and standards achieved by their children in middle schools.

It may be that the reasons for such backward thinking were more to do with fitting into a national two-tier template in order to access public funding and long-term loans for new school buildings, than anything to do with the achievements in the schools. Whatever the reasons for closure it was, in my opinion, a tragic waste of public and private money, in terms of buildings, staff and proven performance.

Existing buildings and staff expertise could have been used to create innovative options in line with the government's aspiration for reform at only a fraction of the cost of returning to an old system with new schools. It would have been possible to:

- develop joined-up provision for 3–9-year olds with better 'wrap-around' care and improved availability of children's centres and services;
- build on the successes of KS 2 and meet the aspirations for KS 3, by developing junior high schools for 9–14-year olds;
- give a clear focus, with dedicated resources, to resolve the issues relating to the education of 14–19-year olds, with academic, applied and vocational education concluding with an appropriately reformed examination system by 2010.

It is apparent that national government and local authorities dancing to a central tune have limited understanding of how effective learning and true transformation of education may occur. We now seem so entrenched in managerial grooves, markets, contracts and private sources of funding that we no longer know what an education service should be about.

Source: Trevor Scholey, School Governor, Former Chief Education Inspector, Northamptonshire.

he was stepping down. He described his achievements of 20 years as a councillor thus, 'I think I've achieved a lot. First of all we've had the single largest reorganization of schools in the country' (Forsyth 2004: 1). The political mindset around achievement is often seen in terms of the size of the single action rather than on the impact of those actions. The systems in themselves are actually not that important. However they can seem to be to politicians who believe that change demonstrates a no-nonsense, sweeping managerial approach to improving things. Unfortunately, many of them are not in office when the impact of such changes are felt, it is the pupils who feel that.

The decade of the 'Great Debate' 1976–1988

It was the famous speech at Ruskin College, Oxford in 1976 by the Labour Prime Minister, James Callaghan which called for the 'Great Debate' about state education and began the trends that led to moves by successive governments to shift control away from schools and LEAs and centralize educational policy and practices. This speech and the subsequent government centralization of education which followed changed the basis upon which state schools operated. 'Discontent about the appropriateness of comprehensive education for either the pupils or their future employers (the main concern of Callaghan) was translated by the Thatcher (Conservative) government into a series of Education Acts' (McCaig 2001: 199). Successive legislation brought the publication of examination results and the right for parents to challenge the LEAs' decisions on which school their children should attend. It also introduced the National Curriculum and a huge increase in power to the Secretary of State. These changes, spread over a decade, separated the operational remits of state and private schools. The moves to centralize the practices of state schools showed little regard for the established constitutional arrangements which had existed in law. The responsibilities traditionally invested in school governing bodies for setting the strategic direction of their schools were eroded. Schools were given direction and policy by government as it became more directly involved with the operational detail of what schools should teach and later (from 1997), how they should teach it. The established pattern of system management designed to function at the four levels of 'individual', 'school', 'local' and 'national' was being undone, the new direction for state schools came down directly from the national authority. There was little room for ideas other than those that flowed from government.

From a time before 1870, both private schools and state schools had enjoyed huge freedom in their organization and in choosing the curriculum they followed. Providing that most clients and stakeholders were content, then schools in both sectors could largely do as they pleased. Even when things went wrong, ambiguity existed as to who had authority to intervene. It is important to trace the policy changes of successive governments which gradually eroded the responsibilities of the LEA resulting in reduced local participation and opportunities for real consultation.

Systematic centralization

The report on the information collected from LEAs about their policies and practices in curricular matters, *Local Authority Arrangements for the School Curriculum* (DES 1979) affirmed the Secretary of State's position on a number of issues at that time:

- 'Education Acts lay upon Ministers the duty to promote the education of the people in England and Wales...and an inescapable duty to satisfy themselves that the work of the schools matches national needs' (ibid.: 2);
- 'Education Acts lay the responsibility of providing efficient and sufficient primary and secondary education firmly on LEAs' (ibid.: 3);
- 'The summary of responses...suggests that not all authorities have a clear view of the desirable structure of the school curriculum, especially its core elements' (ibid.: 6).

The centralizing intention was open and clear for all to see.

Two years later, the Government's Circular 6/1981 requested that LEAs should undertake consultation on its policies within the light of what the government had published in *The School Curriculum* (DES 1981). Again, two years on, Circular 8/1983 moved things along further by asking LEAs to provide, by April 1984, responses to that Circular which gave details, summarized here, of:

- the progress on drawing up policies for the curriculum;
- descriptions of the roles played in the process of drawing up the policies;
- a statement on the ways in which the policy is being given practical effect in the schools;
- a summary of the steps being taken to ensure the curriculum is planned as a whole, that for each pupil it is balanced, coherent and

suited to his or her ability and aptitude; and that the needs of pupils across the full range of ability are met in both primary and secondary schools;

- a summary of steps being taken to ensure that the curriculum is appropriately related to what happens outside school;
- a statement about the level of available resources.

Given the position from where LEAs were coming, this request for policy and content was ambitious, for some it was unrealistic. Nevertheless, many responded well. In Northamptonshire, for example, a working party, whose remit it was to respond to the first DES circular, was established in 1981. It included politicians, teachers, parents, governors, LEA inspectors and officers and an invited DES observer. Following extensive consultation, *The School Curriculum* (Northamptonshire County Council (NCC) 1984) was produced. This 'framework of principles' was owned by and was meaningful to school communities because their key representatives had created it and their participation was at a high level. In many ways this was a more effective approach to ensuring that the work of the schools matched national requirements than prescribing everything that should be taught, as in the National Curriculum.

Whether a more effective approach or not, the course of history ran the way it did. Local participation in and consultation about education was slashed. The DES was apparently unmoved by the quality of the collective responses by the LEAs to Circular 8/1983. Consequently, government documents and legislation flowed and led to the National Curriculum with its associated regimes of assessment and testing. The Education (No. 2) Act 1986 defined the respective roles of government, LEAs, schools and head teachers; the ERA set the statutory framework for the following decade of so-called school autonomy within national prescription. This included externally driven accountability through the culture of league tables and the Ofsted inspection regime emerging from the Education Act 1992.

A decade of 'fitting in' 1987–1997

By legislating for greater central control of state schools and dramatically increasing accountability, the scope for innovation and diversity of practice was severely reduced. Most state schools were cautious. Even those which were tempted by new 'market independence' did so often with ideas of competitive success and expansion over other schools rather than for motives to innovate. Schools found their own ways of fitting in to the new arrangements, some ventured towards a business model of operation whilst others held on to their ideals of being a part of a welfare state. Either way, they lost influence over the content of the curriculum and increasingly also over how it should be taught. The national system tightened up and schools lost opportunities for creative thinking.

LEAs too were unsure and cautious as the Government changed its mind about what LEAs should be doing. Local Management of Schools (LMS) had given schools greater and welcome autonomy over how they could utilise their budgets but newly delegated powers had little impact over the central legislation now in place. Confusion was caused by the introduction of independent GM schools. LEAs had been charged with taking on a more strategic role but later 'the Government saw a minimal role. LEAs "may have a continuing responsibility for maintaining a number of primary, secondary and special schools if parents decide not to vote for grant maintained status"' (Whitbourn *et al.* 2004: 5 quoting DfE 1992: para. 6.2). Exercising a strategic role for LEAs became difficult. If LEAs tried to take strategic action, for example, removing surplus places, the schools affected could vote to turn to GM and scupper the overall plan. In this way national policy increased parochialism with individual governing bodies acting out of self-interest rather than within the local democratic process.

School improvement work goes private

By 1996 the role of the LEA was seen very much as that of 'mop-up'. As defined by the Department for Education and Employment (DfEE), 'Their role should be to provide those services and undertake those functions which schools cannot carry out for themselves and which no other agency is better placed to carry out' (DfEE 1996: 49). These other agencies were seen to be private sector groups and it was through this period that many LEA advisers saw 'the writing on the wall' and moved across to the private sector or to work independently. Many took on private inspection work through Ofsted and made a good living. The growth of educational businesses was very evident during this time. In due course, many of the smaller groups of educational advisers linked themselves to larger commercial and industrial organizations in readiness for the contractual tendering within the new regime of wide-scale privatization of state education services.

Head teachers, governors, teachers, parents, pupils, advisers and consultants ensured that state schools moved forward. Much was claimed to have been achieved in state education by using these national frameworks and by the changes brought about by centralization and privatization. However the cost was a loss of divergence, originality, local personality and true innovation. Energy and resources were focused on restructuring and installing systems which tended not to innovate but rather to consolidate much of what good LEAs did anyway. People in schools and LEAs became the implementers of the ideas of those in government. The situation was such that eventually the DfES felt the need to create a unit within its own department specifically for 'innovation in education'!

Expectations and standards 1997–2005

As a result of this centralization, a system of national education with an emphasis on measurement and accountability has been created. The system has not been led in ways that have inspired innovation and diversity. The modernizing policy of the 'new' Labour Government in 1997 began with this inheritance from the previous Conservative administration. It continued with the view that centrally directed strategies coupled with commercial private-sector disciplines would be its top priority and bring fundamental improvement. Transformation of education was to be driven by prescription and private contracting rather than through entrepreneurial diversity.

The education rhetoric following the 1997 election of the new Government was all about ensuring that all children should learn to read, write and calculate to high standards before they leave primary school. The operational priority was the implementation of national strategies to achieve ambitious new targets set by the Government. The term 'world class' was frequently used to describe what the education service in England was to become. By 1999, Professor Michael Barber, working for the Government, described the approaches to reform. He was aware that 'electorates are fickle and impatient...and will not wait patiently for five or ten years to see if it (a world class education service) is delivered' (Barber 2000: 5). Haste in delivering visible signs of change and improvement were paramount, 'In my job you are...only as good as your most recent results!' (ibid.: 10). Private education does not work like that. It makes progress gradually, building over decades and recognizing the importance of inheritance.

If it is accepted that real change in education and learning takes time, then the climate and attitude in government are not conducive to it. Barber was conscious to state the government's starting point by drawing on comparative results in a number of areas including low levels of adult literacy in the UK compared to most European countries and Australia. His analysis, of how to get 'High expectations and standards for all, no matter what' (ibid.: 1), made little reference to anyone else's ideas apart from those of government. This disempowered many educationists in other levels of the system.

Although schools and LEAs did sterling work to bring about the improvements that were sought and attempted to achieve the new initiatives of the government, the national targets were not met. Yet, recent observation and commentary show that sports and the arts have been neglected.

It is difficult to identify the contribution which has been made so far by the private sector to claims of high expectations and standards. Certainly, private schools cannot be pointed to as having contributed to any aggregated measure of success – they have not taken part. Most private companies which are now running LEAs have not been doing so for long enough to have made a significant difference.

Looking for some room to reclaim some freedom

Private schools had been left outside the straight jacket of this centralizing legislation. They remained in a sector with the freedom, if not always the financial resources, to innovate. Conversely, state schools, constrained by legislation in the operation of education, received hefty capital amounts from the government for innovative developments in buildings and modern technology. Operational freedoms at school level are very significant in shaping the nature of education that schools might provide. As well as having the liberty to choose major components such as curriculum and teaching strategies, private schools also maintained valuable fieldwork and educational visits as an enriching part of their regular curriculum programmes. Whilst attempts are made in state schools to preserve such features, they are now much reduced. This has occurred for many reasons. The bureaucracy of charging policies and a focus on contractual working hours led to making residential experience very costly. Centralization has closed things down for state schools operationally, whereas Government investment has brought resources in modern technology on a scale not easily available to many parts of the private sector.

With the government now seeking ways to develop and transform education it was faced with having to find ways of freeing schools from the very legislation passed to control them. This freedom has been sought in various ways, not least by creating new categories of state-funded schools which make them independent. Alongside this are calls for schools and LEAs to procure new services from private providers on the small, medium and large scales.

In terms of the chronological history of schools and LEAs, this is the point reached. However, there are other contextual issues which need to be taken into account when considering the contemporary role of the private sector in creating opportunities for new freedom and innovation in state education. Historically, these relate to the place of education as a corporate function of society rather than just as schooling for the individual.

Education within corporate services

State education in LEAs is often seen as separate from other services in local government. Yet, it is the LEA as the local authority that has the duty to contribute towards the development of the wider community. There is a bureaucracy around this which successive governments have caused to spiral. The challenge now is shifting to one which is about ensuring that the duty to contribute across the community is achieved through utilizing both state and private means.

Whilst private schools retain their mottos and their bursars and financial advisers secure successful business plans, state schools have become more adept at producing eloquent words of mission and have raised standards. State schools and LEAs have been required by government to expand these with a plethora of statutory and non-statutory plans. For both schools and LEAs these requirements are numerous and fragmented in their concept.[1] Proposals to reduce this bureaucracy in planning are not before time.

The idea of having a Single Education Plan (SEP) is good although this is likely to move to a statutory plan for children, which would be more consistent with the government's plans contained in the *Five Year Strategy for Children and Learners* (DfES 2004a). Even with much needed and drastic rationalization, the culture towards planning for corporateness in the state sector will be different to that experienced by private schools and private companies, essentially in terms of democratic participation.

The way the performance of the education service is judged, is increasingly dependent upon the corporate success of the local authority. The strategic objective within this move to corporateness is desirable as the aims of education reach out and beyond the conventional parameters created by schools and education systems themselves. Privatized delivery mechanisms for education have not been well positioned to do this. Privatization of frontline corporate service functions is rare; it is more common in back room services such as call centres, communication, personnel and payroll. The cultural move is towards a globalization of corporate educational efficiency rather than to education with local participation.

Gaps in services can also easily open with the implementation of large-scale policies emanating from different government departments. There is often ambiguity where policies seem contradictory. The classic example is that of the 'double harness' of education, discussed in the paragraph below. This needs careful and sensitive local political and professional management. With increasing attempts for policies to be more 'joined-up' there is a tendency to standardize common procedures and so reinforce the status quo rather than moving forward on specific and much needed educational innovation. This scale of wholesale system change does not lend itself to real innovation and to taking the risks that transformation entails. As a result, those fortunately placed 'independent' state schools are being freed from the very statutes and legislation which were designed to control state schools in the first place. It seems unlikely that such freedom will subsequently bring those advantages that are perceived as the imperatives from 'joined-up' Government.

The managerial trend of top-down direction by government means practice tends to continue as before. Adjusting the experiences of the past with new livery and celebrity endorsement is more prevalent than educational innovation. Greater corporateness in the short term is mainly about better coordination of the status quo.

The contemporary double harness of education, 'standards and inclusion'

State education, more than most public sector services, is faced with huge challenges to improve the service it gives to its pupils, its parents and its stakeholders. In most developed societies, education is charged with meeting a dual objective. On the one hand, the objective is to raise the academic and the vocational standards of pupils and students, on the other, it is to promote inclusive practices which are successful in educating those pupils and students who are, or feel, marginalized for reasons of their behaviour, underachievement, SEN or cultural, social or economic circumstances.

This double harness of standards and inclusion is the component which makes education the means of social and economic regeneration in poor communities and is the vehicle through which good health and prosperity are maintained in successful areas. Whereas economic inequalities perpetuate the main social difficulties in societies, economic regeneration has to be the principle objective of education.

Considering the history of educational change, we see that inclusion has neither been a central nor an explicit priority in the transformative process. We are 'increasingly being driven in the direction of *privileging the academic*' (Bagley *et al.* 2001: 305), rather than making social inclusion a priority. The complex issues of addressing the double harness pose new questions for the future:

- How do we improve strategic systems in education and existing practices in our schools to make them inclusive, not sectoral and actually raise standards overall to improve the quality of the lives of all children, students and citizens?
- How do individuals make a real contribution, be they taxpayer, student, parent, teacher, head teacher, business leader, administrator, technician or politician?
- How, during the next decade, do we determine the aims and purposes of local education for an interdependent global society?
- How do we change national and international systems so that they make a real difference to the lives of individuals, who can, in turn, shape competitive yet cooperative economies locally, nationally and globally?

Governments have a fundamental responsibility to promote inclusive education practices in practical and tangible ways that, simultaneously raise academic and vocational standards for all. Educators have responsibility for putting this into practice. History shows that achieving both is difficult. The issues are further complicated by the need for democratic governments to be seen to deliver services that meet the impatient demands of their electorates and of the aspirations of parents of different social classes.

The process of establishing initiatives for inclusion is often excessively separate from the drive to raise standards of attainment when in fact they should be closely complementary. Clearly, it is expedient for schools to be 'selective' over admissions and to concentrate on those subjects which are easy to assess by standardized measures and can be publicized for customer satisfaction, than to tackle inclusion seriously. Promotional statements made by the new private companies tend to emphasize very traditional schooling, for example, that geared to securing subsequent university entrance, rather than face the promotion of vocational, applied and inclusive education for all. This opens considerations about potential conflicts between privatization and citizenship based upon meeting social needs and democratic ideals.

3 Privatization, partnerships, democracy and citizenship

> We will not navigate through the complex environment of the future by peering relentlessly into a rear view mirror...innovation should be seen as functions of all areas of activity and not only as confined to particular people or processes.
>
> (Ken Robinson b. 1953)

As has been outlined, there is an international movement towards providing education through private rather than public means. The role of central and local governments, it is now argued, should be that of making policy whilst keeping in place appropriate safeguards and clear lines of accountability. Government should become less embroiled in the delivery of services even though local government has held such a role for over a century and central government has increased its involvement enormously since the 1980s.

This chapter is based on the hypothesis that social and political participation in education is desirable and that two conditions greatly assist in achieving this. First, that democratically elected governments should earn and receive the support of their professional communities in the implementation of policy and second, that educational standards are raised most effectively by leaders who are close to their constituents, staff, pupils and communities.

The premise generally held by government is that privatization of the state education system will break the status quo and bring both innovation and improved performance. The injection of private investment into schools and state education services will enable the perceived needs for reform to be achieved more quickly than without it. There is a desire to reduce waste and bureaucracy by delegating functions to private providers who are disciplined by market forces. However, market forces that underpin private sector trading activities are not straightforward in a world where education is compulsory and seen as an entitlement for everyone of mandatory school age.

Under the guise of modernization, the drive to raise standards in schools and give parents more choice of schools has become regarded as an accepted and popular view of what the electorate wants. The popularity of this drive with most leading politicians, is equivalent to the goodness of motherhood and apple pie! But the electorate is made up of people who see themselves not only as customers and consumers, but as neighbours and citizens.

Even where schools do not score well in the quasi-market indicators of league table positions and in the judgement grading in their Ofsted reports, parents will often rally to support their local school and take ownership of it; they do not act as consumers of education but rather as citizens and partners in its provision. 'The concept of citizenship entitlement is highly developed in education. Partly because in a democracy all political parties are required to advocate opportunities for social mobility, there is an almost universal expectation that education should be available as a right, not needing to be purchased in the market – though in practice in the UK and some other countries this ideal has been heavily compromised by the existence of fee-paying schools to which many wealthy people send their children' (Crouch 2003: 26). One of the main teaching unions in England, the National Union of Teachers (NUT), has a view that many of the education privatization proposals, for example for London, 'are deeply flawed, and that the growth of academies and involvement of the private sector is creating problems, not solutions' (Stewart 2004b: 15). 'Educational needs are best met by publicly provided-services which are high quality, free and comprehensive' (Sinnott 2004: 15).

Education and its privatization exist therefore within a wide polarization of views with and without free market conditions. Although parents sometimes behave as consumers, they also act as supportive partners of their local schools. Private organizations deal in the business of education as wholly private transactions and within public ownership (Profile exhibit 3.1). Contracts include both capital and service projects. Privatization though is only one aspect of the proposals. The range of partnership schemes that are encouraged to promote improvements in education further complicates the precise contributions made by the private partners and the nature of the education market itself.

Profile exhibit 3.1 Education and the use of private companies

Private companies have different roles in public education in England. They provide certain services such as electricity, school books and equipment, they usually build new schools and do major repairs. That is relatively uncontroversial. Recently PFI contracts are being used for building new schools and the contractor then supplies certain services such as catering, cleaning and site supervision. PFI is really an expensive way of borrowing money but it does get round the capital borrowing limits and places most risk on the contractor. However, it does mean that local government has to be careful over the details of the specification. I suspect the profits from matters like cleaning are not really what the private company winning the contract is really interested in. Projects such as BSF could decouple all that since the opportunity of building or refurbishing a number of schools over a period of time would be attractive to a number of large and successful building companies.

The new practice of involving private companies in helping to provide services such as improving literacy is also acceptable if it is a matter of contracting for that service. Many such companies providing this type of service are employing ex-teachers and they can be judged by results. It is also acceptable for schools, if they so wish, to engage services for personnel or legal advice from outside local government. They, after all, are responsible for their schools' budgets and the actions they take. Services such as payroll for instance can be out-sourced, but schools need to be aware of loss-leaders being used by some companies to attract business. Services in the private sector can be cheaper but not necessarily by offering a quality service or long-term viabilities.

However, controversially the government in 1997 did legislate to bring in the private sector to turn round failing LEAs. Many of these employed ex-education officers who were paid considerably more money to do a similar job to what they had been doing before. The success of this has been limited partly because the arrangements isolated the work from the rest of the Council. LEAs and education departments are part of local government and not some separate body. Successful education departments work very closely with the rest of the council services such as social services and regeneration departments.

Where there was difficulty, such as in Liverpool, the seconding of the Director of Wigan resulted in immediate improvements. Contrast that with Haringey, where it took over 12 months to even let the contract to the private company, Capita. As a result progress was much slower.

What the Local Government Association (LGA) proposed was an intervention strategy which included local government working with a private company. The DfES did not support this idea. However, the twinning of Doncaster with Warwickshire and Blackburn with Rochdale produced solutions for both Doncaster and Rochdale very quickly. The LGA did not have the capacity at the time to develop this approach in all cases but realized that a better solution was to prevent LEAs failing in the first place. By contrast, the experiences of Southwark, Leeds and Bradford all of which were outsourced in various ways, show the variability of success by the private companies set up to do this. The way LEAs have become successful in raising educational standards in schools has shown this privatization approach was misguided and actually more expensive than other more successful interventions such as twinning local authorities with or without a private partner.

One reason why organizations like Eddison showed little inclination to take over schools in the UK was because they could not employ the school staff. Therefore, they could not make a profit which would come from employing fewer staff on higher wages but reducing the wage bill overall. Claims of raising standards in the USA with charter schools are contested by their critics and things have become quieter there on that front.

However, the emergence of academies is the latest variance of a form of privatization. These are schools sponsored by the private sector. For a private sector investment of about £2 million, the government builds a new school or refurbishes the existing one. The schools are independent of the local council and really have become under the auspices of the DfES directly. They are free to set their own conditions of service and pay for staff. Most of the governing body is appointed by the sponsor. Already there are claims that the schools in some cases use the company sponsoring the school from which to buy services. If that is true then conflict of interest considerations should be applied and some of the school governors could find themselves subject to legal investigation.

These arrangements confuse freedom for schools to manage themselves under local management with school autonomy. One of the key ways of raising educational standards in a community is for all the schools to be working together in that locality. Competition between schools results very often in standards declining in some schools, while others prosper.

Competition and autonomy also weakens democratic accountability. LEAs cannot intervene in the case of problems. There is no evidence that such schools will drive up standards but they could make it more difficult for the implementation of a coherent system, for example, 14–19 educational programmes suitable for the twenty-first century. These reforms could widen the choice of the curriculum and opportunities for all the students in that locality if strategically coordinated.

It is alarming that the latest proposals for foundation schools could reduce the number of elected parents on the governing bodies from one-third to either one or none. Local government introduced elected parent governors. The Conservative Government made them mandatory and increased their number. Now the Labour Government looks as though it may remove this right to elect such parents.

Public education should be accountable at local and at national levels to elected politicians. The private sector can play a valuable part in helping to raise standards and provide services. The use of industry in helping specialist schools is focused and helpful. They can supply in some cases effective school governors and help train school staff about the world of work. What it should not do is to control the educational process in a democratic society. We moved away from that approach in the nineteenth century to ensure equal opportunities (EO) for all.

The present educational system is, and should be, varied within its structure but its strength will be undermined if it is not democratically accountable. There is a danger that this will happen if we are not absolutely clear about the principles on which the private sector should be involved.

Source: Councillor Graham Lane, Cabinet Member for Education, London Borough of Newham, Formerly Local Government Association Chair of the Education and Lifelong Learning Executive.

Privatization by stealth or true partnership?

The government insists that the involvement of private firms in education is about creating and developing partnerships with LEAs and schools. Partnerships with the private sector can bring in not only much-needed extra finance but also expertise. If this leads to improving standards in education then the objectives will be met. The mantra of 'what matters is what works' is generally accepted by government and its critics but there is little evidence that privatization is any more successful than public provision, blatantly not so in places such as the London Borough of Southwark, where the private contractor, WS Atkins Ltd, pulled out well short of contract completion. Indeed, more straightforward partnership working without private sector involvement, for example, the EiC scheme, is generally recognized as more successful, even though this scheme does not actually lever in significant private resources at all.

There are moral and ideological objections to privatization. These are based around concerns about loss of democratic accountabilities and the traditions of citizenship responsibilities in a system of education for all. Critics argue that making a profit out of the actual delivery of state education is contrary to the democratic and citizenship ideals upon which the traditionally publicly funded and publicly run education system is based. They perceive privatizing education as a threat to equity, access and social justice. There are many who believe that education should be provided by the state without the entanglements of private sponsorship at all. Within this group of sponsors, of course, there may be benefactors who wish to donate to a local school; donations coming with 'no commercial strings' attached.

Privatizing moves in education, which are part of partnership activity with the public sector, are not equivalent to wholesale outsourcing to a private contractor. Certainly, when I accepted the position of CEO in Walsall in 2001 following the government intervention, I did so in the belief that this privatization move was to achieve a 'Strategic Partnership' between the LEA and the prospective private partner, the idea of drawing the best from both worlds. The job description required the achievement of such a partnership, opportunities rather than threats shaped my perceptions. However, it did not take long before it became apparent that certain civil servants and government advisers seemed distinctly more interested in ensuring the perceived successes of the private firm, no matter which private firm was taken on, rather than the success of any partnership between it and the LEA. This scenario is explored in Chapter 6.

It is important, therefore, when evaluating the relative merits of privatization and partnership workings to attempt to identify, from within the plethora of mixed activities, those elements which are actually about private contribution rather than those aspects of non-commercial collaborative and partnership endeavour.

The Private Finance Initiative (PFI)

Despite a decade of reports from various sources which criticized PFI projects for 'poor quality work, missed deadlines and failure to live up to ministers' claims that they would save taxpayers' money' (Farrell 2003: 6), there is a consensus, promoted by the government, that the later PFI projects are successful. The PFI is central to the UK government policy on capital finance. It forms a huge aspect of bringing new private resources to improving public sector infrastructure in a range of services, including education in extended partnerships. In theory, it does this by having local authorities regulate their own borrowing on the basis of what is affordable over a period of about 30 years. Private sector funding then supports publicly funded capital expenditure for the venture, with the private sector managing, at a profit, the new building, the installation or the refurbishment and the subsequent services that are required such as site management, maintenance, catering and cleaning. The arrangement also shifts the balance of risk onto the private partner.

From its beginnings in 1992, the PFI has had a mixed track record. It is fair to say that PFI projects for education were late entrants. However, since 1999 the PFI has matured into the private partnership world of education and now PFI credits are a widely used form of funding. The PFI is the basis of the government's proposal in 2003 to renew secondary schools across England and BSF.

Capital values for PFI projects can be huge. The one referred to in Profile exhibit 2.1 in Chapter 2, granted to Northamptonshire in 2003 to re-organize schools, exceeded £100 million, whereas the value for a single new secondary school in Walsall, as mentioned in Profile exhibit 3.2, was worth just £11 million. Between 1999 and 2001, the signed PFI contracts in English education alone amounted to well over £1 billion.

As PFI projects are activities that are most often associated with the building and refurbishing of schools, they tend to be amongst the least contentious of the PPP in education. The question of how to justify making a profit out of education does not have the same emotional charge for these projects that deal with building contractors, utilities, educational suppliers and information and communication technology (ICT) installation and maintenance as it does for those initiatives dealing with the leadership and management of schools and the actions of teaching and learning. Nonetheless, there are concerns that the PFI is mortgaging the nation over the next three decades with properties and projects that will not stand the test of time but will provide the private sector multinational companies with ongoing profit levels beyond a reasonable formula of value for money expected by taxpayers.

Profile exhibit 3.2 Getting a new secondary school through a PFI project

It is difficult to write about our PFI project without some background. Only then will you appreciate where the enthusiasm, then the drive, then the determination to get a new building came from.

When I became a governor, the school had just gone GM. You could sense the relief that the governors felt to be 'free'. Before as a voluntary-aided (VA) school, the 'powers that be' had stifled and objected to any initiatives to improve the school. The school was successful and over-subscribed but in poor buildings 50-years old, no longer fit for their purpose and on a split site.

With GM status, architects and other consultants were engaged and bids were submitted. The first snag was that only half the funds requested were granted. The governors built a science block and did some modifications to the existing school. The new building made the old buildings look and seem even worse. There was, however, a 40 per cent increase in the take up of science because of the new building. This made the governors more determined to push on for a new school.

With GM status, the land that once belonged to the LEA were transferred to the governors. Schemes were developed to sell land for buildings. But whatever scheme was proposed it was stopped by the Trustees in the sense they would not say 'yes' but would not say 'no'. This left us in a limbo; it appeared that the schemes were too unconventional for them to support us.

At last we hit upon a good fortune. One of the consultants, well versed both in education matters and our plight made our position known to the DfES in a more direct manner than previously. As a result, we were invited to look to a replacement based on a PFI.

Consultants were again appointed to do the bid. It was obvious to everyone that the buildings were old, hard to maintain, unfit for their purpose, cold in the winter, hot in the summer, unattractive, did not stimulate learning and were on two sites with a bridge connecting over a main road. In addition, Ofsted had commented that it was a good school held back by the quality of accommodation. Despite this, options still had to be prepared for: repairing the building to the minimum health and safety would allow; repairing and adapting to suit modern teaching methods with a complete replacement. Not surprisingly, after the preparation of the options, replacement was deemed to be the best value! The DfES agreed and it was shown that PFI was affordable and the project became 'official'. With that the other stakeholders felt they now had to agree.

The part that made the finances work was the sale of the 'governors'' land. GM has worked after all. Yes, we did have land for the sale and the new school, with plenty left!

A very comprehensive bid document was prepared. Expressions of interest were made by numerous providers and a selection of these chosen to bid. It was a very exciting time. Our consultants were good, both knowledgeable and professional, but we had to get on with them personally as well, because they were with us for a long time. In the end we were sending each other birthday cards!

One advantage of PFI was the range of designs we got to see. When tendering in a traditional way, you tend to get one architect's interpretation of what you can do. That may get modified but that basic design concept never gets dramatically altered, certainly never to the point where you get a fresh piece of paper and start again.

When the bids came in we saw four presentations and four very different designs. One, I remember was fantastic but as it turned out it was totally unaffordable. Two were selected for further development. Then the first blow, the change of government in 1997 and we became a VA school again. The project had to be bid again as the stakeholders had changed. Luckily, those who had been chosen were still interested and eventually a preferred bidder was chosen.

The negotiations started in earnest. The detail mattered a lot and I learnt the meaning of 'the devil is in the detail'. We had to get it right or we would be stuck with it for 25 years. There then followed hours of meetings, quite a few lasting all day and into the evening. Though the different stakeholders shared the services of the project manager and the accountant, they all employed their own legal advisers. So as well as negotiating with the provider's legal team, we as clients had to negotiate amongst ourselves as well. It was very frustrating particularly as we were on the 'same side' yet had seemingly conflicting issues between us.

There always seemed to be one problem after another, and at times it was quite depressing. There was a lot of brinkmanship in the negotiations. We had to remain focused on what the ultimate aim was or it would have been easy to give up.

Finally at the end I thought there would be a great day of signing documents with congratulations all round, but the great day kept being postponed and even when the day arrived, amendments were still being made until the evening and into the next day. Over 60 documents were signed, sealed or initialled. There was more relief than triumph in the end.

How is the PFI going after two years? Quite well! The real test will come when we have no concerns about the contract and we can concentrate on improving standards at the school; that is what we are now about.

I went into the school on the first week of the summer holidays in 2004. The school was two years old and I could smell paint. It was not to cover vandalism or bad workmanship. It was because it was on the maintenance schedule to do, to keep it smart and well maintained. Had it not been a PFI project, I doubt that any maintenance would have been done for years as I suspect I would have heard the line 'you have a new school!'

This PFI project to get a new school took eight years. Children had come to the school and left with the promise of a new school unfulfilled. All the fees spent on the process would have built a primary school. It is to be hoped the process really has improved.

Source: Joe Hawley, Governor and Committee Chair, St Thomas More School, Walsall.

Public Private Partnerships (PPPs)

Leaving the large PFI projects aside, PPPs abound in the operational services of education. The government wishes to make it possible for schools and the education services to establish new partnerships with public, private and voluntary sector bodies for the actual delivery of education. This is especially the case where these could provide strong management support. Attempts at offering education in commercial circumstances and at marrying what have been public service education provisions with private practices have taken a variety of forms.

The partnerships are complex, numerous and sit within a labyrinth of government initiatives and projects such as BSF. The government has set up a joint venture, PfS, to develop effective methods of procuring construction and other services and to turn new educational vision into reality.

Private firms improving the provision of public education

It is argued that, because private sector enterprises are tried and tested in the competitive market, they will generally provide a superior service in terms of school efficiency and effectiveness than the public sector is able to achieve alone. The public sector is essentially characterized as the LEAs and their community schools. As quoted earlier, it is difficult to find tangible evidence to support the notion that private companies or PPPs actually give better service in terms of value for money or more effective programmes. It is, however, the case that government is wedded to the belief that the privatization of the education service is the route to improvement.

Although some private-partnership schemes show early positive signs and promise of success, it is questionable whether such promise is due to private firms actually being involved or private firms simply employing public sector personnel who merely retain most aspects of the best practice from public-sector working.

The notion pursued by the government is that private interests will bring innovation and improvements to the quality of education provided, especially where their contributions are facilitated by partnership arrangements with the public sector. The idea is that, due to competitive pressures, private firms disappear if they are less than efficient or if market conditions change. The private sector carries the risks of either case. It is believed that under competitive pressures the survivors must be efficient. As there is no similar competition in public service, so the potential for inefficiency and ineffectiveness is assumed to be greater. Where market conditions change and demand for a service falls then again the private sector absorbs the risk. This is the case with the change in market conditions for privatized school inspection companies. As Ofsted strikes a 'New Relationship with Schools (NRWS)' and reduces the scale of school inspections, many privatized school inspection agencies and independent inspectors will directly carry the loss.

This argument holds its validity providing pure market forces exist, but it rapidly weakens as the circumstances and requirements of statutory education are considered. Education globally, and particularly in England, contains a rich patchwork of provision in mixed market conditions which alters the simple supply and demand against cost and efficiency equation.

A continuum of private models and partnership popularity

Models of privatization, whether in public partnership or not, exist along a continuum. At one end of the continuum are those minimal privatizing elements. These may be small contributions of sponsorship or professional expertise, for example the sponsorship of academies. At the other end are fully privatized services, such as an LEA, operating under a fully outsourced contract. Privatization exists on a wide variety of scales, from individual schools and associations of schools, through to firms holding contracts to run large-scale local and regional systems and companies buying and running chains of private schools.

Alongside this, in England, is a powerful thrust to run education by central initiatives rather than by local government democracy and initiatives born of genuine school autonomies. This centralizing thrust has not been seen as consistent with the policies of locally managed schools and the notion of 'diversity and choice' within the state sector which the government also strongly promulgates.

At whatever point along the continuum and whatever the scale, the concept of partnering is highly attractive politically. Partnership, like excellence, has become an overused term and is seductive, especially when linked with citizenship, enterprise and entrepreneurship. However, those local democratic controls and accountabilities, applied to education, are weakened when partnership contracts replace direct public services. For example, elected members have a distinct role in monitoring private-sector contracts, but given the duration of these contracts, typically between 5 and 30 years, there is little scope for political initiative to change the nature or direction in the short term. This inability may, of course, be seen as advantageous if parochially orientated politicians are seen as merely interfering in previously agreed strategic commitments. But the question of who actually is in control in a local or national democratic sense is a real issue, especially in those cases of LEA intervention where the government is seen to be pushing the private requirement onto a reluctant council.

National and local democracy and education for citizenship

The tradition of education within local government is a rich one, albeit difficult for it to acknowledge at a time when it has been pursuing a strong centralizing agenda. For over a century, education has been seen as one of those 'citizenship services' provided nationally, for all and by mandate, but under local democratic control.

How does such a service move successfully to a system of provision that is based instead on a commercial model? How does it achieve this in the context of greater independence for schools especially when the Government, in 2003, was so concerned about promoting citizenship education within the curriculum of its schools that it made it a statutory requirement for all secondary pupils? The government is similarly concerned about increasing political participation.

Citizens who are already sceptical, even cynical, about opportunities for real participation in the local politics that matter to them, especially in education, would appear to have justifiable concerns. The tension between the concept of education as a citizenship service and the notion of putting education on a commercial basis is clear. The maximization of markets and private ownership in education conflicts with other social goals. Markets are sectoral and the artificial market created will change the actual nature of the service.

Education is compulsory for the common good. In a true market economy, there is no statutory or compulsory element. However, given that the take-up of the education service is compulsory, this means that the commercial operator has a secure knowledge of the consumer-base upon which to plan for effective and efficient service delivery, even if the ultimate consumers are not the actual customers. The issues move to arguments about efficiency and effectiveness in the context of the loss of democratic public authority and citizenship capacity and to whether the conditions for a full free market economy for education should be created.

Private independent schools

The definitions of private independent schools and state independent school are not simple. As Chapter 2 describes, clarity is blurred because of the historical tradition and the invention of classifications of school status that put the maintenance of state education at a distance from the LEA. However, an adequate working definition of a private independent school, for our purposes, is one at which full-time education is provided but which is not maintained by an LEA and not in receipt of government funding. This means that 'public' schools, private fee-paying schools, charity (not-for-profit) schools and proprietor-owned (for-profit) schools can each be treated as categories of private independent schools. Independent state schools are a difficult breed which are considered later in this chapter and in Chapter 8.

Recalling the history in Chapter 2, an independent school is often described as a 'closed community' because it is 'a private, self-regulating community whose conduct is not specifically regulated by law and which, to that extent, is unaccountable and free to regulate its own affairs within the general framework of the law' (Boyd 2001: 16). Boyd states that the term has important significance in the way these schools have developed, and he goes on to compare characteristics of closed communities such as independent schools, convents and monasteries. He explains that those who join such a community waive a number of their civil liberties, they submit to the jurisdiction of the community but, unlike a cult, they are free to withdraw at any time.

Even today, private independent schools remain largely self-regulating with their own system of ethics, rituals, terminology, rules, sanctions and dress. They are not bound by the National Curriculum or by many of the provisions of the Education Acts. However, they are increasingly affected by legislation in such areas as employment, health and safety and negligence, they are regularly inspected and they have to be responsive to their client group. Therefore, they sit rather more comfortably within a cycle of internal accountability than they do in arguments about democratic authority, citizenship capacity and public accountability. The situation is similar for the predominantly state-funded independent schools, that is, academies, CTCs, foundation schools and independent specialist schools.

'Public' schools in the UK

These historical, often idiosyncratic, private schools in the UK known as 'public' schools sit in quite peculiar market conditions. They are the caricatures that spring to most people's minds when 'private education' is mentioned.

Private education provided by 'public' schools is surely one of the most conservative bastions for the perpetuation of the status quo. Indeed, it is the ancient traditions and cherished practices of many of these historic institutions that attract their clientele. Particular market forces are at work in the top echelons of this traditional private education sector. Whether day or boarding, British public schools enjoy an enviable reputation worldwide. Yet, some recent events erode fundamental educational values and the very basis of these reputations.

During 2003 for instance, some of the most famous public schools were investigated by the Office for Fair Trading for allegations of price fixing. Also, the reporting of the events leading to the departure of the head teacher (known as the head master) from Winchester College depicted a bizarre scene of seeming prejudice and entrenchment. These particular events do not suggest a thoroughly open-minded, transparent and dynamic approach to considerations for change and modernization in education. The government's view of educational improvement and that of the Wykehamists (the name for the people of Winchester College coined after their founder William of Wykeham of 1382) hardly seem congruent, even if the places there are well sought after.

These 'public' schools are clearly elite. Their market is rarefied. Parents who prefer and have access to this type of education for their children can afford to pay fees equivalent to an average annual salary, although one in five parents might receive a scholarship or bursary, providing their children can display appropriate worthiness for admission on criteria determined by the school. Only when these conditions are met can this education be secured. It is difficult to imagine any circumstances where the private provision of the 'public' schools will change significantly in the UK, as those who ascend to the highest political power are usually the products of them.

Arguments about the relative efficiency and effectiveness of such schools are not relevant in the context of the national privatization of education, whether in arrangements of partnership, consortia or sponsorship. These schools often enjoy enormous historic wealth, operate as charities and sell a product that is based on the perpetuation of long-standing tradition; some might say class distinction and snobbery. Even with steep rises in fees, which go towards low pupil–teacher ratios, staff salaries and perks which are usually well above those in the state sector, it is their inherited and capital wealth that fundamentally sustains them. New legislation in the Charities Bill will test the tax breaks some private schools receive by seeking the public benefit they actually offer.

The success of past students in terms of entry into prestigious universities and top jobs secured by their 'old boys' is an impressive measure of their self-perpetuating effectiveness. However, the effectiveness of a national state education system cannot be measured just by the number of university entrants, prime ministers and top corporate directors produced, but an increase in the proportion would be a good sign. As those who ascend to the highest political power are often themselves the products of the elite public schools, it is difficult to imagine any circumstances where the private provision of these schools will change significantly in the UK.

When considering what is meant by 'privatizing education' we are actually envisaging a very different concept indeed to that of the traditional English private schools and the strategic associations in which they sit. The developing proprietor private school and privately sponsored but state independent school cannot be compared with this relatively small-scale model catering predominantly for a particular elite. But some associations are gathering.

Many of the public schools have endowments and special guild interests behind them, particularly the City of London livery companies or religious denominations. As outlined in Chapter 2, many public schools have had commercial support in addition to their income from fees for centuries. Although substantially funded by the DfES through a 'funding agreement', academies, for example, draw their range of policies from this agreement and their school governors from the group of private sponsors rather than from the locally elected members. The expansion of the academies' initiative signals a major shift in sponsorship for state schools from a wider range of sponsors with very different backgrounds which include those with prestigious public school links. Set against this shift is a corresponding decline in the influence of local democracy.

Market forces and private independent education provision

The situation where independent agencies enter the field by offering education on a purely fee-paying basis, is closer to a true market economy. This is quite different from the 'public' school sector described earlier and the large-scale contracting-out of LEA education services and schools, which are dealt with in Chapter 5.

Many examples of such private independent schools and independent school trusts exist and operate on a 'for-profit' or 'not-for-profit' basis. The definition of such schools and services is again, not straightforward. They are usually viable education businesses, sometimes stand-alone firms or institutions, chains of schools and/or other service institutions, or business units within other organizations such as universities or corporate concerns. Whilst there are many such private providers in the UK, for example, Nord Anglia PLC, Capita Strategic Education Services, Cambridge Education Associates and Centre for British Teachers (CfBT), many more operate in other parts of the world where the enrolment into private education is considerably higher than that in the UK. Where the proportion of the private sector school take-up in England is about 7 per cent, in Colombia it is '40 per cent at secondary level; in Argentina and Cote d'Ivoire...30 per cent and 57 per cent respectively' (Tooley 1999: 11). Examples of large-scale education companies reliant entirely on fee income include Objectivo/ UNIP in Brazil, Educor in South Africa and Sabis Education Systems Incorporated in the USA.

Multi-national companies are enlarging as takeovers of smaller firms by larger ones occur, good examples are Serco PLC buying Quality Assurance Associates (QAA) in 2001 and Global Education Management Systems (GEMS) acquiring 3Es Enterprises in 2004 to form 3E-GEMS UK Ltd.

Constant measurement of state education against arbitrary and shifting targets in the UK and elsewhere, coupled with political commentary about the need for improvement in state education, leads to the commonly accepted view that standards are not what they should be. Due to a different set of measures and a different commentary, standards in private independent schools generally are believed to be better. Certainly the practice of maintaining smaller class sizes, a traditional curriculum and a wide extra curricular programme is influential. Whether fact or myth, this view is rarely challenged. Private fee-paying independent schools are popular with politicians; those who believe the myth perpetuate it and those who can afford the private school path often take it. Thus, we have an educational market place highly conducive to the spread of private education and one that clearly motivates 'education-for-profit' proprietor-owned companies.

The profile of such companies shows that they invariably attend to important factors that lead to both educational and business success. They attend to profitability (or at least to securing an annual surplus) and to the innovations that are needed to maintain this. They attend to educational quality by demonstrating performance against specified measures, albeit that those measures are different to those in the state sectors. They attend to codes of fairness and justice within and across the curriculum they deliver.

Medium-sized firms and private provision

An example of a medium-sized, private, 'education-for-profit' firm is GEMS, a subsidiary of the Varkey Group, a Dubai-based firm of private schools, healthcare centres and hospitals owned by Sunny Varkey. In 2003 the UK subsidiary, GEMS UK, owned just two private schools in England,

Bury Lawn School in Milton Keynes and Sherborne School in Hampshire, which were an addition to their ownership of over 30 schools in the United Arab Emirates, the Middle East and the USA. By 2004, GEMS UK had 13 schools in the UK and, with the acquisition of a non-profit company, 3Es, begins 2005 with a much-extended portfolio including significant state school sector contracts and high profile international schools. These acquisitions and others from Nord Anglia PLC make an interesting combination as, whilst GEMS has a home-grown fully private background in Dubai, 3Es had its origins in 1990 as the commercial wing of a state school CTC. It represents the coming together of very different educational cultures and practices.

It is one of GEMS' intentions to establish itself as the largest single provider of private education in the UK. It sees building a chain of affordable private schools in the UK as filling a gap in the education market. The cost of a day-school place at a GEMS' school varies, typically between £5,000 and £10,000 a year (averaging only slightly above the cost of a state secondary school place), compared with almost twice that for a typical private day school and four times that amount in a conventional public boarding school.

An issue for GEMS and for other similar companies is that they do not have the exclusive heritage of the 'public' schools or the reputations of the well-established independent schools. They will need to grow their reputations on the perceived quality of their educational outcomes in these new locations and attempt to preserve something of the ethos of those popular schools they buy, in order to maintain that group of clients and expand it.

The Varkey mission is built around providing good quality services to improve the quality of health care and education, whilst making a commercial profit. The education market in Dubai, of course, is very different from the context of using private firms to improve provision in both the private and the state sectors in England. Nevertheless, there are global affinities. With the current political climate as it is in England encouraging private sponsorship for state independent schools (particularly academies), and with increasing demand from parents for private education, the market opportunities look buoyant. By 2010 the market is likely to be very different. Academies are clearly an attractive proposition to a 'for-profit' organization, not least because the capital costs of setting up new or refurbished prestigious schools are so minimal for the sponsor, as 90 per cent of the costs are met by the taxpayer.

In Dubai, Varkey schools are offered on a differentiated scale of fees, the 'English' schools, with custom-made furniture and 'public' school-type names (Winchester, Westminster and Cambridge) and uniforms, tend to be more expensive than the good quality, but generally larger, 'Indian' schools. with utility furniture, more basic uniform and larger numbers of pupils in the classes. The view is that education can be offered on a star-rating system of schools similar to that used for hotels and restaurants. The provision is shaped to meet the particular market niche in Dubai, and is successful. The same is said for GEMS UK. The analogy reported was that 'schools would provide different levels of service like an airline with a business and "no frills" economy class' (*Times Educational Supplement* 30 July 2004: 7). This service approach will no doubt receive adjustment as GEMS becomes increasingly involved with academies, possibly one in Milton Keynes. The aims of the 200 academies to become excellent schools in those areas of highest disadvantage by 2010 may not fit well alongside a system set upon star-ratings, class differences, screening and not welcoming students with behavioural problems, but time will tell.

However, cross-subsidization of student fees and income to cover overheads across a scale of practice can be a useful model. From within a continuum of provision and fees, education can become privately available to all those in reasonably paid employment. In this model, the poorest are subsidized by the better off, whilst those on lower fees receive decent education but in larger classes with more basic furnishings and equipment, consistent with normal market forces. This practice is effectively internal sponsorship across a group of schools, a fundamental practice in business across profitable and loss-making divisions and across operational practices in a welfare state. This private model clearly has possibilities for successful transfer.

GEMS takes advice from good sources. It has had on its advisory board high profile personnel from Ofsted's past, including former HMCI Mike Tomlinson as the chairman no less, and other well-known names such as Lord David Puttnam and James Sabben-Clare (a former head master of Winchester College) and prominent academics and former civil servants. People who worked for Ofsted in senior roles clearly see big opportunities in this field of private school ownership. Another former HMCI, Chris Woodhead, with his private company Cognita, is also acquiring private schools with an aim not too dissimilar to that of GEMS; it seems that there is going to be a number of large chains of private or independent schools of some sort across England! Cognita has 'a former head of the Walt Disney in Europe among its senior partners and has the broadcaster Sir David Frost on its advisory board' (Stewart 2004a: 8). Association with celebrities has become important in promoting private education it seems, and money attracts. Some would argue that the credibility such names might bring to these chains of school is so far unearned.

GEMS is actively attending to those important factors which bring international confidence in quality assurance, evident in its operational rationale and from its advertising. It brings a well-articulated tradition of 'for-profit' activity based on a fair and just ethic from its track record of private hospital care and international schooling in Dubai and beyond. Cognita also promotes the idea that its schools are to be based on 'traditional values' and deliver the highest possible quality of education using the best possible teachers. As yet there is no track record for Cognita.

However, a visit to some of the Varkey (GEMS) schools in Dubai reveals that many elements of the system are impressive. Most notable is the close attention given to the views of parents. Although resourced without delegation of finance from the company's centre in order to achieve economies of scale (rather like the pre-1988 style LEAs), head teachers are expected to take initiative where they can and get on with the running of their schools. The company provides education for over 40,000 school-aged pupils and students from a variety of nations, many from the Indian subcontinent and some from England, European countries and the USA. Fees range widely from the highest which were almost tenfold that of the cheapest. Education appeared to be of a very acceptable quality across the range, although how schools in this different context would fare against Ofsted criteria is difficult to call, especially with Ofsted using such 'movable' criteria depending upon which sector it is inspecting.

Sponsorship deals in medium-sized privatization arrangements

High levels of awareness and sensitivity relating to social and ethical standards are needed when gaining sponsorship for education and especially within a commercial model. The GEMS model is essentially based on offering school fees fixed against competitive market price levels with corresponding levels of resourcing. Sponsorship is a potential strategy for raising additional resources which can then be used to subsidize the market-cost/price relationship. In order to reduce costs in education significantly, the expenditure on teachers (as they represent by far the most expensive single resource) usually has to be reduced.

Both these elements of class size and sponsorship loomed for GEMS in 2004. At Bury Lawn School it was reported that some parents had removed their children when increases in class sizes were planned to rise from 18 to 24. There were also other expressions of concern. Sponsorship and issues of ethics were raised a month later about GEMS' partnership with a large company with tobacco interests. The partnership was sponsoring fee-paying education in Afghanistan. The tensions are vivid in the reported comments. The words from GEMS chief operating officer emphasized the positive; the project is 'a small step towards achieving a brighter future for the children of Afghanistan. The project reiterates our commitment to spread globally the message of holistic education by instilling ethical values and principles that serve as guiding tools for the next generation to grow into socially responsible citizens' (*Times Educational Supplement* 20 August 2004: 3). The succinct comment from the spokeswoman for Action on Smoking and Health was from a rather different stance. She said that the partnership seemed 'inappropriate at the very least' (ibid.). However, the partnership between the two companies had been forged through other aspects of their mutual business interests in health care and hospitals. Given this, and the immense levels of need for education in Afghanistan, the ethical concerns around such sponsorship reduce in pragmatism, if not in principle.

Any dependency upon sponsorship, especially over the longer term, brings the potential for awkward indebtedness and vulnerability. That accepted, it is best not to be over-precious about sponsorship deals in education. It is inevitable that use of sponsorship in education will expand, as it has in sporting and arts activities. But the educational community is rightly cautious.

When the Reed employment group set aside £500,000 to sponsor schools in their bids for specialist school status, it seemed that the only strings attached were that Reed wished for a strap-line to be added to the schools' letterheads – 'A Reed College of Enterprise'. The request by Reed was small; there were no great expectations such as, for example, wanting the schools to change their names or employ staff through their agencies. The request was that each school, in return for the £50,000 or more sponsorship money, should simply associate their names with Reed in order to promote enterprise. One school's response was that this request was going too far and withdrew. The NUT explained that the problem was that the government was trying to convince people that businesses want to support schools purely out of altruism (*Times Educational Supplement* 17 October 2003: 6). Most head teachers, one might suspect, would have tried to persuade the governors and staff to go with it and print the strap-line on the letterhead. Reed has been successful in helping schools through sponsorship. It has sponsored a number of specialist schools and the academy in Ealing with £2 million.

With government policy favourable to state schools being managed by private firms, and to sponsorship, the future looks positive for medium-sized companies and sponsorship deals in the UK.

Privatization and taxpayers' money

Initiatives, which are wholly private, are quite different from contracted-out public education services and privately funded independent state schools in England, and from charter schools in the USA. In fully private education, taxpayers' money, in whole or in part, is not used to provide the schools. The risks rest entirely with the private company. When services are contracted out to the private sector or when sponsorship funds are central then things become more difficult. In the case of privately contracted-out LEA services, for example, the risk of service failure through less than successful contract delivery remains fundamentally with LEAs or government. It is when there is a mixed economy of private and public money that anxieties are raised.

A concept which persists about extending choice across both private and public schools is the use of vouchers. The idea is that parents might access private provision using state money (in vouchers), which would otherwise be spent on state schools. With the final demise of the assisted places scheme in 2004, vouchers could well re-emerge as a political route to channelling public money towards private school provision. Indeed, although ruled out by the Government in its five-year strategy, it is one of the Conservative opposition promises to provide vouchers of £5,500 for the purchase of private core education. The idea is not unpopular with many parents; it is making such a system work in practice that will continue to challenge those who favour a voucher mechanism. Voucher schemes are easily abused by some users and fail to drive potential investment to where it is needed early enough.

State education in many countries does not come free of costs to families. Although in the UK, parents are used to indirect costs for uniforms, writing and curriculum materials, sports activities and voluntary contributions to educational visits the school might make, in other countries direct costs are frequently levied on basic provision. Incremental rises in fees or charging policies can be successful in raising income without loss of customers once pupils are enrolled. Similar incremental increases are justified for charging for aspects of state education; indeed these have occurred for access to serious instrumental music teaching in many state schools in England.

When relative costs to the taxpayer are examined, it is worth turning ones attention to the fees that are paid to the corporate management and accountancy consultancy firms who advise on system change. These firms are used by government and LEAs to scope and to specify the contractual terms that will lead privatization deals, especially in large-scale transactions. Names such as PWC, KPMG and Deloitte Touche spring up frequently in the literature as highly active in education privatization deals. It is often argued that the fees paid to these firms for the functions they carry out in the technicalities of system change could be better spent directly on the existing system of education.

Market economies and large-scale contracted-out education services

The market-driven economy of private schools is rather different from that of the large-scale provision of statutory state education for all, although government policy towards creating state independent schools is likely to cause large-scale services to diminish. In discussing large-scale education privatization there are perhaps five main considerations.

First, identifying the consumer of the education service is complex. Most teachers and governors will claim it is the pupils; for politicians more likely it is the parents and the taxpayers. However, when it comes to letting education contracts to the private sector, it is the LEAs who will usually hold the contracts, but it is the government, in the form of the DfES, which approve and hold the list of those private firms considered able to tender.

The customer is therefore the government, or at best the LEAs are under government influence. It is possible that the interests of the ultimate consumers, the parents and pupils, may not be best met in this scenario. The local democratic procedure of electing a local council which is held accountable by local voters is bypassed when government, not the actual users of the education service, drives on the establishment of a private contractor provider. There are many situations where the interests of government, local councils (especially where the administration is politically of a different persuasion to that of the government) and parents and pupils are not similar. In these circumstances, the best principles of democracy and participatory citizenship are not upheld.

Second, the point at which strategic leadership of the education service is determined and described is vital. Where the local council is of a different political majority to the government of the day, then there is potential for local stalling on national imperatives. By setting out a contract specification for the private sector which includes strategic leadership, the role of the democratically elected council moves to one of holding accountability for contract monitoring, rather than providing a political steer for its own chief officer to execute by contract or otherwise. Indeed in the early stages of the intervention in Walsall, and the development of the Strategic Partnership, there were immediate differences of opinion over the meaning of the wording of the leadership functions as set out in the new CEO's job description and the expectations of the DfES civil servants. Terms such as 'strategic management' need careful and specific definition when used in the context of PPP in an education department which has corporate responsibilities across the whole council.

Third, the main aim of a private firm is to satisfy shareholders and increase shareholder profit. Although this is a valid aim in the true market-driven argument of retaining high efficiency and effectiveness so as to retain market share and not lose business, it is less convincing when the market is actually a statutory education service. How the original selection of those large companies onto the government list of approved education service providers was made is not clear. It seemingly was based on their success in general management of large strategic projects in a range of commercial and industrial pursuits. Subsequently, these companies often linked up with smaller educational businesses to bring that expertise, for example Serco PLC with QAA. However, with the entry of small to medium-sized educational businesses which have education as their core business, and the unremarkable performances of some of the large companies, such as WS Atkins Ltd, then a shift in direction may result.

Fourth, this selection of private firms onto the approved list of education service providers seems to depend very much on the assumption that general management skills are more important than those educational attributes specific to the service needed to be improved. The large firms bidding for educational services contracts were often without educational expertise.

They needed the transfer of personnel from the public sector to their private company, as it was the public sector which held a virtual monopoly of skills in the education field. It had been the public sector that had made the investment to train and maintain the expertise. Even when a huge and diverse international company like Serco PLC, for example, took over the education services in Bradford and in Walsall, most of its education personnel in these two locations were attracted from the public services. Their personnel were from:

- other LEAs;
- the LEAs being privatized who moved under local Transfer of Undertakings (Protection of Employment) (TUPE) arrangements; or from
- takeovers of other companies, for example, QAA who generally had employed or hired mainstream public education professionals in the first place.

It was factors such as these that gave additional confidence about Serco PLC's ability to succeed in the relatively short term of their initial contract of five years. When large contracts let by the government change hands, for example, in 2004 when Capita Strategic Education Services won the contract and took over from the CfBT for the primary and KS 3 strategies, about 300 staff including the two leading players moved across on identical terms and conditions. The strategic leadership and management framework provided by the private company Capita might be seen as important in the procurement and the contract award and so signal potential improvement, but it is the talents of individuals that are fundamental. The people matter more than who actually employs them. I suspect that the majority of this 300 originally came through the ranks and training provided by LEAs also.

Finally, the success of private firms lies in their ability to identify their target market, as is the case with the English 'public' schools and private independent schools as explained earlier. The option of determining who the private firm wishes its customers to be is not available in the work of delivering national state education in contracted-out provision or independent state schools, unless it views it appropriate that some children should not be offered education at all. This is clearly unacceptable in a contracted-out public education service facing statutory obligations.

In 2001, 11 new education partnerships with the private sector were announced by the then Secretary of State for Education and Skills, with a £1.8 million commitment from taxpayers' money towards set-up costs. These were called New Models Projects but not much was new about them. They appeared to be more of the same private sector names that were already involved in contracted-out provision, but set in a series of government-sponsored partnerships with selected LEAs and groups of LEAs.

State schools and small-scale private partnerships

Since the moves to give some state schools in England more entrepreneurial freedoms by providing GM school status in the early 1990s, there has been a continued impetus by different governments in stimulating small-scale private entrepreneurial endeavour by creating different categories of schools and small-scale formal partnerships. Bidding for money or special status has characterized the process. Those schools with influential associations and the resources to make strong bids have generally been the most successful.

GM schools have now gone but they set up an unhealthy legacy of school against school. Having extra funding, the so-called freedoms from LEA constraints and competitive motives, caused many GM schools to go their own way. Although some were highly successful, the move did little to promote genuinely inclusive education and collaboration between schools.

My experience in 1999 in Bromley LEA, where all but one of the secondary schools had moved to GM status, largely confirmed that feeling. Whereas many were academically successful, issues around inclusion and citizenship demonstrated weaknesses in this type of school autonomy. It was here that the widely reported GM school head teacher had managed to embezzle over £500,000, despite a glowing Ofsted report three years earlier. A one-off, half hour visit to the school (to try to sell LEA services in this supercharged world of GM schools) set alarm bells ringing. In parallel, visits by a member of the LEA finance team and follow-up review by the LEA principal inspector began the uncovering a very sordid story and eventually, with diocesan help, the road to repair for the school. The GM movement was as much about school independence and competition as it was privatization, sponsorship and private business involvement. New moves to increase school autonomy for more schools through 'foundation status' will need better safeguards than those that were in place for GM schools then.

Independent specialist schools and academies are now in the ascendancy. These schemes are based on a different rationale to that of the GM school concept and instead on the positive premise of schools and other agencies working in partnership. There is an important element of private sponsorship, £50,000 for a specialist school bid, and about 10 per cent of private sponsorship for the capital cost an academy proposal. These schools, although in the state sector, enjoy levels of autonomy and independence not associated with a traditional state school.

No school wishes to be seen as 'bog standard', nor should it. The way to avoid such a label is to achieve success for all its students. Achieving specialist school status of some sort becomes the priority for most schools. When the idea of creating specialist schools was first announced it was limited to about 10 per cent of schools and was therefore competitive. This was soon raised to 50 per cent of schools and subsequently to just about all secondary schools. The competitiveness has been removed. The extra funding which schools have received creates a sense that the specialist schools scheme itself has been successful. Yet, it became little more than a label behind which to provide more government resources to schools. Schools with good network connections, capacity and skills to prepare successful bids find bidding straightforward. For those that do not, then the spiral of bidding can work against them further. Raising the £50,000 from private sponsorship in those circumstances simply distracts the school from its true purpose. These issues about academies, specialist schools and special projects such as EAZs are examined further in Chapter 8.

Other partnership schemes operate around outreach work from Beacon Schools, Advanced Beacon Schools and those schools with Advanced Skills Teachers (AST). EAZ and EiC programmes were further examples of partnership and cooperative measures, introduced by the government to improve educational achievement and promote social inclusion in disadvantaged areas. EAZs required private funding contributions, the EiC did not. However, it is reported by Ofsted that it is the EiC programmes that have been more effective in achieving the programme objectives. There is clearly a need to consider the nature of these small-scale private contributions within the state sector and attempt to simplify the range of new categories of schools and the separate sources of funding and the bidding rules attached to them.

Implications for the future

There is a lack of research on the impact of privatization and the range of so-called partnerships in education. Policy in these aspects assumes benefit but with little factual evidence as to whether standards and effectiveness are improving because of these new relationships. With such a clear, determined and democratically elected will to expand private partnerships throughout education, the stakeholders have little alternative but to put effort into those policy directions, whether they prove to be more effective or not. Privatization may strengthen education immeasurably but it also threatens to weaken the leadership of communities of schools and local participation in their traditional LEA and corporate services.

The trend is politically unchallenged; in England it is led by the Labour Government which has broadly adopted similar policies in this regard to the previous Conservative Government. The approach is heavily managerial as it is in the USA, Australia and New Zealand. Global trends and national demands for modernization see PPPs as the way forward. These will need to be implemented and managed effectively by the professional communities working inside their democratic ideals and contract specifications.

The responses to bidding involving private sector input, in England for example in the EAZs, show the difficulties that many private firms envisage in making a profit from running schools and education services, it is the wider associations of major capital schemes and utility service provision in PFI type arrangements that are more attractive to most commercial interests. Capital investment in school buildings in England has increased seven fold in seven years. With such a high level of new building, and the interest and prestige associated with new educational plant, sponsors' attention has been caught. Entrepreneurial activity and investment in fully privatized independent schooling and in sponsoring independent state schools represent different options to those of the time of the EAZs, but not without risk and challenge to those on both sides of the traded relationship.

The use of private sector business relationships with state schools and LEAs change the character of the education service. Private investment and sponsorship increases the education resource but in a relatively small proportion. Privatization is seen to reduce democratic activity, which in turn undermines political interest, entitlement and rights, fundamental elements of participatory citizenship. This is occurring at a time of democratic renewal in local government with, for example, the separation of executive and scrutiny functions in councils and LEAs. Scrutiny roles will be increasingly important in the democratic process.

An in-depth, independent research is due. Research into the comparative levels of fees paid to the large management consultancy firms and lawyers since entering the era of education partnership development could be revealing. Huge amounts have been paid to secure proper procurement of private services, but there is little to indicate that the output by many private firms has brought significant improvement to education that could not have been achieved at less expense.

Researchers often write for each other and remain within the bounds of established academic literature. The impact of private–public partnerships in education has not been probed in breadth or with full academic rigour. On this aspect of policy, we tend to remain at this state of commentary and patchwork opinion. Government inspectorates are rarely independent and free of the baggage of central policy and they often seem impeded by over-scheduling or pre-determined expectation.

One promising research study was started in 2000 by the Open University (OU) on *Reframing Educational Governance at Local Level* (REGALL) (Open University 2000), which is conducting case studies of LEA intervention and outsourcing to private companies. It focuses principally on two (or if grants allow three) new models of service provision closely interlinked with the associated elective structures. It aims to examine local democratic accountability, impact on school performance and the perceived distinctive benefits and disadvantages brought by the private sector organizations. The findings of this type of work, linked to other specific evaluations, such as that being undertaken on academies will provide insight into the best ways for development.

There are many important areas for research to be undertaken into the effectiveness of the performance of partnership and privatized endeavour in school and education services. Indications of significant success from the decade 1995 to 2005 are present but overall are not yet convincing. However, with £51 billion being spent on education in England in 2005, and rising, the preliminary reluctance of the commercial world is perhaps beginning to be overcome. The comparative performance of the private sector in terms of improved educational effectiveness and citizenship participation should interest the world of researchers increasingly.

4 Sources of evidence, audit and inspection of education

> Peace, commerce and honest friendship with all – entangling alliances with none...To seek out the best we must resort to other information, which, from the best of men, acting disinterestedly and with the purest motives is sometimes incorrect.
>
> (Thomas Jefferson 1743–1826)

Private sector participation has had great impact on inspection regimes in England. This chapter includes consideration of the inspection of state and private independent schools, the inspection of LEAs and the inspection of corporate local authority functions. There is a plethora of inspection information, so-called evidence about the performance of schools and education services, coming particularly from the various elements of Ofsted and the AC.

The basic principle of inspection is well accepted, 'inspection has always been close observation exercised with an open mind by persons with appropriate experience and a framework of relevant principles' (Browne 2003: 2).

Inspection has two distinct aspects to its privatized associations.

1 Since 1992, for most state schools, inspection has been a privatized function of Ofsted. Ofsted itself is a non-ministerial government department which, amongst many of its functions, commissions the private sector to carry out inspections of state schools. The extent of this privatized function is seriously receding in 2005. It is these inspections of state schools which have had such a huge impact since they were introduced. Other aspects of Ofsted's work are not privatized. The inspection of LEAs and local councils is provided by the non-privatized parts of Ofsted comprising HMI and supported by other agencies such as the AC.

2 The findings from inspection are of great importance in informing both local and central government decisions about privatizing education

services and about action to be taken where less than satisfactory school or LEA performance is found. The distinction which is necessary is between the non-ministerial government department of Ofsted, termed here 'Ofsted/HMI', and the privatized bodies which tender for their work, termed 'Ofsted/contracted inspectors'. This division and terminology are not commonly used; Ofsted sails under one flag for both parts, in the full spirit of public–private partnership!

The relationships which exist between the inspectors and those inspected and the traditions which have shaped the way inspections are conducted have a mix of origins. The influence of the private sector's involvement is relatively recent. The origins of Ofsted are well documented from different perspectives; see for example, *School Inspection* (Brighouse and Moon 1995). Nevertheless, it is worth clarifying briefly the origins of the different groups of inspectors and how they come to be in this business in the first place.

Her Majesty's Inspectors (HMI) of Schools

HMI have a long tradition which dates back to before the 1870 Education Act. The first HMI were in fact appointed in the 1830s by a King's Council. The principle of this practice has been preserved and it is this direct link to the King or Queen that was claimed to give some assurance of HMI's independence of view that has to be doubtful. 'Never at any point in its history was HMI wholly or constitutionally independent of government' (Woodhead (quoting Bolton) 2002: 106). Nevertheless, these early origins confirm HMI's direct interest in the performance of individual schools. This long history explains something of their guarded traditions and their often perceived squire-like bearing. They pre-date even those early school boards and LEAs. 'HMI have worked to a tradition that long pre-dates Ofsted encapsulated by the notion "doing good as they go"' (Matthews and Sammons 2004: 18). A certain heroism can sometimes be detected in their style.

HMI were, and generally still are, regarded as distinguished educators. Indeed, Leonard Horner, probably the most outstanding of the first group of HMIs, appointed in 1833, and Christian Schiller and Robin Tanner, who became HMIs in the first half of the twentieth century, still resound as revered names around particular sectors of the educational community. Personally, I can remember many HMIs as helpful and as influential on my early teaching career and in my headships. I also have memories of meeting some rather formidable and highly idiosyncratic characters in HMI whose priorities were exclusively their own. HMI do much good work. Their core work though faces government and was always at a level closer to government ministers than to schools and their communities. They did run good quality courses for teachers and regularly shared their regional and national perceptions of educational standards with local advisers.

Local Education Authority (LEA) inspectors and advisers

HMI are not the same as LEA inspectors and advisers. LEA inspectors and advisers are much more 'hands-on' people and are employed in the local government service by the LEAs. As a service they came into being in the early 1900s and had a greater direct impact on schools than HMI, partly because they were clearly good practitioners and mainly because of their ongoing contact with schools in a particular area. It was the LEA role that was the most significant and the most immediate in ensuring continuous improvement in quality, in raising standards and promoting the personal development of pupils and the professional development of staff, at least in some LEAs. Many teachers, myself included, are quick to sing the praises of the influences of LEA advisers on improving their teaching skills. However, the experience of other teachers and head teachers in some LEAs were not similar and they would complain of rarely seeing an inspector or adviser during their years in schools. The system was patchy. It could not be relied upon to report on school performance nor to support or challenge teachers across the 30,000 schools or so across England and Wales.

The Government's actions of the 1990s removed most of the funding base for LEA inspectors and advisers. Why? 'They did it partly out of frustration at the ineffectiveness of the way some LEAs had operated in the matter of school accountability; partly out of the realization that if GM status was to be the means of creating a new market-driven sector in the public education service there had to be some means of informing parents in the market-place about the quality of the goods they were about to purchase; and partly as a further salvo in the long-running battle between central and local government over the balance of power in the control of public services' (DuQuesnay 1995: 105, 106).

As national politics and national politicians have claimed education for their own centre stage, a national system of school inspection, using the newly privatized sector, was seen as the way to gather evidence on school standards. The assumption is that schools should also use the private sector to help with the actions to be taken in response to the key issues that systematic inspection identifies. This expectation increasingly marginalized the role of the remaining LEA advisers to work on only the weakest schools. These advisers are now approaching the point of extinction for secondary schools and heavily reduced for primary schools, yet the entry of alternative providers into this part of the education market has not occurred effectively.

The Audit Commission (AC)

Although the practice of public audit goes back to the 1840s, compared to HMI and LEA inspectors and advisers, the AC is a very new breed with its origins in the 1982 Local Government Finance Act. It operates independently and derives most of its income from the fees charged to audit bodies. Financial regulation is its background, but since 1997 it has had a broader remit which includes appointing LEA local auditors, monitoring performance against simplified indicators and published criteria, leading Best Value reviews and giving guidance on achieving economy, efficiency and effectiveness. The Commission has had little to do with schools directly; education was not the Commission's background. However, in its role of promoting the best use of public money, it has become very much involved in education. HMI have called upon the AC to assist in the inspection of LEAs, a feature which is explained within the case study in Chapter 6.

The arrival of the Office for Standards in Education (Ofsted)

The 1992 Education Act brought about the privatization of a national inspection service for schools which impacted upon the roles of both HMI and LEA inspectors and advisers and drew new alliances with the AC in 1997.

Chris Woodhead became HM Chief Inspector of Schools (HMCI), as the first head of the new Ofsted. Ofsted had a wider brief than just school and LEA inspections but essentially its prime responsibility for which it became best known was for making inspection reports about schools very public. It managed the contracting-out of school inspections and monitored schools causing concern. Responsibilities included advising the Secretary of State and ensuring published inspection reports about:

- the quality and standards of education and the leadership and management of schools;
- whether the financial resources of schools are managed efficiently;
- the spiritual, moral, social and cultural development of pupils.

From 1992, HMI ran Ofsted (Ofsted/HMI) which held the oversight for the national inspection system. The work of carrying out most inspections of state schools (Section 10 inspections) fell to private contractors using independent inspectors (Ofsted/contracted inspectors) who had set themselves up in the newly developing education market place. These contractors employed freelance inspectors to carry out the inspections under contract. Ofsted/HMI maintained a register of the trained lead Ofsted/contracted inspectors, known as registered inspectors (RgIs) who led the inspection teams set up by the contracting companies. The Ofsted/contracted inspectors were often ex-LEA advisers and inspectors and ex-HMI. Many others were actively employed LEA inspectors and advisers who found themselves caught up within the change to a trading culture within their LEAs. Most LEAs were involved in setting up their school improvement functions as trading/business units as a part of their new 'arms-length' role with schools.

The schools were being encouraged, by government, to become ever more autonomous, self-managing and competitive.

The pool of Ofsted/contracted inspectors also had the addition of lay inspectors, a few of whom became lead RgIs. The law required at least one trained lay inspector to be in each school inspection team. 'Lay inspectors were probably created as a symbolic representation of the public interest and as a reminder from government to teachers and inspectors that they should not claim exclusive rights to the ownership of the education process' (Ferguson *et al.* 2000). However, as it turned out, lay inspectors added a clearly positive dimension. 'Headteachers particularly appreciate the lay inspector's ability to ask the unexpected question and their good interpersonal skills' (Ofsted 1995).

Hence the privatization of school inspection had begun. It took the 1992 Education Act and the privatization of the Ofsted school inspection process to bring about the comprehensive inspection of schools in England and Wales and with it a broad constituent membership of the central Ofsted/HMI and the privatized Ofsted/contracted inspectors.

Inspection coverage by Ofsted's two faces

Although much contention surrounded Ofsted inspections, generally they were well received by the schools and by the public. It was the expansion of the privatized side of the regime with the Ofsted/contracted inspectors which made the hugely increased coverage possible. The impact of school inspections was undoubtedly due to the radically different approach brought through the creation of a market and the privatization of this sector of the education service. This was helped by the publication of a series of agreed frameworks for inspection and other openly available supporting documentation.

The positive reception and influence of Ofsted inspections is extensively reported in *Improvement through Inspection: An Evaluation of the Impact of Ofsted's Work* (Matthews and Sammons 2004). This well-researched analysis draws out not only the Ofsted/HMI roles but also the significance of the scale of the contracted out school inspections. This brought about 'a private sector, quality assured market, capable of delivering a wide range of DfES and government initiatives in addition to inspection' (ibid.: 136). These include activities such as performance management, training for head teachers and the assessment of ASTs. The impact of the private dimension to the development of the national inspection system that has developed, is the key to its success. It was privatization that opened up the previously constrained system so dramatically and brought new impetus to the process. The cost has to be measured against a range of indicators and this includes losses in the local inspection and advisory services, which had had their previous government funding 'top-sliced' in order to stimulate a market for their services driven by inspection findings and schools.

Informative though this evaluation (Matthews and Sammons 2004) is, like other Ofsted joint publications, it loses something of its quality of independence and transparency. It was conducted jointly by a commissioned university and Ofsted/HMI itself. Ofsted/HMI does suffer from the accusation of too much 'circularity', that is, it often uses its own information to evaluate its own work. Furthermore, it is too frequently around the full circumference of the circle of educational activity. The extent of the Ofsted database, containing information drawn from thousands of inspections, makes highly reliable sample sizes. Analyses however are weakened when Ofsted/HMI itself tends to lead on them and then use outcomes to inform the synthesis of new ideas which in turn become the subject of further inspection. Commissioning true independents to analyse and synthesize ideas which reliably emerge from the aggregation of their data collection would help transparency.

Ofsted/HMI also retains an outmoded preciousness. For example, requests to have access to a reference source listed in the bibliography of this publicly available evaluation were denied – quaint practice from a so-called open agency close to a government with a modernizing agenda!

Accountability in education has increased hugely and the power and influence of the inspection regimes are infinitely greater now than they used to be, hence the need for crystal transparency and real trust. 'Inspection has an important role in responding to the new forms of questioning, but also in fostering public trust in the nation's schools' (Brighouse and Moon 1995: 174).

Evaluation of Ofsted's work has not objectively ascertained the relative strengths and weaknesses, or the potential for further improvement, of the partnership between the two sides of Ofsted, the 'central' Ofsted/HMI wing and the more flexible and privatized Ofsted/contracted inspector wing. Ofsted has tended to be blurred into one, but these wings have had roles which have been quite different. From 2005, under the Education Act 2005 and a 'new relationship with schools' Ofsted looks set to continue but with the role of the private sector diminished and with the new independent contractors, the Regional Inspection Service Providers (RISPs), almost co-inhabiting the Ofsted/HMI regional offices. The pattern looks good for greater efficiency but maybe not for improved transparency.

Inspection of LEAs

The inspection of LEAs was not a privatized function. Responsibility was given to HMI/Ofsted who retained the function within the 1997 Ofsted arrangements. HMCI arranges inspections of LEAs at his discretion or as requested by the Secretary of State. In these inspection activities Ofsted/HMI work closely with the AC. The first cycle of the 150 LEA inspections was completed by 2001 (when most schools had been inspected twice). It is the critical findings of these inspections that has brought government intervention and the subsequent involvement of the private sector into the running of LEAs, for example in the London Borough of Southwark, Walsall and Bradford. Private sector involvement can clearly help struggling LEAs. However the criteria used by government to weigh inspection 'evidence' and judge whether it warrants intervention or some other form of action is unclear. For intervention to be used in some LEAs and yet not in others which are equally struggling suggests possible motives apart from the expedient improvement of education services.

Ofsted's role in the inspection of state schools

The rules changed frequently through the first decade of Ofsted's existence. For state schools there had been five different versions of the Inspection Framework containing increasingly stringent inspection criteria, with Bell (2004a) announcing a major overhaul with new and very different structures, procedures and criteria from September 2005 (Section 5 inspections). The system has been undoubtedly tough on schools, generally welcomed by them and particularly by those who have fared well, either in the inspections or subsequently.

Schools also have different sorts of exposure to Ofsted. Inspections of state schools were usually carried out by Ofsted/contracted inspectors, whilst follow-up monitoring inspection work in those schools deemed to be causing concern and needing urgent improvement was carried out by HMI/Ofsted. HMI/Ofsted inspects schools too. The system of inspection is undoubtedly very intrusive and many teachers and head teachers had some justifiable complaints to make, some are considered later in this chapter. Nevertheless, this partnership arrangement between the Ofsted/contracted inspectors and Ofsted/HMI parts of the system, operating in tandem, is thought to have worked well. It was certainly known to have rigorous impact on bringing improvement in state schools that caused concern. Clearly more of the same is not needed as Ofsted look to make improvements for the future. However, to diminish the market-driven side of Ofsted for reasons of costcutting expediency defeats the very purpose of the market development. There is a sense that rather than going forward in the newly created market environment, things might slip backwards towards a mechanistic civil service type approach. Some of the fringe non-privatized activity has not been a part of the mainstream success.

Ofsted's role in the inspection of independent private schools

The Ofsted/contracted inspectors have been deployed, almost wholly, in the inspection of state schools and not to private schools. Ofsted/HMI inspects independent schools other than those belonging to the Independent Schools Council (ISC) which are inspected by the Independent Schools Inspectorate (ISI), the operationally independent arm of the Council. Ofsted/HMI monitors these ISI inspections as it does the work of the Ofsted/contracted inspectors of state schools.

At a time when state education is being encouraged to work more closely with the independent sector, and vice versa, it is important to recognize the gaping differences in the standards applied in the different inspection regimes in late 2004. Would independent schools, as they are encouraged to draw closer to the lives of state schools be open to the rigours applied in state school inspection?

The private independent sector 'contains many schools that are very good but it also includes schools that are among the worst in the country. This is so because, for almost 60 years, legislation relating to the registration of independent schools...did not do enough to force such schools either to improve or close...One of the arguments for light regulation in the independent sector was that market forces should result in poor schools going out of business and good schools prospering. But to work effectively a market needs reliable and easily available information...' (Matthews and Sammons 2004: 47).

Following the Education Act 2002, Ofsted/HMI had carried out around 60 inspections of independent schools by July 2004. The DfES subsequently asked 95 per cent of those schools inspected to produce action plans to deal with areas of non-compliance. The market of parental consumer choice seemingly has not held these independent schools to account as rigorously as the inspection regime has for state schools, at least not with regard to statutory compliance. But then is compliance what fee-paying parents want? Indeed is it what parents of state school pupils want?

An increasing number of state schools are being granted 'independent' status (e.g. academies, operating under 'funding agreement' rules which often bypass statutory compliances and government guidance). Even though academies are subject to Ofsted inspection, are there not important issues to consider about the equal application of inspection criteria to independent schools in general? For example, why do Ofsted/contracted inspectors not feature more in the inspection of most independent private schools? Who regulates and moderates the quality of Ofsted/HMI inspection of independent schools? As the private and state systems are drawn closer together there is an urgent need to level the ground from which they are both measured.

The situation reported, by Ofsted/HMI, on the quality of the inspections of independent schools conducted by the ISI show major deficits in this system.

To improve the quality of inspections:

- ISI must ensure that inspectors are aware of the need, not only to cover statutory requirements, but also to emphasize the importance of thorough procedures for doing this.
- ISI should ensure that reporting inspectors and team inspectors have all the necessary information about the nature of the inspection and details about previous inspections.

(Ofsted 2004a: 5)

It would seem that the experience of inspection for independent schools is somewhat lighter and the findings less reliable than for state schools. Compared to state school inspection, the inspections of independent schools appear a little off the pace. Judgements being made on the performance of private independent schools against government requirements, and pupils' achievement and progress against national benchmarks lack the rigour that is needed, if the independent and state school accountabilities are to move closer together. The rigours brought to inspection by the Ofsted/contracted inspector regime is perhaps what needs to be increased in 2005 rather than letting parts of the schooling system slip into a new wave of self-evaluation with little understanding of comparative expectations.

Inspecting performance on bigger ideas

Ofsted/HMI, with the AC, have inspected LEAs since 1997. Although the early experiences were sometimes fraught, especially those of LEAs which became subject to government intervention; overall the process was positive. Following the implementation of the Local Government Act (2000) these inspections focused increasingly on aspects of strategic leadership and particularly community renewal. This has drawn both LEAs and schools into a complex interrelationship in terms of the scrutiny of their strategic impact on tackling the causes of underachievement, social and educational exclusion. Self-managing schools, previously often keen to distance themselves from their former pre-1990 ties with their LEAs have been gradually drawn back to play their part in the modern local governance agenda of community leadership, strategic planning and renewal.

Schools have been drawn back from being expected to be in direct competition with each other. However, a decade which has encouraged keen competitiveness and pitched school against school is not swiftly reduced in the dispositions of many head teachers, governors and parents. A likely invitation to be part of the Local Strategic Partnership (LSP) of community stakeholders is a pale influence compared to that of the motivation for school expansion or survival.

Due to this broader interest in services to the community and since the Education Act 2002, the use of inspection has extended considerably. It has moved well beyond the classroom, the school and the education department within the LEA and the independent school sector. It has moved into inquiry about the quality of local government and the participation by local people in determining their needs and priorities. The Government's *Five Year Strategy for Children and Learners* (DfES 2004a) takes on these wider notions of community well-being and confirms the need for measures of performance within this extended education service concept.

The changes in the Ofsted frameworks for the inspection of schools and the inspection of LEAs reflect these moves. Greater emphasis is placed on making judgements about the quality of a school's partnerships with parents, with other schools and community stakeholders, and for LEAs on their councils' corporate structures, strategic planning and partnership arrangements. There can be no question that this is anything other than a positive development. Schools and education services have essentially a leading role in improving relationships and building capacity for community regeneration. Schools know the theory of this very well, but the competitive imperatives placed upon them by successive political leaderships over more than a decade have taught them to seek other measures of success as their priority.

Communities need to draw confidence from the findings of their inspections and be motivated to improve the quality of life for their constituents by wanting to participate and act upon recommendations. Given the great complexity of this, the flexibility of the private sector probably provides more opportunity for fresh thinking about how this might be achieved than in the status quo of the current inspection and audit regimes. Producing more layers of similar enquiry with even greater rhetoric about the importance of self-evaluation than before, is not the best way forward. More involvement of locally elected representatives in determining the development of new independent inspection approaches for a much wider vision is due.

Shifts in inspection emphasis

A more coordinated approach is needed. Aspirations for more effective 'joined-up working' in line with the agenda for the reform of public services are voiced. However, it will take radical changes in the ethos of school inspection and the inspection of the education services to respond adequately and sufficiently quickly to the rigours of these community-orientated criteria.

System changes brought from the private sector may accelerate moves towards greater commitment to economic and community regeneration but the measures of success for this, like those for social inclusion, are very different from those conventionally used by Ofsted to measure achievement and attainment. There is little problem in convincing school governors and head teachers of the philosophical argument that schools should and do make significant contributions to community regeneration. Many schools, with open attitudes, help to build social and economic capacity very effectively. A good school is the sort of place 'where family and friendship networks are developed; through being a place where shared values and mutual respect are actively promoted, and through being a place where more vulnerable parents and pupils can feel safe enough to go for help' (Allen 2003: 7). This aspiration, however, is not characterized by perceptions generally held about the key criteria which influence Ofsted's main judgements and schools' league table positions.

People affected by inspection know how improvements in attainment scores and comparative measures of achievement dominate the reports written about their schools and services. Also, perceptions of the ethos of private commercial companies and contract-driven practices do not fit comfortably with this greater aspiration. The popular managerial approach that prevails in this whole environment does not raise levels of confidence about shifting this dominance.

A widely accepted and promoted principle of school improvement is that it should be based on evidence about relative performance in comparative situations. This is fine whilst the focus of education is on specifics, for example, improving reading competence or raising attainment scores in mathematics. But when the aspirations are wider reaching then judgements based on comparative performance can be too constraining unless highly sophisticated sets of information are used.

Reliance on data

The prescription of inspection, and in the criteria used in making judgements, highlight the difficulty schools and school systems can have in adjusting their aims and priorities according to real social and educational need. There is often a contradiction between what is called for in education and what is measured and reported upon in inspections. For example, a positive feature of many schools is success with social and educational inclusion of pupils, with pupils, for example who do not take to school easily.

There is, however, wide disparity between schools. On the one hand, there are schools which frequently admit pupils who have been excluded from other schools and integrate pupils from special schools. On the other, there are schools which, in a desire to protect their attainment ratings, are selective in the pupils they admit.

Socially inclusive schools design educational programmes around their pupils' needs and trust that the outcomes are sufficient to show up well in real terms and possibly in the various league tables. Of course, these improvements often do not show in the league tables. The outcomes, for example, can be very successful in terms of better attendance, lower rates of exclusion and improved social and educational adjustment for pupils, who have had difficulty in even attending schools elsewhere and in behaving appropriately. Although pupils' spiritual, moral, social and cultural development is judged in school inspection reports, they are not shown in the league tables of schools' performance. Even where outcomes are not that good, these schools can still be much better places for pupils than those of their previous experiences.

It can be difficult to write up the true successes of such schools in Ofsted reports. This is because the emphasis in the inspection framework is on analysing comparative performance against the previous report, against all other schools and against the so-called similar schools. The 'similarities' of so-called similar schools exist often only in the government's classification figures, drawn from census material, which are confined to eligibility levels for free school meals and past academic performance data. Similarities in ethos, philosophy, perceived purpose and the approaches employed by such schools to deal with the needs of children who present for school (or who do not present), often difficult young people from very different circumstances, do not feature in the data-driven comparative gradings. It is also interesting to compare the changes in the classification grades when the source of comparative information shifted from the 1991 census to the 2001 census. Comparative data from the new decade often put schools in a very different light to the one shone for the previous year!

It is for the inspection team to tease out the arguments for a school's success and explain away any backdrop of attainment at C, D or E grades produced by the data for fictionally averaged similar schools! This can be infinitely more difficult than simply plumping for 'serious weaknesses' or 'special measures', when the grade comparisons suggest that judgements might go in that direction. In fairness, work to improve the comparative performance and assessment data about schools is set to influence the inspection process positively, post 2005.

It is for these reasons that it is unwise to pursue a path for inspection which diminishes the role of the team of inspectors in school and relies over-heavily on data and information analysis. There are many examples reported of the 'iniquity of Ofsted', especially where schools have made relatively successful attempts at inclusion. 'Labelling a struggling school as being in special measures is draconian and counter productive . . . the treachery is in inverse proportion to the help and support previously offered to the school' (Taylor 2004: 21). Whether private teams or HMI conduct inspections in the future, the resources to do so must include sufficient time in school for careful observation and analysis of what the school is actually achieving and not rely on the neat data crunching and self-review documentation which can be highly unreliable.

Changes in the inspection relationships

With the launch of *A New Relationship with Schools* (NRWS) (Ofsted 2004d), a climate of greater trust between schools and the Government, and a light touch inspection regime which will place greater emphasis on schools' self-evaluations (an aspiration incidentally of frameworks since 2000 not convincingly realized) is heralded. Nevertheless, the national policies which steer schools and LEAs and which are the basis on which they are inspected remain contradictory. This contradiction is over what the inspection process is really seeking to report. It is not genuinely reporting on schools' abilities to build social capital (e.g. networks for families and friends, promotion of mutual respect, places where the vulnerable might be supported). It continues the trend of reporting on attainment outcomes based on comparisons of their test results against other schools and on broad principles listed in *Every Child Matters* (DFES 2004b), principles which do begin to shift the focus in the right direction.

There is also the contradiction about new inspection procedures acknowledging the spirit of 'this new relationship with schools'. The new relationship is characterized by a model of increased professionalism, the schools' own self-evaluation procedures being presented as integral and essential to the inspection process; yet the new inspection system for 2005 is still heavily managerialism in its assumption. Claims are made that no matter how much the government claims to trust schools, these changes do not reflect that trust enough.

Furthermore, the idea of head teachers offering each other challenging advice, as 'school improvement partners', has been introduced alongside inspection. Although these notions of head teachers offering each other 'peer challenges' may go some way towards indicating a growth in trust in their abilities to help with their professional development, such challenges will not be received by the public or by some sectors of the education community as practical or convincing in terms of true accountability. Cosy pairings are the likely options to be taken. Schools are probably still too competitive in their dispositions (due to their experiences of the 1990s) to move to significantly trusting collaboration and rigorous challenge, especially when considering the latest inspection criteria and continued public reporting. LEA advisers who will be replaced by 'peer challengers', and HMIs returning to lead inspections, are also likely to be somewhat sceptical about the depth of trust in these new relationships.

These changes in relationships point away from the private sector's involvement in school evaluation and accountability. The relationships proposed are inward looking. 'Peer challengers' and 'school improvement partners' are similar practices to those adopted for private school inspections where head teachers contribute to each other's inspections. Here in the private school system, the criteria for the inspection and the nature of inspection reports are rather different to those in state schools. Serious adjustments in the state sector's rules of engagement for inspection would be necessary to make such a move workable. Perhaps in the new environment of 'independent schools in the state sector', it may be possible to launch some form of 'peer challenge' with some degree of credibility across this group of schools, with a climate of increasing independence that seems doubtful, however, unless soft and within some kind of professional or class enclave.

Reducing the role private companies have in school inspection

With the shift away from the privatized Ofsted/contracted inspectors in the inspection service, will more centrally led Ofsted/HMI inspections, with less observation of subjects and lessons, be more reliable and more effective in giving schools accurate and constructive feedback and so help to improve the education system? It is doubtful. As inspection becomes more remote from the actions of teaching and learning, then the greater the influence will be of those who know much about business efficiency, but little about the nature of education. Education and growth is organic, its true measurement and evaluation has to use many subjective and dynamic qualities of judgement in addition to success in examinations and in the reaching of attainment targets in English, maths and science.

Nevertheless, for the years post 2005, the system for the inspection of schools is to be hauled back from the private contractors and into the hands of HMI within Ofsted in sizeable proportion.

In HMCI's letter, *Improving Ofsted and the Future of Inspections* (Bell 2004b), one reason for this claw back and reduction in the role of the private sector is made plain, it is 'a response to the Government's review of efficiency' (ibid.: 1). Clearly, in facing the squeeze on the number of centrally employed civil servants, part of the chosen management strategy is to cut back on the privatized dimensions to protect the HMI core of employees. This move reverses the purpose of privatizing the service in the first place. To attempt to improve government departmental efficiency by reducing the role of the private sector with its competitive checks and balances, signals a major change of direction. HMI remain protected from market forces and market constraints. Indeed, HMI's tendency to use expensive hotels, whilst private sector inspectors doss in the equivalent of a local hostelry, is a frequent gripe amongst Ofsted/contracted inspection team members. A cost analysis and a comparison of expenses between the two would be interesting.

Proposals for September 2005 required legislative changes. HMCI continues: 'While the initial intention of the legislation was to ensure that the registered inspector was independent of the school being inspected, in practice the legislation prevents me as HMCI, being responsible for the inspection report. I feel this is a weakness' (ibid.: 2). This alters the whole basis of a privatized service and points back to a centralized system. Most Ofsted/contracted inspectors I think believed that HMCI was ultimately responsible for their reports as HMCI withdrew those that, for whatever reason, did not make the grade. Technicalities and 'get outs' to justify these changes to a more centralized operational system surround all this.

The private sector's future role

By September 2005 there are plans to have only six RISPs working in pairs and covering three regions nationally, north, midlands and south. These six RISPs were selected, via bid application, from over 20 existing inspection contractors and will work closely with HMI on inspections. Through collaborative bidding, only some of the contractors will be successful in gaining a role in the RISPs. What HMI will do as opposed to what the RISPs will do, at the time of writing, is uncertain, but it seems likely that HMI will lead about 80 per cent of secondary inspections and about 20 per cent of primary inspections. The leadership of other state school inspections will remain in the hands of the private sector side of the RISPs, whilst HMI are likely to retain work overseas and in the private school sector. Quality assurance procedures and performance management for inspectors will use the same standards of output. The Ofsted register of freelance lead or RgIs is to cease in September 2005. It is not clear at the time of writing how lead inspectors will be identified for the 80 per cent of primary inspections or the 20 per cent of secondary inspections.

The privatized system has certainly served its purpose well in being subject to the changing demands of the market. The tariff for inspections from September 2005 is dramatically reduced, with the private sector taking the brunt of the reduction. In HMCI's words, 'For example in a large primary school, where we would expect under the current Framework to see 14 inspector days in the school, for the new Framework six days will be needed; in a secondary school, under the current arrangements 48 inspector days would have been spent inspecting, but we expect this to take nine in future' (Bell 2004b: 5). A reduction of 57 and 81 per cent respectively is achievable because of the flexibility provided by a contracted privatized service, subject to market pressures. It is doubtful that any outcomes of the Government's review of efficiency will be able to match figures like these.

Market forces in the business of school and LEA inspections are therefore not being allowed to run and to develop. After a decade of market practice, the civil servant hand of HMI is retrieving much of the business. This has caused the number of contractors to be reduced and those that are successful and remain to be placed in a second-class relationship behind HMI who will, it appears, 'cherry-pick' inspection activity. Dramatic reductions in the number of private inspectors available within the system will reduce long-term flexibility and remove market competition.

Some privatized successes

Sensitivities around inspections will prevail. Privatized contracting is a good strategy to deploy in an activity like inspection as it builds in contractual layers for the effective handling of complaints and adjudications. Having a purchaser group which sits independently of the contracted inspection teams is helpful.

Contrary to much popular opinion, most evidence suggests that schools and teachers do not object to the principle of cyclical inspection or to the open publication of reports. Ofsted/contracted inspectors have won overwhelming support from governors, head teachers, staff, parents and pupils for the way in which inspections have been carried out. The situation is similar for officers and politicians within LEAs.

Old or new, 1992 or 2005, most features of inspection are seen as positive. Most teachers, for example, think that a couple of hours of observations of their teaching by an external inspector, whether every six years or three years is reasonable, they recognize that the producing of extra documentation for the inspection is often more associated with their own need to feel well prepared rather than the actual demands of the process – teachers, as a matter of routine, have to digest huge amounts of documentation generated by different government departments anyway, so this is only seen as part of the new culture.

The inspection of state schools is increasingly based on straightforward self-evaluation forms. Where schools have maintained a current up-to-date version that truly reflects their school's work, and which shows a generally satisfactory or better performance against comparative indicators, then inspection is not overburdensome. Many LEAs have facilitated the use of highly sophisticated information on pupil performance. Some, for example Buckinghamshire, have even produced good quality guides to help schools maintain an up-to-date set of evaluation forms. With increasingly sophisticated self-evaluation data available to schools, and inspections being carried out without notice, issues of burdensome preparation will no longer apply.

Thousands of inspections have reported that teachers and head teachers are doing a good job, hundreds similarly for LEAs. Even where messages are critical, those who work in education are usually able to take the messages on board and act on the issues quickly and effectively despite the fact it might mean departure for certain staff members.

Of course there are weak teachers and head teachers. Inspection does rightly identify shortcomings so that action can be taken and this is overwhelmingly supported. On the whole, the education community is not fearful of such objective evaluation. In private conversations rather than public displays, teachers, head teachers and LEAs usually agree that the vast majority of inspections are done very professionally and that a cycle of inspection is necessary in a regulatory world. They often see inspection as an opportunity to have their efforts validated externally and to help them adjust their priorities and their actions in relation to the findings of a team with a wider external perspective perhaps different from their own. Parents hold a similar view. They welcome the information that the Ofsted reports bring, are quick to recognize contextual issues which may have particular bearings on their school, and are pleased when issues of concern to them are examined and, where agreed, become a key issue for action.

There is much evidence to support this view. In reply to a letter arguing that inspection should be abolished, which appeared in *The Guardian* newspaper, the Director of Inspection of a private company (Tribal PPI) wrote 'Inspections are carried out by professionals who are human and fallible. In my career as a local authority inspector, an HMI and now as director of inspection for Tribal PPI providing more than 500 inspections annually, my overwhelming experience is of professional inspectors working conscientiously' (Whitburn 2004: 29).

Problems however, do begin to emerge around some areas of criticism. These occur in inspections and in reports where:

1 there is a mismatch between what the inspection actually reports upon and what the schools or LEAs see as their major purpose or priority;
2 there is perceived to be gross unfairness in the way opinion is presented as fact.

Cultural prejudices and constraints within inspection

The inspection system since 1992 has been based on the careful use of managerial measures and from an express desire to sort out what was seen as a previous failure, or complacency, or inability by HMI to sort out the complexities of determining educational truths; 'there was more than a grain of truth in the accusation that HMI...had like the proverbial dog, failed to bark in the night' (Woodhead 2002: 102). The power of the managerial message created its own version of truths against those attainment and outcome indicators which are most easily measured. The system was set up to measure against nationally designed criteria which had not previously existed. Diversity of purpose in schools was rapidly constrained to the national purpose set in various schedules. The ranges of educational truths, and the complexity of determining them, which perhaps had caused HMI to be previously more cautious in declaring sweeping failure, were a lesser part of this new inspection culture. Whether for schools or LEAs, the managerial formula for producing a report was the interpretation of school performance against comparative data from other schools and, in the second cycle, improvement since the last inspection, albeit that the ground rules upon which judgements were made had changed very significantly.

In gathering 'facts' the inspection regime had very neatly assimilated into the 'managerialist' culture of the 1990s. In its early days, the regime of Ofsted was seen very much as about 'blowing the whistle on failing teachers' and 'seeking out under achievement'. It seemed often to be about denting the self-confidence and challenging perceived complacency of the educational establishment. The understanding of these 'facts' and the way in which they were used and presented took little account of any features of the 'professional' model. To quote the then HMCI '...our job, as I saw it, was to gather the facts and then to make sure that their significance was understood by everyone who had an interest in our schools. If this upset some academics and politicians, then my attitude was, frankly, so be it' (ibid.).

So, what is the significance of these problems? They are significant where:

• practice is judged to be failing because there is a mismatch over the views held by the school or LEA and those of the inspection team, about the school's or LEA's central purpose;

- the forced consequence is a shift in direction from much needed features of 'professional judgement and diversity' to features of 'uniform managerialism';
- views, prejudiced by the nature of the model, obscure transparent fairness in the approach to the inspection;
- there are wide variations in judgements that are supposedly based on tightly defined criteria.

These problems manifest themselves sometimes through other forms of weakness in the inspection culture.

Mending weaknesses through modern privatized methods

Even problems such as these are tolerated when they are managed with sensitivity. It is when these problems occur and are then handled badly that cause frustrations. The main faults include:

- features of arrogance;
- inconsistencies in the way the process of inspection is applied;
- superficial information gathering and assuming premature judgements;
- changing inspection criteria between inspections without open acknowledgement which in turn leads to misleading statements in the reporting of progress.

These weaknesses raise justifiable concerns about the processes of inspection.

It is worth looking at four of these areas where a fresh approach from the private sector may bring about a swift mend to nagging faults which have their roots in the public 'governmental' culture of centralized agencies.

1. *Arrogance by inspectors and the popular concept of 'denial'* A traditional feature of some Ofsted/HMIs has been a not-rarely assumed tendency for arrogance in their professional style. High-handedness is a danger of supreme confidence borne out of successful experience and very senior position.

I can recall, during some Ofsted training in the early 1990s, witnessing an HMI reporting the inspection team's findings to an unconvinced head teacher. The HMI concluded with the words – 'Do you recognize your school Mr Jones?' Mr Jones clearly did not but he was too polite to say so outright and to her face, and especially not in front of all of the on-looking trainees! It was as well he did not, I had heard that line and the follow-up before from HMI. If the head teacher replied something along the lines of 'Oh yes, I do see all your perceptive insights', then all was rosy – the HMI and team glowed in the knowledge that they had helped the head teacher to see their school in a new and a more objective way which would lead the school forward. In truth they probably had! If however the head teacher replied 'Oh no, you have got it wrong' then the likely advice retorted would be that the head teacher must try to avoid denial and accept the 'truth' of the judgements as presented. It would be explained that the role of head teacher was to help others to see the wisdom of the inspection findings!

As a general rule, teams of inspectors do get the judgements right, usually they are certainly near enough to the truth to be helpful in moving schools forward. However, they occasionally do not. Over the last 15 years I believe that more than a few inspectors have used such a line in feedback to school staff 'do you recognize your school?' or 'do you recognize your department?' and then retorted 'you're in denial' when heads or heads of department challenge. It is a weakness from a former institutional norm. Being described as 'in denial' seriously weakens the position of the head teacher and their professional objectivity. It is certainly less personally damaging not to argue in these situations. 'Take what's there with a smile and get on with the issues for action' were the pragmatic words of one head to his governors when receiving a critical report. The advice was most certainly expedient, but was it wise or hypocritical and cowardly?

This type of exchange between some inspectors and head teachers has created some tensions around the inspection regimes. It is parallel to assuming to know what is best for everyone, from on high or from a view drawn from particular elicited information. The serious shortcoming in this is that it does not help generate a culture which questions inspection findings openly and readily. Nor does it achieve a 'doing it with' rather than 'doing it to' approach to external inspection. 'Doing it with' is supposed to be the desired style, as external inspection draws closer to internal school self-evaluation. The attitude of 'best to agree rather than be accused of being in denial' is not one that should continue. People in education rarely assume positions of unjustified denial. Sometimes there might be parochialism; perhaps a lack of broad experience which hinders understanding, or even outright prejudice. The way to real improvement is through discussion and argument not arrogant charges of denial and privatized contracted inspectors know this better than those within the government agencies.

Challenges do occur. One widely reported case was about a secondary school in a south London Borough which soon after having had a clear bill of health from an inspection by an Ofsted/contracted team, was revisited by Ofsted/HMI who carried out an additional inspection. This found the school to be warranting special measures! The LEA and school had to go to the door of the courtroom before the attempt to re-designate the school as being in special measures was dropped and the original report findings were allowed to stand.

More recently, in the spring of 2004, the HMCI seemed to have a rather difficult couple of months when having to account for a range of happenings at Ofsted/HMI. In April, he wrote a short press article entitled 'We will continue to tackle bullying and harassment' (Bell 2004c: 8). I assumed from the title that the article was to be about bullying in schools, but on closer examination found it referred to concerns and fears expressed by staff working at Ofsted! Apparently, over 20 per cent of staff felt they had been bullied by their manager and over 60 per cent said they felt unable to speak freely at work or share ideas about changing the way work was done. Again in May, he was reported as admitting that Ofsted teams were damning schools unjustifiably. The arrogance and high-handedness described earlier finds a resonance in these statements.

Having detected such weaknesses in the organizational climate within Ofsted/HMI, it would seem that the better road to improvement would be to expand the work allocation to the infinitely more flexible privatized Ofsted/contracted inspectors, rather than trying the reverse.

2. *Inconsistent judgements about different schools and LEAs* Despite efforts to moderate inspection practices through the initial and ongoing training of inspectors and the monitoring of inspection practice and report writing, it is plain that reports on different schools and LEAs are pitched with different degrees of rigour. The presumption is that inspection criteria are set against a form of national calibration but that the task of moderating the practice of school and LEA inspections and the reports is hugely difficult.

Even taking 'similar school' indicators into account, a teacher may be a 'star' in one school but unable to maintain a satisfactory performance in another due to different prevailing circumstances. It is easier to score well in some classrooms than in others. It might appear easier to get a good teaching grade in some private schools than in some state schools and more difficult in some urban comprehensives than in selective grammar schools.

It can be argued that reports do not need moderation providing that the report helps the individual school or LEA to move forward. Whilst true to a degree, too much is riding on the inspection findings for this to be accepted by most groups in the educational community. Generally, because inspectors are fair-minded and credible people and because teachers and LEA personnel are quick to recognize and accept their shortcomings, the majority do not get over-concerned about inconsistencies across inspections providing they get at least a satisfactory report.

However, some groups do get concerned. Those responsible at LEA level for school improvement get concerned. Sometimes there is great relief when a school, known to have serious weaknesses by the LEA team, scrapes through its Ofsted inspection with a clean bill of health. Sometimes though, there is frustration (even anger) when this happens, especially if the school is not serving its pupils well and is not serious enough about taking effective action to improve things. It is difficult to quantify the degree to which moderation fails and where this is significant.

From my experience in senior roles in three different LEAs since 1993, I would suggest that such failure does not reach 5 per cent. Two examples however stand out. One primary school, with severely low-attainment performance (19 per cent level 4+ compared with 80 per cent average), with obviously low achievement and with management in considerable disarray received a report judging it to be satisfactory. Consequently, there had been no Ofsted/HMI follow-up and no central resources from any of the government's 'schools in difficulty funds' to help it. Conversely, another school not far away, which had been deemed as in need of 'special measures' in its report more than 12 months earlier, was still receiving weighty monitoring visits by HMI and yet the school, by comparison with many, shone as a beacon of success. To their credit, Ofsted/HMI did re-inspect the former and cease the monitoring visits at the latter immediately upon the request by the LEA to do so, but the system should not have allowed that differential of calibration in the first place. Aspects of LEPs using privatized advisory teams could be effective in resolving this kind of weakness in the system.

3. *Pre-determined conclusions from pre-inspection data*   Inspectors begin a school inspection by establishing a baseline evaluation based on the previous inspection report and by analyzing existing documents which indicate the performance of the school in comparison with all schools nationally and the so-called similar schools. Similar schools are those with similar proportions of pupils entitled to free school meals and those with similar attainment levels on entry. The main information provided by the Government is the Performance and Assessment (PANDA) document. Using this and the set of self-evaluation forms and the response to the questionnaires received from 'stakeholders' an analysis is produced and used to form a series of hypothesis in a pre-inspection commentary (PIC) that guide the inspection team once it arrives in the school. The process is similar for the inspection of an LEA.

The simplicity of the approach is reassuring. It has validity but is one which is heavily managerial and so, by virtue of its nature, creates data and rankings which are presented as 'truth' rather than hypotheses. Inspectors usually understand the shortcomings that can exist in this kind of data and are at pains to uncover anomalies during the inspection visit. These efforts can only occur during the inspectors' time in schools. For example, they might include finding out whether the data performance ranking is based on an untypical group of students, or whether the school promotes inclusion for pupils with learning or behavioural difficulties which impacts negatively on the attainment grades achieved by the school in the PANDA, or that comparative census data was only valid a decade earlier.

A report by the National Audit Office (TES 28 November 2003: 1, 22) indicated that a significant number of schools were being assessed using raw scores only with no reference to value-added data that was available. Reports failed to acknowledge the extent to which schools had overcome low-prior attainment and disadvantage. It was found that 10 per cent of schools reported in the bottom fifth should in fact have been rated in the top fifth for effectiveness in GCSE once such background factors had been taken into account. Raw data can lead to misinterpretation. As inspections become shorter and of a lighter touch, less time is available to probe such issues. Heavy work schedules for inspection teams, linked in some cases to rather arrogant stances, can lead to judgements which err towards the 'given truth' of data rather than to the 'actual truth' revealed by close inspection.

A similar perception was reported in June 2004 when a school in Worcestershire complained that a privatized contractor team had treated the school unfairly because the team had based their PIC on data relating to another school. It appeared that, in using a computer, the data had been cut and pasted in error. Mistakes happen, the PIC is sent to the school prior to the inspection and it would seem that it should not be difficult for the school and the team to correct any difficulties or misunderstanding immediately. The head teacher's reported comment at the time is very telling; 'Inspectors arrived with the wrong impression of the school. It was almost as if the team were trying to justify the incorrect pre-inspection commentary. It was not a fair process' (Graham 2004: 3). This perception is not rare.

The cases where schools make actual improvements but, because the inspection criteria have changed since they were last inspected, are reported as having stood still or even deteriorated. Whilst hiking standards up (and therefore, the associated judgement criteria in line with the rate of continuous improvement) is acceptable, the reporting should be open enough to spell that out but the reports usually do not.

Inspectors have to listen hard and probe deeply if they are to explain why their inspection findings may differ from the pre-inspection data indicators. Whether LEA or school inspection, private contractor team or HMI team, sufficient time must be given to direct observation if judgements are to be accurate and the inspection process is to be valid, accurate and valued.

Will privately contracted inspection or more government inspection help achieve this and drive further towards an accurate version of truth? Probably neither if inspection becomes increasingly about matching performance data to the schools' self-evaluations and the validation of the fit. The reductions in the inspection regime planned for autumn 2005 in England would seem to indicate a shift to greater dependency on the use of data measures. With Ofsted contracting out less of its work to the private sector and with few HMI at the centre leading more of the inspections, then it is likely that there will be more dependency on judgements being based on pre-inspection data than before. The flexibility provided by contracted inspectors may be useful to federations of schools in countering these problems from the outset.

4. *Questionnaires and reliance on statistical generalizations* As inspections become increasingly of a lighter touch then the reliance on responses to questionnaires and surveys will increase. To gain an idea about general trends of opinion, a well-constructed survey is a useful device. Pollsters, for example, well understand the use of such methods and the various forms and degrees of their validity and statistical reliabilities. The ways these devices are constructed are all important if the responses are to be meaningful.

Similarly, the style of presentation to the user groups and the methods of distribution are highly influential in shaping the nature of the responses on completion and return.

The design, construction, use and interpretation of parent and pupil questionnaires in school inspections, and head teacher and stakeholder questionnaires in LEA inspections, have scope for considerable improvement. The expertise for making these improvements probably resides in the private sector rather more than with HMI and the AC. Parent and pupil questionnaires used in school inspections are considered later; questionnaires used in LEA inspections are covered in Chapter 6.

Feedback from pupils and parents is vital in any school inspection but the questionnaire approach used to probe the issues that really matter is weak. Fundamental rules of questionnaire construction are broken. When more than one element is placed within a single question then tick box answers are meaningless. For example, responding to the statement in the parents' survey: 'I feel comfortable about approaching the school with questions or a problem or complaint', can be tricky to respond to with a single tick. Approaching the school with an enquiry about a child's work or their needs for a PE lesson can be of a very different order to approaching with a complaint about the deputy head. Similarly difficult is the question for the pupils: 'Are your lessons interesting and fun?' As a leading education professor and humorist writes, 'lessons can be interesting, but serious; fun but not interesting in subject terms, because three pupils are tying the teacher to a chair!' (Wragg 2003: 32).

Questionnaires of this kind do not contribute reliably to inspection findings. The responses gained may suggest areas for enquiry and set up some ideas for face-to-face questioning, but that is all. Parents and pupils make their feelings and opinions known best through openly written or spoken exchanges. Artificial questionnaires and opinion-gathering devices, which lend themselves to mass data processing, give simplistic trend information but are less communicative about important facets about growth and nurturing. When inspectors are available then parents and pupils can talk to them and good sense can prevail. This is the basis of real communication about qualities in education.

Formal meetings for all parents and guardians, meetings with governors, informal conversations around the school and the playground are infinitely more informative about the complexities of issues that go to make up a school, than the responses on questionnaires and surveys. Evaluating a school is not equivalent to an exit poll or a product survey. If inspectors are to be swiftly in and out of schools and base their views on the responses from surveys previously drawn up and gathered in by the schools, then quality will be compromised and the confidence of parents in the system eventually reduced.

It is a strange phenomenon that, occasionally in schools, where parents and pupils are delighted with things, some inspectors feel the need to mark down the grade simply because there is an absence of a formal system of regular opinion gathering through surveys. Expectations have become so bureaucratic around education that we are in danger of diminishing the nature of real engagement and genuine satisfaction in favour of the allure of quasi-scientific methodologies.

A similar but unrelated issue applies to the summary table of main inspection judgements which are presented on the last page of school inspection reports, at least up until August 2005. The table gives the summary of the main numerical inspection judgements (using a 7 point scale) in the five main areas reported upon, along with 24 sub-category judgements. These 24 numerical grades are a summary of the internal record of corporate judgements made by the inspection team, which contains well over 100 numerical judgement grades for the school as a whole, and many multiples of these when subject and key stage judgements are added in.

The weakness of numerical summaries is that they can be totally misleading, particularly when the summary table combines different elements into single categories. Take, for example, where the combination is 'accommodation and resources'. A school may have poor accommodation (dilapidated mobile classrooms and limited space) graded 6 (poor) in the report detail, and very good learning resources (computers, books and maths equipment) graded 2 (very good), and yet receive an averaged grade 4 (satisfactory) in the report summary. In these circumstances the summary is quite meaningless. Despite this, those who drive on audit and inspection seem keen on using simplified numerical generalizations. Giving numerical grades suits measuring for compliance, data crunching and produces what seems to be expedient and quasi-scientific quality control indicators. Such numerical oversimplifications also assist those quarters of the media interested in commentating and headline reporting rather more than they are in assisting schools, parents and learners in making improvements.

Privatized contracted inspectors have a role in improving these situations. If utilized effectively in LEPs, perhaps initially as agents of opinion gathering and interpretation in the capacity of championing the interests of pupils and parents, then their impact could seriously improve the system over time and remove the weaknesses characterized by these examples.

Management pressures and controls in inspection regimes

As the commissioner of school inspections, Ofsted/HMI has stood one step removed from Ofsted/contractors. Ofsted/HMI has been the agent responsible for ensuring that the inspection reports meet satisfactory standards defined by the contract. This is the strength of the privatized system in that it builds in clear layers of responsibility – Ofsted/HMI determine the cycle of schools to be inspected, are responsible for maintaining and monitoring the system which is, in turn, let to Ofsted/contracted inspectors who operate in the market environment.

When inspection teams are accused of doing a less than satisfactory job, it is for the contractor to resolve with their teams in the first instance. Ofsted/HMI holds the power of decision over the contractor as to whether the report has been produced to a standard that meets requirements. In the example of the school from Worcestershire quoted earlier, it was Ofsted/HMI that responded to the complaint by apologizing to the school and asking the contractor to make amendments to the report, even though it had already been published. Although slow to take action in this case, the accountability for quality assurance was clearly with the contractor, held to account by Ofsted/HMI.

This is not the case where Ofsted/HMI does inspections directly. The 'arrogance factor' here weighs in heavily. Some schools in special measures 'enjoy' or 'tolerate' very many monitoring visits by HMI, with the school realizing there is no arbitrator to whom they can turn. Ofsted/HMI is actually more legitimate and effective in the role of quality assurer of the work of its contractors than it ever can be of its own work. The role of the LEA in these situations will become increasingly interesting as, in the future, they become champions of parents and pupils.

The changing viability of the market for privatized inspection

Markets are created by demand, sometimes by artificial demand. The education inspection market was stimulated in England and Wales in the early 1990s by the government of the day wishing to introduce a comprehensive and a systematic school inspection programme across all schools. It wanted to do this as part of a political ideology which favoured the privatization of public services and also to increase the public accountability of state schools.

The first cycle of inspections established a 'supposed' national baseline. Cycles of inspection will have run about three times for most schools by the time of the planned changes in 2005.

Market conditions had changed in that time. A large number of small inspection contractors tendered to carry out the work in the mid-1990s. By 2004, there were only 13 bidders for the new RISP contracts. Many of the original Ofsted/contracted inspector teams in 1993 were made up of newly independent inspectors; many others were within, or linked to, LEA school improvement services. Fees from inspections carried out by these LEA teams were ploughed back into the LEA's 'service units' which had to maintain trading viability without subsidy from other LEA service areas. In this respect the market was internal.

Local government employees (the LEA inspectors) worked on government-let inspection contracts to retrieve the income that had been top sliced for inspection, income which had previously gone to the LEAs for their school inspectors' salaries. LEAs were expected to become more focused on their so-called core business of SEN, access and school transport, educating excluded pupils and pupil welfare. Their more minimalist school improvement role of tackling school failure in inverse proportion to success caused LEA trading units of this kind to fall away simply because only a small proportion of their schools were failing. Because of this, many school advisers moved at some stage to work in the private sector, except for those nominated for the local implementation of the government's national strategies, or those who have subsequently moved from schools to undertake those roles.

As a consequence, where LEA school improvement trading units have survived, they have often done so with much reduced capacity. Where they themselves continue to trade then they often suffer accusations that such trading interests inhibit the LEA's ability to give independent advice to schools about best value procurement in their access to wider sources of school improvement services. This is because the LEA is a competitor in the market itself. The fact that the market has little else to offer does not seem to influence those who make those judgements.

Financial viabilities, rates and fees

Initial inspection work in the privatized world of Ofsted/contracted inspectors in the mid-1990s was quite attractive, financially. An RgI, leading a team, could afford to spend the number of days required to carry out inspections and write the reports. Doing about ten inspections over a year, the earned fees could match or exceed the full-time salary that he or she may have earned in their earlier LEA or HMI role or their previous school headship. Fee levels and quality controls in inspection are a delicate balance; it is more cost-effective to write to the given data about a school or a service, than spend time and effort arguing a more rounded truth.

By 2003, market pressures had created a squeeze on that balance of supply and demand. Fewer inspection contractors existed and evidence showed that these contractors were paying less for work of similar quality to that carried out in the late 1990s. '(T)here is evidence in the terms published by SERCO QAA for September 2004 to July 2005 of a reduction in their rates and fees' (NAEIAC 2004: 1). 'The average cost per pupil in 1999 was £2.10 compared to £1.83 in 2003' (Matthews and Sammons 2004: 143). Contractors tried and succeeded in maintaining and improving quality by more effective-working practice. However markets change quickly,

> Market forces reflecting the availability and cost of suitably qualified professionals to act as inspectors have recently driven up the cost of school inspections. Ofsted believes that...(T)he greater focus on inspection quality has meant that the most competent and effective inspectors are in demand and can charge premium rates. There is a smaller pool of inspectors and less competition for work. Moreover many inspectors are more attracted to more lucrative work in other parts of the education system.
>
> (Matthews and Sammons 2004: 144)

With the civil service cutbacks and the DfES closing down its key education units, it is evident that Ofsted/HMI will reduce its commissioning role for inspections in drastic proportions. More inspections will be led by Ofsted/HMI itself in the future and fewer will be let through private contractors. Hence, the viability of the market for privatized inspection does not appear to be sustained. The direction set for national inspection is against the trend of privatization of local services.

With this trend and a much reduced resource, there is a danger that resulting pressures will cause there to be a more mechanistic approach to inspection and to reporting. There is likely to be an even more managerialist character to school inspection and reporting than before. For the reasons explained, it is difficult to see how such a shift will help inspection to become a continuous self-improving factor in the future improvement of education. Much of the documentation which Ofsted produces is of a very good quality. However, on its own this will not bring radical moves towards serious transformational change in schooling. For this to be achieved then more professional flexibility in the inspection regime will be required, not less.

5 Local education partnerships, government intervention and participation

> Strategic leadership requires one other skill. It is a readiness to look personally foolish; a readiness to discuss half-baked ideas, since most fully baked ideas start out in that form; total honesty, a readiness to admit you got it wrong.
>
> (Sir John Hoskins b. 1927)

So far, what has been described is the privatization of education through ad hoc decision making. Whether LEAs and schools have come to use private companies has depended either on local will or government intervention. There has been little strategic shape to the wide range of partnerships and combinations of public and private provision which have emerged since 1997. Through a political ideology that has favoured markets and contracts, the provision of state education has changed, partly by choice, with initiative being taken in response to government encouragement and partly by force through government intervention.

There is a hotchpotch of arrangements. The government is pushing for wider service competition using internal and external markets across education, whilst LEAs attempt to meet their current responsibilities for maintaining state school provision, by utilizing the various combinations which have developed within and around them. These include:

- PFI projects;
- privately contracted-out service providers;
- strategic partnerships and partnership forums of different kinds with the private and voluntary sectors;
- 14–19 collaboration with the Learning and Skills Council (LSC);
- school federations;
- innovative arrangements with private schools and liaison with the category of newly created independent schools within the state sector.

LEAs have had success. Many have brought the private sector on board and to good effect. Some have joined the trading ranks themselves in providing services for school improvement beyond their own LEAs whilst managing their responsibilities for school access, pupil welfare and SEN and their contribution to local strategic leadership to high standards within their own councils. Using inspection grades (Ofsted 2002/03) from the second cycle of LEA inspections as a measure, over 20 per cent of LEAs are judged to be very effective and over 80 per cent at least satisfactory in their overall effectiveness, a vast improvement on the first cycle of grades in 2001 which showed less than 10 per cent as very effective and 50 per cent as unsatisfactory.

Success breeds success. It is apparent for both LEAs and private providers; although for some LEAs and private companies it has been easier than for others. Where market conditions have been less favourable (perhaps because delivering a statutory service for all is not a true market condition anyway) both LEAs and private sector providers have been seen to fail.

People are not opposed to government involvement in influencing services at local level. In a survey of the general public, over half the respondents thought that 'Government should do more to control organisations that provide public services' (Steele and Corrigan 2001: 5) yet less than 10 per cent thought that government should exert less control. Events since 2001, however, make it doubtful that this would be the opinion poll result in 2005. Confidence in local democratic processes has risen relatively although not for undemocratically elected regional assemblies. Intervention involves one tier of the democratically elected government intruding in the affairs of another local tier 'which raises difficult questions of democratic legitimacy and accountability. These questions arise because the electoral process has proved slow to produce change, even where councils have provided poor services for many years' (Audit Commission 2001: 5).

The protagonists for government intervention argue (especially where turnout in the national elections is significantly higher than in local elections) that its national democratic mandate gives it a legitimate role in addressing failures in local priority services. Whilst this may well be true, the mechanisms for ensuring that PPPs work well must be properly conceived and be able to operate effectively. The more genuine the support mustered from the local political representatives and stakeholders, the greater the chances of success. Given the nature of intervention, however, getting such support is usually difficult. Even though it is the local council which formally holds the contract with the provider, the choice of provider can be limited to the government's list. With intervention the council has severely limited choice due to the constraints of a short list of government options, exacerbated until recently by cautiousness on the part of private companies reluctant to enter the risks of a business in which they have little or no direct experience.

Two distinct strands emerge:

1   Consideration is needed about whether and how a more coherent national framework for the development of models for private sector partnerships might help to improve the education services on a national

scale. Though within a national framework, these services need to be available locally. The usual market pressures of geographical distribution come into play. Schools concentrated in urban areas or in regions of high population density represent better market opportunities than those more widely spread. Communities which are 'joined-up' by the installation and use of ICT facilities might help, but education tends to be a face-to-face business. This is being tackled in 2005 by the development of LEPs of very different styles and shapes.

2   There is a need to consider the future role of government interventions and their validity in the so-called failing LEAs, those LEAs in fact which invariably face the most difficult and intransigent urban issues and often in need of serious social regeneration. Some interventions since 1997 have been particularly clumsy. Not only have they cut across the principles of local democratic ownership, but also have appeared to slow the rates of improvement when significant and effective action to bring about improvement had begun.

Each of these strands, both LEPs and the future of government intervention are now considered.

Local Education Partnerships (LEPs)

In 2003, in a joint venture, the DfES and Partnership UK (PUK) set up PfS, initially to manage the delivery of the BSF programme. PfS had been working in shadow form, prior to that time, with a private company and a number of so-called pathfinder LEAs to develop such a model, essentially 'a local delivery vehicle through which the strategic capital investment made available by BSF can be efficiently and effectively deployed by local authorities into their secondary school estate' (Partnership4schools 2004: 4). The model was simply another form of PPP, which existed to assist in establishing investment, procurement and project management, for other PPPs at LEA level, the LEPs.

Whilst emerging through the strategic focus on the renewal of England's secondary schools, the development of PfS came to include more than just the provision of secondary school buildings. It set out to enable successful management and delivery of large complex investment programmes at the local level through more effective partnership working between government, local education and diocesan authorities and the private sector. This meant that, in addition to new school buildings and physical upgrades (e.g. refurbishing for new curriculum demands in ICT and vocational education), advisory services related to BSF were to be included.

This was a significant introduction as it linked the major capital investment strategy for new secondary school building with a single point of contact for the procurement and delivery of the services needed for design, construction and ICT support and also brought in opportunities for the private sector to bid for new school improvement services which had traditionally been supplied, albeit depleting, by LEAs. It created the possibility, at national level, of a mechanism being available for LEAs to engage in the procurement of private sector services through a mix of procurement routes, for example, PFI, outsourcing and those more conventional funding channels.

Given that services such as building new schools and the provision of associated services by the private sector are relatively uncontroversial, it is the role of the PfS in working with the local authorities and other stakeholders to develop strategic investment plans in the education advisory services which becomes the focus of interest. As the original projects were conceived through BSF (essentially for secondary schools) where, for example, will the advisory services for primary schools and special schools fit?

At the time of writing, the PfS framework is in its early stages with private companies still in the preliminary rounds of bidding for education advice and support services. Terminology used in their documentation is new and not well defined. This will improve no doubt as PfS sets up its specifications for LEAs and stakeholders to work together in helping to identify the solutions that might resolve the issues that different authorities face. Clear definition needs to emerge for some of the ideas, such as 'personalized learning' and 'flexible, inclusive spaces', as bids come in and are selected against whatever form the criteria takes. These ideas are different to what has been happening in the recent past and, whilst cloudy, look promising. The Secondary Heads Association (SHA) and the Specialist Schools Trust are jointly active in developing some of these ideas.

On the PfS web site, there is call for new ambition in education with a place for the LEA stakeholders within government policy, 'funding allocations will address whole areas, demanding profound reshaping of local educational visions. LEAs and communities will be guided by government education policy, taking into account what is required today and can be adapted for future needs' (info@p4s.org.uk 2004). The process places LEAs' procurement activities within a national framework and as such is an improvement on previous arrangements. Such a process could be of particular help to those LEAs which had a poor track record of performance. It is certainly a different concept of approach to piecemeal intervention by government into those weak LEAs subsequently held to the behest of a range of consultancy firms with the monopoly of knowledge about procurement following government intervention.

Pushing the boundaries

At the heart of this twenty-first century vision for LEPs is a desire not only to rebuild schools, but to improve services to local communities for decades to come. As the BSF programme is pitched over 15 years, and as many early PFI projects run for 30 years, we are presumably envisaging the educational world for the decade 2020–2030. PfS is approaching the aspects of the process of developing and delivering new schools with such questions as:

- What do we want education to be in the twenty-first century?
- How can we learn from the best of our current schools?
- What is the right pattern of local provision (e.g. the location and size of schools, or the relationship between primary, secondary and post 16 provision)? A limit on thinking is that the age of transfer from primary to secondary seems fixed at 11 however;
- How can we best translate the vision into specific schemes and projects?
- What kind of leadership is needed to achieve this?
- How can we best involve schools and communities along the way?
- How can we create the most productive partnerships with the private sector? (info@p4s.org.uk 2004)

For many LEAs this is the approach that they have previously adopted but which they now find the need to curtail. The Profile exhibit 2.1 in Chapter 2, for example, describes how and why a particular system of schooling was introduced in Northampton in the 1970s and seen as the right pattern for local provision. New pressures to conform to particular national systems, and planning and funding application requirements led to the loss of much former capital and human investment in education, which is now thought not to fit with the expected norms. Innovation and compliance are not comfortable partners.

Four simple key ideas are claimed to have emerged from the preparatory research by PfS and these have formed a framework for their approach:

- Look – how has education been delivered around the world? What could schools be? What works and why?
- Listen – how can we give a significant voice to parents and pupils, teachers and governors, communities and other stakeholders?
- Link – what does it take to create successful partnerships, particularly with the private sector?
- Lead – are there effective ways of developing the leadership skills and styles needed to succeed during the different stages of scheme development?

Though not new, these ideas are sound enough, looking, listening, linking and leading are fine things to do.

What will emerge as the vision for education by 2030? Will we by then still have a continuation of the managerial mantra of target-setting and accountability through the measurement of academic outcomes? There are other social and emotional imperatives that need greater attention within the double harness of schooling, than the obsessive preoccupation with academic attainment outcomes. Smug accountability through the use of safe and conventional academic measures is simply not good enough anymore. We need education to face the cultural and the economic changes which are happening all around us through the acceleration of new technologies. This educational provision will need rather more divergence in the ways it is held to account than those used at present.

Thinking differently

In his book *Out of our Minds, Learning to be Creative*, Ken Robinson (2001) argues that we think too narrowly about education. 'It makes you wonder why we insist on sustaining an education system that is narrow, partial, entirely inappropriate for the twenty-first century and deeply destructive of human potential when human beings have so much latent creative ability to offer' (Wally Olins in Robinson 2001: back cover).

Whilst Robinson sees one of the essential tasks of education as the development of academic ability to the best standards possible for everyone, he sees much more the need to educate people differently. 'There is an intriguing ambiguity in the idea of academic ability. On the one hand it is thought to be absolutely essential to individual success and to national survival. If academic standards are thought to be falling, the popular press beats its chest and politicians become resolute. On the other hand, "academic" is used as a polite form of abuse. Professional academics are thought to live in ivory towers and have no practical understanding of the real world at all. An easy way to dismiss any argument is to say that it is merely academic' (Robinson 2001: 7). The constant drive for ever higher academic results alone will not solve the problems we face now, never mind in 2030. More thinking is needed outside the box.

Unless the vision for education is raised then there is a real danger of slipping into new contractual relationships which will have little effect. It will be the contracts and the configurations themselves that will be new, not the match of service to new need. The danger is that contracts will be tied in to provide more of the status quo but in new schools and from within a new configuration of local authority partnerships.

Private sector contributions give an opportunity for a different kind of empowerment and for greater creative ability to be harnessed. 'Creativity is a prominent issue in educational policy...One of the key motors driving the keen interest in and beyond the education system is the perception that the contemporary economy requires continual innovation and learning... But it is not only economic rationales that are driving the burgeoning creativity discourse' (Woods and Woods 2002: 3).

Woods and Woods argue that there is a concern for achieving 'creativity for empowerment'. Such empowerment would facilitate personal contributions to organizational and cultural values and the means to their implementation. Fostering self-determination and feelings of control and personal ownership within the corporate drive are qualities that have been forced to one side in the enthusiasm for accountability against narrow definitions, specifications and ranks of test scores. 'To move forward we need a fresh understanding of intelligence, of human capacity and of the nature of creativity' (Robinson 2001: 9).

So, will the contracts let through PfS help us to form fresh approaches befitting education for now and the new advisory services which will help to shape that understanding for the next quarter of the century? There are signs that they might. The education advisory services framework agreements are of two basic types:

- local authority advice and support;
- national education advice and support, which is service required by government and other organizations such as DfES and PfS.

Local education advice and support

The services for which tenders are sought for LEPs are predictably within many recurring and well-known themes, for example:

- assessment of the current situation on standards of pupil attainment;
- weak or failing schools;
- strength of leadership at LEA and school levels;
- local curriculum strengths and weaknesses.

Though on the agenda that is well known, this is fine; a stock take is a wise starting point and what has to be faced is a fact of life. However, as the list continues into more detail, the classification used is not fresh. It is for the consideration of well-trodden key policies relating to:

- school improvement;
- raising levels of pupils' attainment which again are for very predictable themes;
- ICT;
- the 14–19 curriculum;
- assessment;
- SEN;
- diversity and equality;
- school workforce remodelling.

There is little in the list to suggest scope for much 'blue sky thinking', but there are a few breaks in the cloud. LEPs, for example, that get seriously into consideration of extended full service education and community use of schools, the design of teaching spaces with flexibility for a changing curriculum, the characteristics of inclusive schools, the design of social spaces contributing to improved behaviour and the identification of education-related evaluation criteria, may well begin to change the culture of education in a sensible direction.

Overall, the tender opportunities listed are status quo, but then new approaches to doing things with the private sector might have to begin on known ground, these are early steps in forming new ways of LEAs and the private sector working in partnership. The breaking of new ground for schools and learners can only come subsequently. The initial agenda proposed by PfS for joint working is hopeful.

National education advice and support

Here, the service themes are more promising. PfS are seeking advice in many fresh and challenging areas.

Top of the list of services is provision of policy and implementation support for delivering transformational educational change. Though the rhetoric is certainly dated, the opportunity to contribute to policy is welcome. The reality of educational change since 1988 has been prescriptive and far from transformational. The increments of progress have been on a narrow range of core subject or examination pursuits.

Second on the list is to develop and challenge statements of local educational vision with appropriate evaluation of such statements. As LEPs will work with the local authorities and other stakeholders and address the key requirements of each to develop strategic plans (SPs), and act as the single point of contact for the procurement and delivery of services, the opportunities to create a different kind of education service befitting the needs of the future are very real. Some challenge of the statements of educational vision at national level may be helpful too.

This local and national approach to involving the private sector in the strategic development and the operational delivery of education is a vast improvement on the practice of government intervention in failing authorities.

Government intervention in failing local government services

Prior to developing the idea of LEPs, the government had as one of its key strategies to improving public services the notion of 'intervening' at local level. 'Where a council or service is poor or failing we will expect councils to act to put things right and where necessary we will take decisive and tough action' (DTLR 2001: 3).

This 'decisive and tough action' took a number of forms within a hierarchy of alternatives, but the most severe was where the government insisted through statutory powers (Section 497 of the Education Act 1996) that local authorities should outsource particular parts of their functions to a private contractor, or operate within a partnership board or with imposed assistance from other LEAs. In many respects, this 'tough action' was seen by some as simply part of the predictable style being adopted by a government which had a large majority.

The processes which led to government intervention might be described at best as murky. There is little to give confidence about any consistent baseline for intervention or even-handedness either in the degree to which councils were deemed to be failing or in the reasons for determining the nature of the tough action. 'Between 1997 and 2001 in England there were 20 interventions in council education departments' (Audit Commission 2002: 3). Walsall, the case study presented in Chapter 6, was one of these 20 severe interventions which occurred following a critical Ofsted report of the Borough in 1999, the year in fact which saw interventions peak to their highest level prior to that year and since.

Internal markets and school improvement services

One of the central tensions in whether an LEA is deemed to be successful or otherwise is the performance of its schools. Although many indicators are used, school performance is measured essentially in terms of averaged attainment outcomes. The aggregation of these results, set alongside the performance of the LEA in its functions in the Fair Funding categories form the basis for judging performance. If performance is low, then of these functions, school improvement services are generally seen as those likely to be the most attractive to private companies, or to the internal schools market itself (Profile exhibit 5.1). As schools become increasingly autonomous and self-managing, the attractiveness of the private sector strengthens. Schools are to be helped to a position where they are not dependent on their LEA for this range of services, as LEAs will not be staffed to provide them.

The government has expected LEAs to devolve the maximum amount of their funding to schools directly, in excess of 85 per cent since 2000, often reaching 87 per cent, sometimes even 90 per cent. In theory, this allows schools the freedom to choose where they buy those educational advice and support services they need. 'LEAs are expected to help schools to be "informed purchasers" and they are responsible and accountable for the quality of education services, without necessarily providing them directly' (Audit Commission 2001: 6). This effectively leads the LEA away from providing school improvement services and instead faces it towards becoming yet another agency for judging the comparative quality of services taken by schools. This is consistent with the LEAs' role in challenging schools, championing the interests of children and parents and less so with school support; this pattern is the declared direction for the future.

In the previous chapter, it was argued that even the major inspection regimes are not particularly reliable in making close judgements for comparing one institution to another, or a particular service to another. Therefore, it is unrealistic to expect this of many LEAs, especially those which may have employed staff with excellent service delivery skills and knowledge and understanding of school improvement but less expertise in the evaluation of such provision by others. Not to presume to be able to do so, as others may

Profile exhibit 5.1 Internal markets, outsourcing and school improvement
services

Wider service 'contestability' through the introduction, albeit in
different forms and to different degrees, of internal market competition to aspects of the secondary education system emerged as a principal feature of the Government's *Five Year Strategy for Children and
Learners* and related initiatives in 2004. Proposals for more independently managed academies; easier school transition to a highly
autonomous 'foundation status'; notions of head teachers offering
each other 'peer challenge' in place of professional LEA advisers;
'lighter touch' Ofsted inspections; a unified school improvement grant
largely under head teacher control; and Children's Trusts to 'commission' local school support services, pointed firmly in this direction.
Some months earlier, Professor Julian LeGrand of the London School
of Economics had joined the Prime Minister's team of advisers and
visited several educational institutions. His association with the concept of internal markets within public services dates back over a
decade, to his book *Quasi-Markets and Social Policy* (LeGrand and
Bartlett 1993) and doubtless influenced this shift in DfES policy.

The overall direction was not new. Specialist schools and the first
academies had already attracted controversy and several new models,
including direct outsourcing to private companies, had been encouraged for selected LEA school improvement services. The Indepen and
Bannock Consulting *Evaluation of New Ways of Working in LEAs*,
commissioned by DfES, concluded that:

> The development of the market has been less than was hoped by
> policy makers and remains patchy in terms of the range of services
> available and in terms of geographical distribution. There are several
> possible reasons for this but a significant and valid concern among
> potential procurers was that markets had not developed sufficiently
> for effective competition to be relied on, with the consequent risk
> that the objective of risk transfer might not be met. If it remains gov-
> ernment policy to stimulate the entry of alternative providers into
> the market, procurers will need more encouragement to take the
> necessary risks and more support in how to do this effectively.
>
> (Bannock Consulting 2003)

Additional efforts have been made to connect private interests with
external school improvement activity. One example is the Government's recent BSF initiative. The related PfS guidance on the new
LEPs, designed to structure these linkages, stated:

> Core LEP services will deal with programme and project
> management around the new investment into secondary school

buildings – that is it will deal with building, Facilities Management, ICT and related services. Where local authorities (LAs) believe it is good value to seek a broader scope of services from the LEP (e.g. educational support, school transport), these can be incorporated into the scope of services to be provided by the LEP. There will be no obligation on LAs to transfer existing educational support services to the LEP but all LAs will be expected to demonstrate in the strategic business case that measures to ensure transformational educational delivery in the classroom will accompany the investment in transformational learning environments.

(Partnership4schools 2004)

Quality of management

A key question is whether involving the private sector generates a higher quality of service management. Private sector claims to greater managerial efficiency sometimes rest on speedier decision-making processes, unencumbered by the formal accountability to elected mechanisms, however, should still operate in connection with such major public concerns as standards of attainment in local schools.

The aforementioned Indepen and Bannock evaluation of outsourcing and other experimental models for reshaping LEA work with schools noted that 'in most cases, the individuals in or appointed to key posts, including interim appointments, were major factors in determining the success of a new way of working'. However, the same report recognized a likely 'constraint' with regard to 'the availability of qualified consultants with a track record in the field' and it is true that the pool of experienced leaders in the specialist arena of external school improvement services is a small one. This renders sectoral claims to higher-quality management in this field difficult to justify. Changes in organizational culture and in management methods inside such small local services, may be associated with leading personalities, as opposed to issues of legal ownership, confirming the view of some economists since the London Business School study by J. Kay and M. R. Bishop, *Does Privatisation Work? Lessons from the UK* (1988).

Cultural change is indeed important for these specialist services, which require the deployment of key inter-personal skills to influence school performance without the benefit of line management authority over school leaderships. The government's endorsement, two years ago, of the first National Standards for School Improvement Professionals (NSSIPs), drawing on the earlier National Association of Educational Inspectors and Advisers and Consultants' (NAEIAC) framework of competencies for advisers, has proved helpful in enhancing the status of LEA advisory officers' work. *The Annual Report of*

Her Majesty's Chief Inspector of Schools (Ofsted 2004b), summarizing the conclusions of Ofsted inspections of LEAs, reflected this positive picture. NSSIPs have provided a much-needed national focus on those specific qualities required to perform the advisory role and influenced the content of relevant job descriptions and performance management systems. Skills-based NAEIAC training for school improvement staffs, based on NSSIPs, is now widely commissioned by LEAs. This process of change is largely 'owned' by the practitioners in the field, since their regular work is closely linked to concepts of organizational and staff development and their own professional association is helping to drive the process.

This heightened investment of time and resources in refining the educational advisers' role and honing their specialist skills, points the way towards ensuring consistently high-quality service delivery. Indeed, such longer-term capacity-building should inform relevant government policy in relation to school workforces as well. A daunting list of significant DfES reforms directly affecting schools – including 14–19 curriculum and qualification changes, school workforce remodelling, more integrated childrens' services and the SEN strategy – confirms the need for effective external support and challenge for schools, delivered by highly trained professionals, if real progress is to be sustained.

Source: John Chowcat, General Secretary, NAEIAC.

be inclined to do, is healthy. To attempt to evaluate the quality of private sector service provision availability with any reliability, given the state of the market, is to get ahead of the services actually becoming available. The enthusiasm to evaluate often seems greater than the willingness to face and actually do the work itself especially where there are difficult jobs.

When one is faced with a range of bids that are more costly than services already provided by an LEA and where the output specifications are across narrowly conceived performance indicators, it can become difficult to get enthusiastic about outsourcing. Millions of pounds have been paid out by LEAs to test private sector feasibilities and much of the expenditure has come to nothing. Helping schools to get better is a difficult business, the idea of helping schools to be 'informed purchasers' is abstract and it is particularly slippery with such patchy market conditions prevailing. Perhaps, by removing the LEAs from the operational role of delivering services and placing them in the role of champions of parents and pupils and acting as strategic leaders in their area will remove some complications and help the education market to mature. Educators as taxpayers worry when they see options that may only hold service at the level of the status quo cost much more.

The aim of all this, we must remember, is actually to make things better for pupils, to raise their achievement and so improve the quality of their learning and the lives of those in the communities in which they live. It is not to create the privatization of education services just for the sake of it.

The private sector at this time is perhaps more likely to make a more significant contribution to the rationalization of joined-up planning and priority-setting for education across council services, than it is to go peddling around schools with enticing school improvement products.

Retaining services in successful LEAs

Given that the private sector market is severely underdeveloped in providing advice on curriculum, teaching and learning issues, it is not surprising that many LEAs have retained their own services to sell to schools. In these situations, providing the schools choose to buy these services, then LEAs can claim some success in supporting schools; at least that is, if the schools' performances are high in the national tables! However, if the schools do not do well in these terms, then such a claim is difficult. Either way, to draw a direct link to the quality of the services is not necessarily reliable. Due to the perpetual difficulties in trying to link cause and effect relationships of these kinds, it is wise to be cautious about them.

Many successful LEAs which sell their own services to schools, who in turn achieve well against national comparisons, have been criticized in their Ofsted/AC inspections because they have assumed themselves to be the most cost-effective provider. It is not difficult to understand why these LEAs are not proactive in developing a culture of informed procurement across schools. As providers themselves, why should they want to promote the competition? Are the private companies that are running LEAs committed to this practice of helping schools to become 'informed purchasers'? Not really, they are intrinsically interested in selling their own.

In many areas, the services are simply not in the market place to be procured. Buying services from the LEA or the option not to buy may be the realistic extent of purchasing choice for schools. Other options are useful. Self-help and cluster work is usually very valuable but use of this exclusively can lead to parochialism. Sharing expertise across groups of schools is the basis for many state schemes, EiCs, for example, and new proposals for 'peer challengers' and 'school improvement partners' shape up in that direction.

Global ICT online facilities increasingly offer training opportunities linked to curriculum materials for schools. Whilst these are useful to disseminate information and open 'professional chat-room' dialogue and virtual experience, ICT training has limited impact on changing real educational practice other than in using ICT applications themselves. However, using online educational products as an alternative to traditional schooling is likely to increase, but there is a danger of this turning education into a global oversimplified interactive commodity which becomes increasingly similar, hypnotic and bland.

For an LEA to be judged successful by the Ofsted/AC inspection teams in achieving good local education results there needs to be evidence of schools choosing from more than one service provider. By outsourcing or privatizing the school improvement services for which they are responsible, LEAs could improve market conditions, increase capacity and flexibility and so genuinely lead the way for schools to have the conditions to become informed purchasers. In many respects, the initiative for swift and effective intervention sits with the successful LEAs stimulating both sides of the private education market.

LEA failure and types of intervention

It is unlikely that a failing LEA will be trading successfully with its school or helping them to procure services wisely. Although there may well be pockets of excellent service available, for the government to intervene, the problems the LEA faces are likely to be of a much more fundamental nature. Once an LEA is deemed to be failing and in need of intervention, then the choice as to the form of intervention to employ rests essentially with the DfES although, as the LEA will hold the resulting contract, negotiation around the options is usual.

An intervention is likely to begin with the LEA receiving a critical Ofsted/ AC report. 'The DfES would then appoint consultants to advise on the action that should be taken to address the problems identified. The intervention action finally recommended would depend on the circumstances of the council' (Audit Commission 2001: 8). It is this process from inspection to the securing of a lead private sector provider in outsourcing, which is fraught with difficulties and anomalies.

Outsourcing LEA services to the private sector is not the only course of action when the government intervenes, although it is most common. Of the 20 interventions referred to earlier, 50 per cent were outsourcings. Other alternatives used were, the setting up of a partnership board (10 per cent), providing support from another LEA (10 per cent) and providing close DfES monitoring and support (30 per cent).

The outsourcing option   is dealt with in the Chapter 6 as a case study. It provides a detailed account of a partial outsourcing following government intervention and the move to extend the outsourcing of the rest of the LEA services subsequently. The account indicates the inadequacy of the process in terms of effectiveness in time and in the utilization of available human resources in those circumstances.

Partnership boards   have a mixed history and a range of models. After some slow starts there has been some success, though rigorous research on relative effectiveness is lacking. For example, Leicester City LEA used a partnership board solution, which seemed to earn a positive second round

Ofsted/AC inspection report. Partnership boards are sometimes used in conjunction with other external providers, private and otherwise, to varying degrees of success.

Providing support from another LEA is perhaps the most effective option reported. Graham Lane, in his Profile exhibit 3.1 in Chapter 3, is unequivocal that support from good LEAs, through twinning arrangements, has proved to be more effective than outsourcing to private companies. He cites the examples of Blackburn twinning with Rochdale and Warwickshire with Doncaster as evidence of this success. Indeed, in the case study of Walsall intervention which follows, the suggestion is that the good work put in by other LEAs during the long procurement process to identify a reliable private sector partner was not properly recognized in the second round Ofsted/AC inspection, not that this option was ever recommended in their management report as a possibility.

Close monitoring and support by the DfES is parallel in many respects to the action taken by Ofsted/HMI with a failing school. As such, the DfES engages directly in a process which moves beyond monitoring to actually providing evaluation and a relationship purporting as help. The DfES is not the same as Ofsted/HMI. Questions arise about 'fitness for purpose'. This particular process is more recognizable as a means of holding a lower political tier to account through the civil service. It is an attempt by government to evaluate the rate of improvement brought about by the local democratic authority and its officers.

This process is an extension of the problem caused by the only slender recognition that responsibilities for exercising leadership and judgement in education are spread in a balanced way across individual parents, schools, local education authorities and national government. Intervention gives legitimacy to the government's concentration on process and enthusiasm to get involved with local detail which gives rise in turn to 'the steady disempowerment of those working at every other level in the system who are cast increasingly in the role as "implementers" ' (Wilkins 2004: 7).

Forms of intervention other than full outsourcing may seem less intrusive on the principle of local democratic control, but as contracts are with the local authority in all the circumstances, the democratic accountability is actually maintained. The track record of many private companies in education is becoming more convincing but others have already failed quite badly. The original ascendancy to the government's list of less than 20 potential private sector providers did not get the process off to the best of starts.

Participation following intervention

Intervention is necessary where councils fail to take action when there is serious service failure, it is necessary because without intervention action will not happen. The attempt should be to bring people with the appropriate expertise together in order to stimulate change in the best forms possible, whether from public or private sectors. Neither sector has the monopoly of best practice. There is a continuum of possibilities with partnerships comprising different proportions of activity. The permutations that exist within this continuum have not been fully explored; the political will of the future may well turn towards such an exploration. A democratic and a citizenship dimension is important in being seen to be prominent in considerations of education interventions. Broad political and community engagement is central to success. If elected members and their constituents who vote for them sense a sidelining of their influence through contract specification inflexibilities, then confidence in democratic accountability is reduced.

Terms used in intervention processes such as 'compulsion' and 'threat' do not sit comfortably with people who see themselves and their local representatives of whatever political persuasion, as peaceful and law-abiding citizens. Although suspicion might abound, there is usually a working level of trust between groups because of their shared interests in the local context.

Intervention is described by the AC in three phases as shown in Table 5.1. 'Phase One' is reminiscent of the high-handed arrogance described in inspection feedback. It does little to clarify; the assumption is that failing local government departments will deny any failure anyway. This is an inadequate assumption, as are the stages of compulsion and threat. These may well become reality in this model because of the highly confrontational style of its design. When people's understandings are low, then their natural reaction is to retreat, when they are compelled they resist, when they are threatened, they fight. Confrontation coupled with low performance and brief explanation is not the best way to bring creative change. It is the basis of social exclusion. What is more, it flies in the face of the very purpose of education. The recognition of democratic change strategy and fundamental human psychology in Phase One are sadly lacking, the overall assumption of needing to overcome denial which is faulty.

Phase Two and Phase Three are more reliable processes. Phase One might actually be about 'Challenge', the subsequent processes then determined by the reaction to that challenge.

Table 5.1 Phases of intervention – hostile

Phase One: overcoming denial			
Challenge	Persuasion	Compulsion	Threat
Phase Two: taking action			
Impetus	External solutions	Setting and monitoring targets	Building capacity
Phase Three: exit			
Intervener trusts council	Monitoring/special measures cease		

Source: Adapted from Audit Commission (2002: 26).

Table 5.2 Phases of intervention – developmental

Phase One: challenge			
Demonstration of validity	Clarification of failings	Clarification of options framework	Deadline set for an option choice
Phase Two: taking action				
Impetus	Setting targets	External solutions	Building capacity	Monitoring targets
Phase Three: exit		
Intervener trusts council	Monitoring/special measures cease	

Source: Adapted from Audit Commission (2002: 26).

A more helpful alternative to the model given earlier might be as those found in Table 5.2.

This provides a less hostile entry. Such a revised model reduces assumption, increases understanding, improves democratic ownership and stands more chances of achieving impetus of action and earlier trust across the stakeholders.

Strategic planning, ownership and new models

Government intervention is most common where the failings in LEAs are perceived to be in strategic planning, either at political, community or executive levels. The expectation on the private sector is to create more coherent and corporate approaches to strategic planning in order to improve effectiveness by reducing duplication and other inefficiencies. The aim though is simple. It is to produce plans that are fit for purpose, engaging of the community and accessible to a wide audience.

In 2001, the DfES launched the small New Model Projects (worth only £1.8 million for the first 11 projects) which brought joint public/private sector activity to a total of 17 participating LEAs in a range of different relationships with 12 private sector companies and with the University of Wolverhampton.

Evaluation of these projects suggests that where LEAs take the initiative in establishing partnerships, this results in good ownership by the community. In the case of the Black Country School Improvement Partnership (BCSIP) of Walsall, Sandwell, Dudley and Wolverhampton LEAs with the University of Wolverhampton Leadership Centre, there is an interesting component. The partnership included the outsourced aspects of Walsall's education services to SercoQAA who provided, by secondment, the partnership's director. As the partnership was focused on setting up a school improvement traded services agency which would provide services across the LEAs, the scene was very much the reverse of what is seen in the usual LEA. Here, a private firm was leading a project with LEAs to provide a choice of viable procurement options for schools. This bodes well. It begins to answer in a curiously reversed context, the criticism made by Ofsted of successful LEA trading units where LEAs have assumed to be the cost-effective provider and have not been proactive in developing a greater culture of informed procurement across their schools.

It also suggests that the development of a viable and robust market for the trading of education services will develop more readily, where LEA and private sector providers choose to become involved in the strategic planning of such services mutually, rather than having the private sector forced in through intervention (Profile exhibit 5.2). This needs to be the recurring theme throughout the establishment of LEPs.

Profile exhibit 5.2 Privatization: imposed or embraced?

When the creeping tentacles of privatization began to impinge on the consciousness of schools, the initial reaction was largely negative. Whatever schools' relationships with their LEAs (which varied from the mutually respectful and supportive, to an almost total breakdown of trust), schools were used to dealing with people they knew and to having direct lines of communication to them. This feeling of having some control was removed when, for instance, a commercial organization was brought in to take over some or all of an LEA's services, often as a result of a poor inspection report from Ofsted.

Schools viewed with some scepticism the prospect of a private company, with little, if any, experience of the education service, being the right vehicle to improve services and raise standards in schools. The situation was exacerbated further by some companies taking on the very staff who had come out badly in an inspection, thus using people who were perceived to be part of the problem and expecting them to become part of the solution simply because they were now working for a different organization. In a few cases, the doubts expressed by schools have proved to be justified, as companies brought in to improve services have themselves had to be taken over when they discovered that the task was beyond them.

The PFI is another aspect of PPPs, which has had a mixed reception from schools. On the one hand, some schools have reaped the benefits of gaining new facilities, in the form of buildings or refurbishments they would not otherwise have acquired. On the other, there have been frustrations caused by being less able to influence the design of any new facility, by the cumbersome procedures that may be in place before repairs can be carried out, or when they have been locked in to a long-term commitment over which they have little control. This is particularly serious when the private company itself runs into financial difficulties, leaving the council and its schools in a very precarious situation.

What is common to the elements of privatization that have been discussed so far is that schools have felt that the changes have been imposed upon them. However, with fresh demands being made on schools to extend and change their roles, attitudes are beginning to shift as schools take greater control of their links with commercial companies.

In its *Five Year Strategy for Children and Young Learners* (DfES 2004a), the Government has set out a vision that increases substantially the expectations of what schools will deliver.

The majority of secondary schools, for instance, are becoming specialist schools and they are also being encouraged to seek foundation status. This will make them more independent of the LEA, while tying them in more closely to the business world. Meanwhile, the growing number of academies is described as 'independent schools within the state system' (DfES 2004a: 45) and they will have even closer links with business.

As for primary schools, they will be at the heart of the government's drive to offer a combination of education and social care to the very young, working closely with other agencies to provide for the needs of children and families. Some schools are becoming children's centres. Others are establishing nurseries for babies from 6 weeks old upwards. This has led them to seek out private providers to help them run these new facilities, for, in this case, it is the private organizations rather than the schools that have the necessary experience, so schools are choosing to work in partnership with them.

At least one successful council (as opposed to those previously referred to that take the privatization route in the wake of an unsatisfactory inspection report), has decided to outsource its services to a private company and hopes to win contracts from other authorities, as well as providing a wider range of services for its own schools in a new type of PPP. Some schools already sell online courses to other schools, while others are considering offering a range of services in the future. The blurring of the boundaries between public and private providers is likely to continue.

Schools are in a period of such rapid change that school leaders have to be prepared to think about how to engage with an increasing number of other organizations, including those in the commercial world. While the priority will remain the education of pupils, new ways of working across boundaries in the interests of children, families and communities will have to be discovered and nurtured.

Source: Rona Tutt, President of the National Association of Head Teachers (NAHT), 2004–2005.

Rationalizing plans

A serious rationalization of planning requirements, along the lines of achieving an SEP is likely to assist the development of LEPs in bringing new solutions to old problems. To improve the quality of strategic planning and to improve public service most rapidly, private sector providers might examine the opportunities, within bidding for LEPs, to draw together the priorities emerging from the local strategic audits which local authorities and stakeholders identify in their LSPs. Education, health, social services, crime reduction partnerships, the LSC and regeneration boards are not well placed to maximize action on shared and overlapping elements of their different priorities. Early work undertaken between 2002 and 2004 in the five LEAs involved in the Local education strategy (LES), and moves to create the SEP, are ripe for private sector facilitation. Yet, in late 2004, there is little guidance material in the bidding information on LEPs for prospective private sector companies about these dimensions.

The SEP could become an important device in creating a framework on which to shape the potential contributions from a wide spectrum of providers. 'The DfES should work with the authorities and other partners in order to agree criteria for an effective, overarching strategic plan (SP), disseminate good practice and facilitate the sharing of innovative and imaginative approaches' (Ofsted 2004c: para. 18). Such action could facilitate the role of the private sector's contribution to the education service, in the context of local council priorities and clarify mechanisms for achieving 'big picture' outcomes. Greater purpose could also be achieved through new tendering opportunities. Rationalization of the many plans in and around education is long overdue, specifically, for example, in 14–19 education and more generally in plans such as those for the reduction of youth crime.

Historically, there has been too little cooperation between different sectors of the public services, though there is often willingness. The overarching functions are not in the working traditions. Contracting private sector providers systematically to carry out strategic functions of this nature is an option. For them to coordinate priority action across different sections of public service, especially where LEAs know this to be a weakness, would bring a fresh approach to a challenge which has not been faced particularly well so far. 'Even in the five LEAs involved in the LES project, there was a disappointingly low sharing of good practice' (Ofsted 2004c: para. 40).

Positive directions

On balance, the opportunities to develop new local partnerships within a national framework and to increase participation at different levels in the processes are realistic. It will be important to break the mould of current limited thinking about educational measurement, both at the levels of schools and LEAs. Measurement, assessment, evaluation and reporting need considerable modernization, in order to strike more qualitative tones with more inclusive indicators of success. The public as represented by parents do not want global ratings about services and schools; they want to experience high quality locally available, personal services at fair cost. The efficiencies sometimes claimed in the name of change and modernization do not necessarily sit as well in such fundamental activity as raising and educating young people in schools and communities, as they do in some other aspects of life.

Ambition needs to be raised and to go beyond the government's strategies laid out for 2005–2010. Some fundamentally different thinking is required about how to educate, for the rapidly changing world of the future. An approach by the government that establishes, for example, 'a unit for innovation' misses the point completely; these qualities sought are developed through encouraging an open and divergent set of attitudes and skills and not by forcing a culture of compliance and of 'fitting in'.

Pupils in schools and in the wider 'learning establishment' as Malcolm and Maggie Greenhalgh describe it in Profile exhibit 0.1 in Introduction, need to be creative, innovative and flexible. Market products need not be about the profit motive entirely. Caution though over the impact of contract-led education is needed here. The more takers of one product specification, the more cost effective that product is likely to be – a basic market incentive. The product has to be about utilizing collective human potential in the process, not reducing it to the most profitable product that global consumers will take.

As private sector methods and resources become more available and as market conditions mature, the view should be on the educational scenario for 2020–2030 as this is the timescale set for the currently high investment in education at this time. Spending on education is unlikely to be sustained at these real levels after 2010, by then the cycle of political priorities will have turned.

Confrontational government intervention in local service failure is not the way forward. Since the peak years of 1999 and 2000, these interventions have declined anyway. Other approaches will be found to be more successful and LEPs are likely to be one such approach.

Chapter 6 offers a case study of the intervention in Walsall's education department and serves as an illustration of why government intervention as a process is not to be recommended even though the resulting privatization gave eventual potential for the creation of new solutions across the education service.

6 Government intervention
A case study

Your legacy should be that you made it better than it was when you got it.
(Lee Iacocco b. 1924)

This case study is a personal account of the key events of the government intervention in Walsall LEA from 1999 to 2002. The intervention by the government required significant and specific outsourcing of education services to the private sector. The account is based on my involvement, as the statutory CEO from 2000. As such it is my story of events and therefore it is interpretative and partial. Nevertheless, partial as it may be, given the perspective of a new CEO, free of any 'baggage' from Walsall's past, and with a previous decade of working in successful LEA and traded partnerships, this view is probably more complete and balanced than most. For a parallel point of view from a legal perspective, the Profile exhibit 6.1 by George Curran at the end of this chapter offers a solicitor's view on the wider situation and the subsequent government intervention across the Council as a whole.

There was very little sense of any denial in Walsall, people knew things had to change. Aspects of the processes of intervention caused other concerns, but the drive from stakeholders, schools, councillors, officers and parents was about putting things right for schools and the education service as a whole within the Council.

A deal had been struck between Walsall Borough Council and the DfES that there should be a partnership approach to bringing improvement. I accepted the job on the basis that a private sector 'Strategic Partner' was required to work with retained service provider units within the LEA, together – the 'Strategic Partnership'. That was the agreed and declared plan by all involved, reflected in the job description and the contract specifications that were developed. However, it was clear from the outset that the Strategic Partnership was very much a negotiated outcome, preferred and achieved by the LEA. A greater degree of outsourcing to the private sector had obviously been the preference of the DfEE. The thorny issue was about where the control of strategic management of the education functions should lie.

Since 1988, with the start of LMS and the trading of educational services, looking towards the use of business models and partnerships in education, to improve rates of progress and get better results, had been a consistent feature of my work with two other LEAs. Determined, as I was, to make such a partnership work well for the communities across Walsall Borough, it was the experience of managing the post-intervention transactions that led me to believe that statutory government intervention is not the best way to approach things. The interest from government officials seemed to be consistently about achieving the maximum amount of private sector involvement in the new partnership, no matter what. Remedying service delivery failings requires more than chasing a current politic dogma. It was certainly not the most expedient way to move things forward, nor was it efficient on the use of available human resources.

People need to feel that they are genuinely a part of the solution. Step change is possible without reducing participation. Bureaucratic procedures involved in procurement and contract specification and confusion caused over roles and lines of democratic and professional accountability are only part of the hindrance. An injustice about true opportunity for participation in the process lurks. Problems in education and in the social turbulence of towns and cities need to be worked on by citizens within those communities. Sweeping intervention by government ministers may well be a necessary catalyst when there are deep-seated failings and change is overdue. But wielding a private sector market solution, long before the market is ready, can be less than cost-effective.

The origins of the intervention begin well before the inspection of the LEA in 1999 but the report from that inspection provides a good starting point.

Ofsted/AC inspection of the LEA: 1999

Government intervention is usually triggered by a critical inspection report; for Walsall this arrived in December 1999. 'The inspection report concluded that a large range of services carried out by the LEA were performing inadequately and that there was need to develop a response for rapid improvement of the future management, structure and delivery of these services to support school improvement' (PricewaterhouseCoopers (PWC) 2000: 1). Forty-four high-level recommendations were made. Criticism was summarized into three broad areas:

- hesitancy to define and pick up action on needs identified by the national agenda;
- confused leadership of the service which failed to give either clear strategic direction or adequate operational control;
- inept development of new relations with schools which are at the centre of the Government's Code of Practice on LEA–School Relations.

'Given the opportunity to put the sour legacy of earlier politics firmly behind it, the LEA has so far failed to translate an ambition to work more productively with schools into convincing practice' (Ofsted 1999: 6). Serious stuff! The Chief Executive took decisive action by removing the senior management team of the LEA and appointing an interim CEO pending further action.

Intervention: what option for Walsall?

Consistent with usual government intervention practice, the Council, working with the Secretary of State, appointed PWC in February 2000 as the management consultant to support the LEA and to advise on how it should respond to the Ofsted recommendations. By September of that year, seven months after their appointment, the consultant report listed four options, none of which included the use of expertise from other LEAs.

The options presented were:

1   reformed in-house
2   strategic partnership
3   joint venture
4   external provider.

It recommended that 'As the agenda for change is so fundamental, and so contrary to the historic role of the LEA, we do not believe that current in-house service delivery mechanisms provide a viable option to bring about the fundamental and rapid changes required' (PWC 2000: 2). It seemed little account had been taken of the work of those LEAs, which had made the shifts from historic to contemporary practice and the possibility of utilizing that huge pool of expertise. Throughout the process I felt an underlying, even prejudiced, assumption that 'LEA' was regarded as synonymous with 'backward looking' and that intervention from the private sector was the only sure way to 'modernize'. But there was very little convincing evidence of private practice being successful on this scale elsewhere at this time. Apart from ventures in Westminster, Haringey and Sandwell by Nord Anglia, in Waltham Forest by Education Ltd (Nord Anglia and Amey), in Islington by Cambridge Education Associates and in Southwark by WS Atkins Ltd, other private sector endeavour was relatively small or very much focused on school inspection or the delivery of new national training programmes for head teachers or aspiring heads. If anything, the evidence pointed to a distinct lack of success by the private sector in taking over front line duties of LEAs on a large scale.

From PWC's appraisal of the four options, the report stated that 'the joint venture option provides the best combination of benefits and the reformed in-house the least' (PWC 2000: 3). However, the preferred model negotiated between the Council and the DfEE was to use a private sector provider within this Strategic Partnership arrangement where there would be outsourcing of some functions and retention by the LEA of others. PWC reported that 'In May 2000, the local elections resulted in a change in the political leadership of the Council and, following discussions between the Council and the DfEE, a decision to proceed with a strategic partnership was agreed' (ibid.).

The Strategic Partnership model

The Council wasted no time in taking action. Within the month of receiving the report it had advertised for a CEO to lead the recovery and 'actively develop the relationship with the Strategic Partner'. By the beginning of October, after the usual rounds of interviews, I was offered the job as Director of Education and Community Services, the statutory CEO role, to commence in January 2000. Although the portfolio coverage was quite standard, primarily the job in this case was to achieve a successful partnership for the LEA with the private sector.

Celebrations were cautious; three separate interviewers for local newspapers and radio used the term 'poisoned chalice' as part of their questions about my new job, as did one of the local MPs, in jocular fashion, soon after I started. Obviously, some turbulent history lay behind the words 'sour legacy of earlier politics' and 'political instability . . . culminating at one stage in the virtual paralysis of the decision-making process, has handicapped practical action on education' (Ofsted 1999: 5).

Radical changes were necessary, from reading reports and from conversations with wide-ranging groups of stakeholders, and there was an accepted recognition that things needed dramatic improvement. Education plans had not benefited from adequate exposure across the Council and to wider interest groups. Links, for example, to the Single Regeneration Budget (SRB) programmes were not made well enough in advance and so impeded subsequent actions in reaching potential.

There had been over-inspection and audit in Walsall. Reports were piling high. For example, by 2002 in addition to two Ofsted/AC reports and the follow-up management reports by PWC, the pile included many routine evaluations by District Audit, the long-term joint review by the Social Services Inspectorate, the contributions of the government imposed Supervisory Board, the evaluative contributions of the DfES Standards and Effectiveness Unit Adviser and other DfES civil servants, consultancy audits by the Improvement and Development Agency (IDeA) and the AC's Corporate Governance Report. As reported at the time, 'there has been no shortage of audit in Walsall Metropolitan Borough Council (MBC) recently. Repetition of critical messages is quite demotivating. Sometimes their recommendations have appeared contradictory and this has caused some confusion, even suspicion' (Williams 2001: 22). Ofsted, for example, cited that the LEA education advisory service had the capacity to deliver the Education

Development Plan (EDP) whereas PWC specified that this service should be the main activity for the Strategic Partner. Presumably, their thinking was that it would be this advisory service that the private sector would find most attractive, because it was the area of advisory services that represented a more developed and commercially lucrative part of the market than other services such as SEN and access. Things needed clarifying, there was a 'need to get behind these audit headlines and draw out a valid interpretation which is understood across the educational community. This will inform planning which must then directly translate into clear and effective action' (Green 2001a).

However, any denial of problems by officers or members that may have existed earlier seemed to have been overcome, Phase One, 'Overcoming Denial' of the AC's three phases of intervention had been accomplished. Its component parts of, 'challenge, persuasion, compulsion and threat' (Audit Commission 2001: 26), uncivilized as they sound in an educated world, had run their course and the Council was clearly up for Phase Two 'Taking Action'.

Difficulties over the bias for action

Throughout the documentation and guidance which dealt with recovery, there was a recurring emphasis on the importance of impetus. The PWC management report used the term 'rapidity'. 'The preferred option must be able to be capable of delivering change quickly and effectively' (PWC 2000: 39). This was agreed with completely, by elected members, professional colleagues and the school communities across Walsall. The report went on, 'it is likely that the implementation time-scales would be between six and nine months (although there is potential for significant delay if procurement problems arise)' (ibid.).

However, it was getting 'rapidity' that was the problem. The tension was between getting on with the improvement process urgently and yet allowing for the time it would take for the procurement of the private sector strategic partner. The difficulty was simple. The LEA was keen to get on with the improvements called for, but the more progress the LEA made prior to the appointment of the private sector Strategic Partner, the less scope the Strategic Partner would have in shaping the new foundations of the overall service. The differences that had been settled between the LEA and the DfEE at an earlier stage of negotiation were becoming a root cause of tension and delay. The DfEE clearly wanted to see the private sector partner in a stronger strategic role than the LEA and this immediately surfaced as a brake on the recognized need for impetus.

In five days of preliminary work I did with Walsall prior to my official start date (bought in fact as a consultancy service from Bromley LEA), a paper was prepared outlining some initial 'firming-up' of the leadership team for those areas not to be outsourced. The DfEE applied a firm delaying hand to what was proposed. Following a meeting about this at the DfEE with senior civil servants, my letter of follow-up to them and their letter to me, crossed in the post. The letter I received was quite emphatic on one particular point; it read 'I just wanted to confirm our understanding of the outcome. Your paper will be delayed until we have had chance to assess the bids for the contract and identified a preferred bidder' (Crowne 2000). The earliest this could have been was April 2001, at least four months away, and with the stated delays anticipated by PWC, it turned out to be July, seven months later! My letter to them spelt out my concerns about such a delay. 'I do not want to find myself in the position as the CEO in Walsall in autumn 2001, two and a half years after the original Ofsted inspection of the Authority, with little evidence of improvement outcomes and only a rudimentary installation of the Strategic Partner. We will not be able to tolerate another damning report' (Green 2000a: 2). With the benefit of hindsight, and despite a series of achievements and improvement trends, that is how Ofsted chose to report on things one year later.

Even though the proportion of the outsourcing was to be considerably less than half the education service, it was the outsourcing of strategic management that presented anomalies and which caused the DfEE to press for delay. The issue was visible from all sides. The actions taken by the LEA following intervention were seen in part as needing to satisfy the DfEE expectation; the LEA was after all the subject of intervention. So, without DfEE agreement, the Council understandably felt the need to hold back. We did not want to pre-empt the role to be played by the Strategic Partner, we genuinely wanted the partnership to work well for the benefit of the people and children of Walsall. To go ahead would alienate the basis of that new partnership. It was clear that there would be lengthy delay and that the delay was likely to be reported as continuing ineptitude on the part of the LEA! The alternative taken was to continue and extend the very adequate interim senior management arrangements that had been put in place by the interim CEO. This had utilized expertise from other LEAs.

Buying expertise from other LEAs

Progress was achieved by employing consultant managers from other LEA traded services units, principally Birmingham and Lancashire to provide emergency leadership and management and begin to establish new and better systems at strategic and operational levels. As well as the routine business of running the education service, these included stakeholder negotiations for setting up the procurement process for selecting the private sector Strategic Partner and the construction and implementation of the Post Ofsted Action Plan.

Progress was evident in key strategic areas:

- budget and management planning;
- support for the few primary schools in special measures and other schools causing concern;

- consultation arrangements with stakeholders, especially head teachers, parents and governors and with strategic groups for crime reduction and health;
- coordinating with the LSC and other LEAs the construction of the 16–19 area-wide review action plan.

Practical action brought improved outcomes in a number of key indicators:

- performance outcomes had improved significantly in schools upon the previous year's results in both GCSEs and KS 2;
- Walsall was the fifth most improved authority in mathematics and the ninth in English;
- the one secondary school that had been in special measures had made sufficient progress to be removed from that status and, although serious difficulties existed in another secondary school, it was not in special measures.

The management report by PWC had also reported some of the successful key aspects of the LEA's performance as reported by Ofsted. These represented significant areas such as:

- school admissions;
- curriculum support for ICT and primary numeracy;
- the extent to which the LEA had defined monitoring, challenge and intervention;
- support for ethnic minority pupils.

The picture was not all gloom. This emphasis was perhaps a deliberate ploy by PWC in an attempt to make the idea of working in Walsall more attractive to potential staff and particularly to private sector interests.

The action taken to use the expertise from other LEAs highlighted the absence of this alternative in the PWC options review. Not only had the idea of using expertise from other LEAs gained favour in Walsall as an interim solution, evidence showed that, for some aspects at least, things were moving in the right direction. With PWC support, this strategy was being used effectively to bring about conditions favourable to the procurement of the private sector Strategic Partner, although it was taking too long. The strategy was also effective in planning and acting on the recovery priorities set out in the Post Ofsted Action Plan.

The interim management team brought experience and know-how. They put the beginnings of essential strategic and operational structures in place. Birmingham and Lancashire, after all, were highly successful LEAs running large and viable support services in the modern and the contemporary culture of trading educational services.

Given the extent of the difficulties facing the education department in Walsall, the list of priorities in education alone was long. Perhaps not enough time was found to work on wider strategic issues across the Council with the Walsall Strategic Executive Team. The weakness was that although these consultants' services were bought in for well over a year in some cases, they were there as a temporary stop gap with a tight education brief. They were seen that way by the educational community and therefore not integrated into cross-council leadership as much as the modernizing agenda for local government set out. Consequently, the contribution by the education department to moving the corporate leadership of the Council forward was not as great as it would have been, had substantive appointments been in place. The temporary status of senior leaders in education meant too little engagement on corporate Council matters.

The community had expected more 'rapidity' in getting over the already lengthy transition. 'Ministerial promises for change and progress led head teachers in Walsall to have very high expectations about the speed of developments' (Green 2001b: 2), yet the procurement process in such new market conditions had to take time, as PWC had indicated from the outset. Delay compounded further delay in getting the urgently needed capacity to tackle work on many fronts. The process of procurement meant temporary consultants were engaged in that process, whilst still having to run the education department. The intervention had worked against the serious call for 'rapidity'.

Not a new problem, it has always been and remains so; it is notoriously difficult for lower tiers in any walk of life to meet the artificially raised expectations created by those in tiers above them. Confusion occurs where lines of accountability are crossed and where external advice does not contain a comprehensive range of the real options available. In the harvest of confusion, the finger of blame will invariably point to those in the lower tier, in this case the local government service. The process at every turn seemed to set that up. The Walsall team (whether employed or bought in from other LEAs) could not be seen to be successful. It had to be shown that private intervention was necessary and the private sector had to be seen to be the solution.

This was not anything other than that which had been expected. The task was to secure a good Strategic Partner from the private sector. There were three very capable private sector organizations lining up in the short-list with bids to be Walsall's Strategic Partner. The sense that the private partner had to be seen to be saving element of the LEA was generally accepted as a fact of life across the LEA staff. Full effort was given to securing the best fit from the three short-listed companies for Walsall.

The procurement process and identifying the preferred bidder

Differences of perception about the robustness of the education market showed around this time. Whilst those stakeholders in Walsall approached the selection of the preferred bidder as an increasingly rigorous competition which they saw each company as eager to win, PWC and DfEE officials were very aware of the risks to these companies as private providers in an uncertain market. They were highly aware of the dangers of collapse should these bidders walk away during the later stages. Had Walsall not been fully committed to the Strategic Partnership and had the bidders lost confidence and withdrawn, then this could have brought the whole process to an abrupt end.

Extreme care was taken to ensure that the procurement process was scrupulously thorough and professional. The LEA consultant bought in from Lancashire led the process meticulously with technical support from legal and finance colleagues and from PWC. Decisions taken had to be seen to be made in a fair and equitable manner and they were. The competitive process ran its course. The evaluation was demanding as it had to evaluate quality in many complex areas and ensure an effective and affordable value-for-money outcome for the Council at the end of the process. The stakeholder forums and working groups and the Education Committee faced up to hefty strategic decisions on the quality and viability of the bids in ways that did not reflect the levels of weakness reported in the previous Ofsted report.

Respecting commercial confidentialities, all three short-listed bidders, Nord Anglia Education PLC, Prospects Education Services and Serco with Quality Assurance Associates (SercoQAA) offered strong, though different, proposals. Just two, Nord Anglia Education PLC and SercoQAA were taken on to the final Invitation to Negotiate (ITN) and to bid at the Best and Final Offer (BAFO) stage.

Following these BAFO submissions and the scored evaluations against tightly prescribed criteria, the preferred bidder, selected in April and to take preliminary effect from July was SercoQAA. They would take contract commencement from September 2001. The dates are important. The next inspection of the LEA was looming and the CEO statement was due in October 2001. Urgent planning with the new Strategic Partner was long overdue and, with this result, there was now a Strategic Partner to work with.

SercoQAA is successful

The two companies in the successful joint bid had agreed 'heads of terms' for Serco to acquire QAA prior to a final contract award. Serco, a £700 million group, described itself as an international task management contractor to government and industry. A company with a wide-ranging portfolio, 80 per cent of its business came from the public sector and 90 per cent of its staff had worked in it. It had contracts to manage prisons, hospitals, leisure centres, light railways, air traffic control and housing and maintenance services, and operated research and training facilities. It would gain its core expertise in education by buying out QAA and by transferring across over 100 of Walsall's LEA staff (under TUPE arrangements). QAA, by contrast, was a smaller group of capable inspectors and advisers, mainly from LEA backgrounds and with successes in Ofsted school inspections, performance management work in schools, training of head teachers and small-scale LEA reviews in partnership with KPMG. QAA staff and their associated network of consultants would join the 27,000 staff employed by Serco, who were spread across 35 countries on seven continents.

Despite the size of the joint organization and the strength of the bid when evaluated against the bid evaluation criteria, it presented with an appealing quality. Those leading the bid presentation, mainly from the QAA side, were sensitive to enter the Strategic Partnership under a low profile and understood the need for Walsall's educational community to be prominent within the partnership on its traditional patch. Hence 'Walsall Education', 'WE' as the logo read, was the first brand name of the LEA and SercoQAA in partnership. The style of nomenclature was repeated in reverse, when Serco soon after won the contract to run Bradford LEA. It was named 'Education Bradford'. Subsequently, as their role became greater and different in Walsall, the change to 'Education Walsall' was made. The name was to be significant.

The capacity of this new Strategic Partner to inject capital, expertise and innovative systems was evident. Hopes were high. Serco/QAA claimed competencies including:

- high quality service delivery in education;
- strength in change management;
- effective contract management processes;
- extensive and successful experience of dealing with public sector customers from local and central government and skill in transferring staff from the public sector under TUPE;
- experience in gaining quality accreditation and delivering results through a culture of performance management;
- use of effective management information systems;
- experience of working in multi-stakeholder environments;
- operating on a daily basis through a devolved management structure (SercoQAA undated: 2).

These competencies, at high order levels, were the very ones needed to get the strategic shape and delivery pattern to Walsall LEA's performance and particularly to its work in improving school effectiveness.

Whilst the SercoQAA contract was hugely symbolic and very important to Walsall LEA and its schools, it was relatively small. Compared to the contract SercoQAA won with Bradford LEA only weeks later, the largest of its kind, the Walsall contract was only a sixth of its size.

Getting the partnership started

Although the lead from Serco was immediately helpful and positive, with the internal adjustments necessary for Serco to acquire QAA, there were distractions in that direction and away from the immediate business at hand for the newly establishing partnership of identifying the Strategic Partner's Director of Strategy and School Effectiveness (DSSE). The DSSE would have a key leading role in the new partnership between Walsall LEA and Serco (the partnership of Walsall Education). This in fact would be the long-awaited lead from the private sector.

A number of well-qualified people were approached by Serco who made visits and considered their options. But more time was being lost in what was becoming a further protraction of the process. To speed things up, the role was taken on by the founding managing director of QAA who, in the acquisition by Serco, had retained a working interest with the company. With his strong LEA background and understanding of the context, early progress was rapid in agreeing draft protocols and partnership practices. These, as with other shared developments, went for scrutiny and approval to the Partnership Board, to which the DfEE were invited. Clarity was established over the roles to be filled within the partnership structure and moves to create a substantive management team and to pick up the now advancing work of the consultants forming the interim senior management began. Finally, a DSSE was appointed before the commencement of the contract in September 2001. In the four months between the award of the contract in April and contract commencement the following September, as CEO, I had worked with three different leads from the private side. It was the LEA management team that kept the impetus of improvement through to well after-contract commencement, in September 2001.

In addition to assisting with the internal adjustments within Serco and the associated induction and orientation needs, the LEA with help from PWC was in the throes of transferring its staff to Serco. It was necessary to establish a baseline from which the transfer of 105 staff could be achieved under 'TUPE' requirements. The demands created by organizing and providing the necessary induction for the partnership and the TUPE transfer coupled with service planning and implementation were huge. Added to this was the evaluation of progress on the improvement agenda already set in train. As the contract swung into full operation in September 2001, there was only four weeks before the Ofsted/AC team would require the Authority's self evaluation for the re-inspection, scheduled for the following January 2002. Quite literally, Serco had less than one term to become involved and begin contract delivery before the inspection that would measure progress since 1999.

In the spirit of partnership and pragmatism, the LEA handed as much of the contract work to SercoQAA as was realistic. However it continued, with interim and newly appointed substantive staff, to fulfil many areas of work which should have gone to the private sector side as specified in the contract, whilst delivering its own service provision unit responsibilities. The main priorities had become very much about maintaining the momentum of improvement which had started, and building a constructive and effective partnership which avoided 'contract-picking' in the early weeks. It was apparent that SercoQAA was not in a position to marshal full expertise (to the degree specified in the contract) to Walsall from 'day one'; although they did do well with their extensive network of school improvement consultants and redeployed 'TUPE' staff. Contractor monitoring against penalties was two years away anyway and the desire to see those real improvements (across the service and in schools), which had begun to continue was genuine across the partnership networks. So commonsense and team work was the tone rather than tight contract adherence in that first term.

Predictable ripples

Alongside these developments in Walsall, SercoQAA was busy setting up arrangements in Bradford. If the winning of their first education contract in Walsall and their second more major contract in Bradford in close succession had caused them to be somewhat overstretched, then no one was admitting to it.

However, some concerns were fuelled when confusions about quite fundamental earlier agreements began to creep in. For example, the DfEE copied me into correspondence between themselves and Serco (Williams 2002), which indicated very basic confusions about agreed high level partnership arrangements. The confusion was over the role of the Walsall Education 'Partnership Board', the agreed body to have oversight of the top level work of both the Strategic Partners in Walsall. This was an important area and one that deserved better care than the sending of confused messages to government departments directly and without the other partner's knowledge. There were other examples of clumsy information transfer on e-mails which I received in error. There did seem to be a desire on the part of some people in the private partnership to try to appear to the DfEE that they understood particular aspects when they clearly did not.

One of the difficulties of trying to resolve serious service deficits locally by using a network of people nationally is around maintaining a 'finger on the pulse'. No matter how good a provider is on big picture issues, to set effective strategy and high quality operational delivery across diverse local communities within a single metropolitan borough requires well-developed local knowledge. Responses sometimes have to be face to face. Telephone, e-mail and web-page communications are good in fair times but not always in times of difficulty. The integrity of the local parts of the new partnership was seen in many ways as more important than in its more distant national and multi-national dimensions. Problems encountered were only ripples in the pool. Overall, there was great confidence that the Strategic Partnership had the potential to be highly successful in moving Walsall forward and this attracted new high-quality staff to be appointed to both sides of the partnership.

Ofsted/AC re-inspection 2002: the process

The re-inspection of the LEA in January coincided with the new *Framework for the Inspection of Local Education Authorities* January 2002 (Ofsted 2002c), but the approaches followed were a mix of this and the earlier version of the framework in use to December 2001. Corporate strategic planning issues brought by the implementation of the Local Government Act (2000) were in some flux nationally; new elective arrangements were being installed and different inspection regimes were attempting to become more coordinated in their activities. Uncertainty over what was intended to happen under the new arrangements for January showed during set-up. Regardless of whatever turmoil Walsall LEA may have been in at this time, there was plenty of ambiguity over the changes in the inspection framework and the new arrangements.

This caused a number of operational problems from the outset. For example, unbeknownst to the LEA, the AC had sent out to schools their pre-inspection questionnaires 18 weeks before the inspection, long before the guidance had indicated. Consequently, this pre-empted arrangement made for the staff in the new partnership of 'Walsall Education' to talk through perceptions about service changes at the round of meetings already planned for head teachers. Disgruntled feelings existed around schools for sure, many about government initiatives which the LEA had successfully moved forward, bringing an (City) academy to Walsall, for example, was not seen as the most popular thing to do in some quarters. Along with justifiable dissatisfaction over service quality, the successes of the LEA in moving forward the government's agenda were ironically destined to produce even lower satisfaction rates. Yet the chance to discuss such issues with head teachers before the questionnaires were due for return was wiped away.

There were other examples. As a part of the general trend in inspections, the Ofsted/AC inspection team's reading of pre-inspection documentation had been lightened, principally it was reduced to the CEO statement and the summary self-evaluation grading forms. Due to traffic congestion, the Ofsted/AC team arrived very late on the first morning of the inspection and lost hours of planned reading and orientation time, including the slot arranged for their briefing discussions with the education management team. We cobbled together a meeting over lunch instead.

Punctuality seemed an ongoing problem for the inspection team and so the time lost never seemed to be made up. This manifested itself in the same questions being repeated time and again by different inspectors during interviews which were designed for other purposes. Questions also often sought clarification about either the changing arrangements in the elective structures and the developments associated with the LSP, or the nature of the Strategic Partnership itself between SercoQAA and the LEA. The team had insufficient time to sort out the complexities of who was doing what in this very different environment and in the very early days of contract commencement.

Ofsted/AC inspection 2002: the report

When the draft report was produced following the inspection there was a particularly glaring error in paragraph 19. The error indicated that there really had been serious confusion over 'who was who' and 'who was doing what'.

The paragraph showed confusion over the new service title for the partnership. The new title of 'Walsall Education', had been misunderstood as being synonymous with 'SercoQAA'. This was quite wrong, of course, and caused the Walsall side of the partnership more than a little concern.

The error was corrected by wording dictated to the inspection team at the preliminary feedback meeting. From saying in the draft report, 'The(se) services managed by the contractor (SercoQAA) have been re-branded as Walsall Education' (Ofsted 2002a), it was corrected in the final report to saying, 'The joint partnership of the LEA and the contractor has been re-branded as Walsall Education' (Ofsted 2002b). Although this correction was fine in itself, the consequences of that misunderstanding on the judgements made and on what was said throughout the report were not amended.

The implications from this were huge. When head teachers and stakeholders had been reporting the more positive aspects of the most recent work of both sides of the partnership, and using the term 'Walsall Education' (we had all worked hard to encourage the use of the new name for the branding of the whole partnership), the inspection team were hearing it and taking it to mean the private sector partner only, SercoQAA. Whilst the error in paragraph 19 was easily corrected, the same was not true about the critical judgements about the LEA side of the partnership throughout the report.

Apart from that and the operational weaknesses that had existed, the main problem was that the Council had undergone a Corporate Governance inspection six months earlier. This was known to be critical but had not been published prior to the inspection of the education service. Sir Andrew Foster, the Controller of the AC, said on 16 January 2002, the middle day of the education inspection, 'Walsall Council has failed local people. The council has considerable political and financial problems resulting in poorly run services and wasted taxpayers' money' (Foster 2002). The headline announcement of that Corporate Governance inspection, from the previous July, was indeed very badly timed for the education service. Any progress that was being recognized, however small, during the preliminary part of the education service inspection was not heard again following that announcement. Two year's work in education by the LEA, to create a springboard for fundamental change would have been difficult for anyone to report against that backdrop, let alone members of Andrew Foster's own AC team working in the Ofsted team.

There was an interesting attempt however. Particular paragraphs in the report gave some quite positive judgements, but they singled out this work as that of SercoQAA as the new private contractor. 'The contractor is leading on the development of the second EDP...This process has been rigorous and draws on a more comprehensive range of achievement, inspection and comparative data than before. Communication and consultation with headteachers and other stakeholders have been managed effectively. There is broad support for the three local priorities, in particular, the priority to enhance inclusive education' (Ofsted 2002b: para. 32).

To credit these examples specifically to SercoQAA was particularly inappropriate. These priorities had been identified as urgent in correspondence to all head teachers in Walsall in December 2000, 18 months earlier (Green 2000b). Significant action had been taken in these areas long before SercoQAA was even identified as the preferred bidder. True, SercoQAA were leading on these developments by the time the inspection came around, but the judgement was really about the achievement of the interim LEA team who had passed over to SercoQAA, work that had been in progress for almost two years. In some ways this was seen as inevitable, given the situation. Pragmatically, it did not really matter that much, SercoQAA were getting into the job successfully and the positive words about them in the report were good for them and for their future, but there was a sense that the people on the LEA side had been 'stitched up'.

Misleading spin

Whether an approach which assigned strengths largely to the private sector was the only 'politically' acceptable way of presenting the findings of the LEA report within the context of the critical Corporate Governance report, or whether there was confusion over who had actually done what, is not that important. The spirit of the new partnership was about the partnership succeeding. The fallacies in the apportionment of credit were obvious. To suggest that the scale of such activity as 'achieving greater rigour in the use of a more comprehensive range of data', 'managing communication and consultation with the community' and 'gaining support for three local EDP priorities' could be achieved by the contractor from a standing start in just a few weeks was nonsense and could be seen to be so. Paragraphs such as this helped the cause of the private sector considerably and no one can blame it for gaining a high-market profile from riding on the wave. Nevertheless, many members of the new partnership who had been heavily committed to making improvements on all sides throughout the process, on seeing the report and the spin that resulted lost a lot of faith in the processes.

What did matter and what is wrong, is the subsequent political spin and exaggeration given to such bias. The government press release quoted Estelle Morris, then Secretary of State for Education and Skills, 'Ofsted has commended the rapid progress made by Serco/QAA since September last year in structuring and redefining the services to support schools, and in the quality of service delivery. But the LEA has not made the improvements expected of it' (DfES 2002: 1). The DfES advisers who drafted that had made a leap of very questionable ethic. By any stretch of emotion, value or judgement, the injustice of that conclusion was grave.

Particularly where support for the private sector exists within the public sector and where public service effort and support to bring the private sector on board is so constructive, such misrepresentation is highly damaging to participatory democracy in the longer term, and the public are the losers in that. The process of reporting the bringing of the private sector into state education should be better than this.

Taking stock

Despite inspection reports not choosing to include them, the drive for greater joined-up strategic working across Council services and the public and private sectors, had produced some very tangible and positive results. Drawing together large-scale strategic schemes with different origins and with less than complementary priorities is not a short-term challenge. However, by focusing actions on education, with a view to achieving social and economic regeneration and to make real improvements in the quality of life, there were achievements.

- Political decision-making had clearly improved with a unanimous vote for the acceptance of the Strategic Partnership.
- Attainment trends in schools were improving at high rates well above average with good evaluations of the national strategies in literacy and numeracy.
- The LEA had agreed a coordinated strategy with secondary schools to apply for specialist school status. At that time, because government was intending to facilitate only 50 per cent of schools to that status, options were planned in Walsall for local community specialisms. Supply of the unconditional private sector sponsorship needed by schools to apply was secured to £100,000, enough for two schools, through a link with one of the sponsors of the academy.
- The establishment of Walsall Academy was a rapid win in itself, with the sensitive issue of the alignment of the Academy's admissions criteria within the pattern for the Borough well placed.
- The School Organization Plan (SOP) for the LEA and the removal of surplus places was in good order.
- Withdrawal of delegated powers from the one failing secondary school, had been carried out with the Governing Body's cooperation and

foundations laid for a neighbouring school to work in tandem, later developing into a new federation arrangement.

- A major improvement in the budget allocation for social inclusion through education initiatives was secured.
- Education's leadership in the reduction of youth crime, in out-of-school hours provision including entitlement to cultural and art through joint schemes by the DfES and the Department for Culture, Media and Sport (DCMS) were successful.
- Walsall contribution was instrumental in preparing the 16–19 area-wide review post inspection action plan with the LSC.

In short, progress was visible on many strategic fronts.

With the next round of continuing intervention and the dismantling of the Strategic Partnership in favour of seeking full outsourcing to SercoQAA (whilst observing again all the proper procurement procedures), the ground was already set and boded well for the rate of progress to be maintained. Given the new starting point, the chance for SercoQAA to perform very well in the coming years were exceptional. They could build on successes and improve services and perhaps prove just how successful a private firm can be in leading an LEA service. We will never know whether success could have been achieved by the Strategic Partnership or by twinning arrangements with other LEAs. I suspect that either would have been equally successful had a fair opportunity been allowed.

Full outsourcing: some losses and some gains

The losses were around human resource and the impetus of change. Faith and trust in government departments and agencies slipped. Levels of confidence that had been built into a real belief that the public and private sectors could work effectively together to bring service improvement took a blow. None of the newly appointed senior managers to the Strategic Partnership on the retained LEA side sought transfer to SercoQAA; they left Walsall altogether for what they saw as better options elsewhere. These were top professionals, accomplished in education policy and practice, not in any way people who could be stereotyped or labelled as 'part of a problem'; they were new appointments creating the solutions that were credited elsewhere. In authorities with challenges like those in Walsall, people of this calibre are badly needed. It is high levels of expertise that bring improvements, not ideological prejudices for private over public; or commercial contract over working agreement or vice versa. Moving from the Strategic Partnership to full outsourcing had to delay the progress being made. The gain was the expansion of the service contract to SercoQAA, a company in which there was confidence about its capacity to serve education well.

The next inspection report on the education service in Walsall is due in 2005. This will be on the contract delivery by SercoQAA. With time to establish implementation based on better strategic approaches and with rises in Council Tax, the judgements about improvements and the value-for-money of the education service goes full circle. It will be a great surprise if SercoQAA does not achieve very well. The potential to show progress and 'value-added' improvements is particularly good. However, whether it will contribute significantly to improvements in the Council's services as a whole is more doubtful. The fully privatized nature of the education service being a discrete outsourced contract and not within the original concept of a Strategic Partnership is likely to inhibit progress on that front. Nevertheless, the citizens, consumers, parents and pupils of Walsall, its teachers and governors, SercoQAA and its TUPE staff deserve whatever progress has been made this time to be recognized fully. No matter what is achieved there will always remain a lot more to be done.

Profile exhibit 6.1 The questionable benefits of corporate intervention

For a significant period before the turn of the millennium, Walsall Metropolitan District Council was a turbulent council with frequent change in political control and regular changes in the leadership of the main political parties. Sometimes, changes were during the municipal year.

The wish to retain political control was, therefore, reflected in expediency such that major decisions were approached in ways considered necessary, so as to retain the political vote at the ballot box. Due to this and for what some perceived as doctrinal reasons, the previous healthy financial reserves of the council were depleted while increases in the council tax (or its equivalent) and council house rents were minimized.

The council's strategic direction in the delivery of services and financial stability was perceived as uncertain. In this environment, officers had to exercise care to avoid creating 'political' problems, yet strive to deliver services while keeping a close eye on expenditure.

An authority in this situation is likely to be the object of forensic examination; and indeed it was.

Receipt of a critical Ofsted report in 1999 resulted in Government intervention and a structural change to the senior management team of the council, the appointment of a new CEO and the privatization of a significant part of the education service.

The council received management letters from the District Auditor criticizing the council's lack of adequate financial reserves. Further, adverse reports were received following inspections of Trading Standards and Environmental Services. These outlined corporate and services weaknesses. By July 2001, the whole council was subject to a corporate governance inspection by the AC. Their report, published during the second Ofsted inspection of the LEA, found weaknesses in the political and management processes leading to the delivery of poor services. These failures were considered to be systemic. Such was the position that they said that the authority could not be left to itself to resolve the problems.

The path to recovery was laid out to include:

- a supervisory board of external officials but no elected councillors;
- support from the Improvement and Development Agency for Local Government;
- political mentors for each political group;
- assistance in performance management and community planning;
- a package totalling £400,000 for 6 months.

Perhaps the question to be considered is whether a council can recover from such a position in such a period of time. Is recovery in that frame actually a realistic prospect?

The council engaged in a wide range of activity to address the recommendations. Hardly any additional staffing resources were provided, and the external support was at times more obstructive than helpful. Change and improvement were top priority but this was in addition to the 'day job'.

From December 2001, the Supervisory Board met monthly in private and received reports from the Chief Executive and the political group leaders (there being no overall political control). However, there was no feedback from the Board on the rate of progress being achieved, its appropriateness or its acceptability. Such a relationship is unlikely to produce the best results.

In May 2002, the Board reported to the AC on progress. This acknowledged significant progress in four important areas, but two areas of failure were identified together with three less significant areas where recommendations had not been achieved.

Unfortunately, in the meanwhile, there had been an inspection of Social Services and a further Ofsted inspection. Both reports were critical in terms of corporate management and service delivery. In terms of education, the CEO had been in post for less than two years and had in that time been successful in gaining and in inducting a private sector provider, in response to the earlier education intervention of 2000.

One conclusion of the report was that 'the council needed some robust interim management arrangements to provide leadership and capacity to deliver the recovery plan whilst the new executive team was appointed and established itself'.

An earlier part of the report had said that the collective and individual competencies of the existing executive team should have been externally evaluated but this had not happened. It seems that irrespective of the relative strengths of those employees, they had to go. However the democratically elected decision-makers, the councillors were not equivalently challenged.

It was the view of the AC that the council retained its employment responsibilities although this was not the view of the Board of the Commission. The council apparently had to make the decisions, but did it have freedom to act as it wished; or was it subject to political influence from the centre?

There was regular communication between the council and the central government. The council was reminded that if they did not make appropriate decisions the Secretary of State would be invited to take formal action. Whether he would do so and the form of any such action was of course a matter for him. The message was clear. Ultimately, the council decided 'to let the executive team go' but it has to be a matter of conjecture as to the degree of government influence.

In *The Times* (12 December 2002), it was reported that the government was planning 'to send hit squads to take over the worst councils'. It is questionable whether the government should be running local councils in this way and over-riding democratically locally elected councillors. These planning proposals envisaged having 'up to 8 weeks to prepare recovery plans and then 2 to 3 months to see if they worked!'

There are clearly issues of democratic concern even if the intention is to improve performance rapidly. It is said that 'excellent' councils tend to have political leadership that is strategic, clear and focused on it priorities. These priorities are then successfully communicated to officials and percolate down to council staff; clearly laudable objectives following unsatisfactory inspections. It may be that the corporate inspection regime may secure swiftly enhanced performance, but there must be recognition that genuine improvements require an adequate resource of time.

The government intervention was lifted in August 2003 but *Housing Today* (2 April 2004) reported that Walsall 'was awarded no stars for its strategic housing services by the Audit Commission' in their 30 March 2004 report. The fully privatized education service however is expected to do much better.

Whether intervention on this scale works is therefore still undecided.

Source: George Curran, Solicitor, National Secretary of Solicitors in Local Government 2005.

7 Parents, choice and information

> I was at Eton, yes for four or five years. I didn't like it, and I have been blamed for putting in Who's Who that I obtained my education in the holidays from Eton.
>
> (Sir Osbert Sitwell 1892–1969)

The vast majority of parents send their children to their local schools. They do not seek other options. Having a choice is often not even considered, it is thought that the district school is the only feasible place for their children to go. However, in many places, particularly urban areas, the schools available are not deemed to be good enough by increasing numbers of parents and so parents go to great lengths to find alternatives.

Launching plans for ten new schools to be built across five London Boroughs (within a federation enabling pupils at one school to attend lessons at another) the Prime Minister said 'There are parents who feel the schools in their area are inadequate' (Blair: 2003). It is in inner city and urban areas like these where the crux of the problem lies. The strategy of creating sponsored specialist schools is an attempt to resolve the problem. The protagonists of specialist schools know the issues well.

> Choice is an emotive word in English education circles. To many supporters of equal opportunities, choice often means privilege and the ability to pay for a private school education for one's children, or to attend a good school because you live in a socially advantaged, leafy suburb where the cost of housing is higher.
>
> (Taylor and Ryan 2005: 83)

Sometimes the lengths that parents go to in order to secure a place at a school, especially in the London Boroughs, receive sensational media attention. In late 2003 the UK Shadow Home Secretary, Oliver Letwin, himself educated at England's most famous 'public' (that is private) school, Eton, was reported as saying that if necessary he would rather go out on the streets and beg than send his children to the state secondary school next to where he lived in the London Borough of Lambeth. He made the point that parents with enough money end up getting their children into good fee-paying schools, whilst those that do not are forced to use state schools. His point was that all parents should be given the choice of sending their children to good schools; the less well-off should not be left with a poor second best. That is agreed all round. It is how to go about achieving that situation which presents difficulties.

Scarcity of places and contradiction

A few months after Oliver Letwin made these remarks, a major British TV channel ran a two-part programme about a small primary school in the London Borough of Bromley. During prime-time viewing the broadcaster, Trevor McDonald, told the story of how some parents had gone to great trouble and expense to buy houses with addresses very near to the school, and had even attempted to bribe the head teacher in order to get their children into this particular school. The school was in a good social area and maintained very high test results. What the TV programme did not show was that, whilst the school was high achieving and socially well placed, it was also part of the South East of England Virtual Education Action Zone (SEEVEAZ). This meant it was within the government's EAZ scheme, a scheme designed to tackle underachievement and promote inclusion in areas where disadvantage was at its keenest. The additional resources the school received as a part of the scheme, coupled with the very highly sought after status it enjoyed, presented a contradictory scenario to what one might have expected.

Those interested in seeing strategies to improve schools in disadvantaged areas, actually match the purpose for which these strategies were designed, argue about how a good match might be made. They argue either that a socially advantaged school such as this one in Bromley should be included in the EAZ on the grounds that it provides a model of high attainment and parental popularity and so may help the other schools in the zone or, conversely, that it should not be, so that extra resources attached to the EAZ could be more prudently and appropriately focused on those schools in real need and therefore not diluted in this way.

Where scarcity of places at oversubscribed schools is the critical factor, as in this case, a mix of factors and tensions comes into play in varying proportions and at different times. Schools which are sought after often enjoyed success during the highly competitive era of the GM schools in the 1990s. School was often pitted against school driven by a market philosophy that the weak and less popular schools would close and the others would expand. It can be quite a shift in philosophical stance for some schools in moving from that idea to a genuinely more collaborative practice of the sort now extolled. The pedigree of the Specialist Schools Trust with its original associations within that era fails to raise a genuine confidence for many.

The fact that some schools are in great demand and that shortages of places exist can in itself make these schools seem better and more attractive than they really are. However, if other schools in the area which could provide places are perceived to be inadequate, whether they are, then the problem persists and intensifies. Giving real choice to parents has never been achieved for the majority of the population, nor has it been demanded. But expectations are changing. The situation has become most visible in those disadvantaged urban areas where pockets of regeneration and the gentrification of older housing have brought higher social expectations from new householders on the local schools.

Expressed simply, more and more families see their choice as between using a 'low class' state school or paying fees to use private education. Many parents believe that private education is superior to state education automatically, the logic being that otherwise it would not sell over the competition which is free. Access to private education at independent day schools range widely but costs of around £8,000 a year are not untypical. If a parent can afford to pay for education twice, once in taxes and then again in school fees then the private option might well be taken but there are sound arguments as to why taxpayers should not have to pay twice for a decent school that meets their requirements. Hence, the political preoccupation by recent governments to attempt to find ways to give more freedom of choice across the system and, within that process, break the cycle of underachievement associated with social disadvantage.

Overcoming scarcity of places

The way forward is seen as bringing the private and public sectors closer together in providing school places. Lots of ideas swill around about how this might be achieved. The population of parents, whether viewed locally or internationally, is made up of hugely varying groups. As debates unfold about educational choice and the rights of parents, then the interests of individual families are framed by national and even global terms. Work on parent choice in Canada and the USA parallels the situation in the UK. '(I)t is wrong to assume that "parents" comprise a unified constituency with similar interests in relation to education or that they can and do take up identical positions in the contemporary politics of school reform' (Dehli 2000: 1997). This is an understatement, but it confirms that privatization has to mean either choice for parents or a single good quality option that appeals to a broad constituency.

Schemes for choosing schools are well developed in North America. The use of vouchers, to be spent on any school of choice, has been tried extensively in the USA, most notably in Milwaukee, Wisconsin, Cleveland, Ohio and in parts of Florida. In England the use of a voucher scheme was flirted with for access to nursery school places but was quickly dropped. Generally speaking voucher schemes are viewed as not being particularly successful, partly because their use are easily open to abuse, but more crucially, because they do not lead to the creation of new schools in the most disadvantaged areas where they are most needed.

Charter schools in the USA are seen, instead, as a more tangible way of 'harnessing the best aspects of the market and the public sector while mitigating the shortcomings of both' (Rotherham 2003: 21). Rotherham reports that whilst, like state schools, charter schools receive government funding for each student, unlike state schools they can be set up and operated by a wide range of community organizations; thus increasing pluralism and community involvement. There is bipartisan support for charter schools with 41 states having passed legislation to allow them. There are almost 3,000 charter schools around the USA prevalent in poor neighbourhoods where educational problems are most acute.

However, there are issues about the supply of education not matching greatest demand, whether from those holding vouchers or those interested in starting charter schools. Shifts from voucher schemes to charter programmes are complicated by the relative value of the vouchers and the levels of public accountability placed on charter schools. The concerns are similar to those in the UK about how educational success is measured and whether particular enclaves wish to exercise their own ideas about this. 'Voucher schools in Cleveland and...Milwaukee...are not required to submit their students to state tests, and have generally refused to do so' (Carnoy 2000: 15). Typical alternatives to state schools are often charter schools formed by religious groups that tend to resist usual public accountabilities. Questions about quality and equity prevail, 'in a market you could get choice *and* the same amount of education for *fewer* resources, but not necessarily better education for the same resources' (ibid.: 15, 16).

Though different in concept and scale, there are some parallels between charter schools in the USA and the development of academies in England. The direction that academies take is to have publicly funded, privately run schools which provide places in often new high-quality buildings, in areas where schools have not been popular. There is a real sense of economic and social regeneration in the areas of these schools, emanating from the schools. Parents are keen to seek places for their children at these academies; many are disappointed. In proportion to the taxpayers' investment in state schools, academies are expensive but then they are being established in those areas of most disadvantage and where fresh approaches to secondary education are most needed. Despite the claims about private sponsorship and their independent status, academies are almost totally funded by the taxpayer.

Suspicions about whether privatization actually improves choice

In England, as private schools and private companies become increasingly involved in state school provision, either through sharing expertise or bringing sponsorship, concerns lurk in two dimensions.

1   There is concern about the ease with which sponsors can gain influence and direct control over state education. With the drive in secondary education towards 200 new academies with independent status by 2010 and over 2,000 independent specialist schools by 2006, all requiring some level of private sponsorship, then the fundamental character of state education, which is traditionally funded by direct taxation and maintained by democratically elected local councils is set to change.
2   As private firms become involved, they are often perceived as buying their way in to state education and to the benefits that may bring them, very cheaply. With less than 10 per cent investment of capital costs or a £50,000 one-off sponsorship donation then the private sector's relationship with a school can be forged. Subsequent influences on budget decisions over the huge-funding streams to schools, which flow from taxpayers' money, move significantly to those with private sector interests. This concern is succinctly expressed by a professional association representative, 'Academies were supposed to lever private finance into public education, not lever public money into private pockets' (Evans 2004: 1).

There are few reasons to believe that, with due probity, private sector companies and private schools will be anything other than ethical and upright in their dealings with and in state schools and so bring a positive influence and give parents better choice. The capital investment from the private sector in supporting 200 academies and an additional 1,000 specialist schools by 2010 would amount to about £450 million, a small but not an insignificant amount. More importantly is the investment of corporate and personal energy that the private sector is thought to bring to the leadership and the management of state schools. New ideas and insights and the ambition and determination to succeed (even in areas of disadvantage) are traits often perceived to be more prevalent in private sector leadership than in the public service routes. This emphasis is, however, on the impact of high-level management rather than on greater engagement of local constituents.

Looking back to the charter school movement, it is not high-level management impact that is driving the movement, but more of the different parochial interest of those that seek to set up the school. Views about radical steps to break the cycle of educational underachievement come in different ideological and practical packages, yet it is the labels of privatization and independence that draws them into the same frame.

So, both the public and the private sectors are seen as having legitimate roles to play in improving the educational provision available, which includes fair access to decent schools. Participation is at the level of individual action, group interest and at the highest levels of policy formation. The hunt for alternatives is led in different ways, at different levels and from different starting points by government, LEAs, private sector companies, particular interest groups, head teachers and governors and by parents. Suspicions abound around what is actually going on!

- How are parents engaged in the process of determining state educational provision and improving its quality?
- How do parents find out about schools in order to exercise any choice of school that might exist?
- What perceptions do they gain from the information that is available?
- How reliable is information about school performance and what messages are conveyed by its presentation?

Much has been done in the last quarter century to involve parents in the processes of developing state education and concerns about a reduction in democratic participation are real.

Parents' involvement: participants, partners and consumers

In England, following the Education Act 1980, parents gained significantly more representation in the governance of state schools. They gained greater representation on school governing bodies and education committees. This was a tangible manifestation of their involvement in local democratic structures. Their role and influence in state education has continued to grow since and this has been a good thing.[1]

However, there is a precarious balance in the emphasis placed on trying to engage the whole community of parents as helpful citizens and neighbourly contributors to their community of schools, against the consumer-type role for parents of holding schools to account against published performance data. Where is the line clarifying the role for parents between 'partnership and engagement' from 'consumerism and accountability'?

Loyalty, voice and exit

When parents who become involved in partnership work with a school and, for whatever reason, feel the need to withdraw their children yet continue with their partnership work, the unease created in the partnership can be very real. Partnership as we know it and accountability as it has been developed for schools can form a counter-productive process. The circumstances which prevail within the continuum of 'loyalty' (where parents tend not to complain but support the school with their children remaining in it despite difficulties), 'voice' (where parents complain) and 'exit' (where parents withdraw their children) has been well documented by academics for decades. Many parents feel uncomfortable in adopting what they feel might be the right position on this continuum at different times in their children's school careers simply because of uncertainty. Should they behave as engaged citizens and partners with the school and face issues in that role or should they behave as consumers and hold the school to account by complaint and withdrawal of their business?

The system in which parents find themselves is predicated on division. They perceive this division in the types of schools presented to them, the relative status afforded to different schools, especially where they are selective or fee-paying, and by governments' obsessions to publish schools' performance results in ranked league tables. It is more comfortable to make a partnership contribution, or be satisfied with your consumer choice, on the high side of the performance divide. Yet, it is the low side of the divide that needs the time and attention of our most talented parent population.

Parent Partnership Services (PPS)

Much good work has been achieved by these services. However, the scale of engaging the wide population of mainstream parents is a huge and a nebulous task. This has not been the central feature of their practice. PPS have usually been about helping parents of children with SEN. The services were set up from 1994, usually in an arms-length relationship with LEAs, and evolved with the aim, 'to ensure parents of children with special needs, including the very young, have access to information, advice and guidance in relation to the educational needs of their children so they can make appropriate, informed decisions' (DfES 2001b: para. 2.19).

It was, as Sheila Wolfendale puts it, 'Because a number of surveys of the 1980s attested to parental dissatisfaction with the apparently slow realization of partnership in practice, Parent Partnership Services were created to accelerate cooperative working practices' (Wolfendale 2002: 6). She goes on, 'A linked concept to "partnership" is that of "empowerment" which can be viewed as the active manifestation of a partnership relationship, wherein all parties mandate each other to exercise their rights and responsibilities' (ibid.). These issues about partnership and empowerment are complicated by political manoeuvring which attempts to appeal to the middle class voters and by professional interest groups who are in the front line facing very different demands from politicians and parents. 'The challenge is to enable and empower families but are we ready to align professional practice with family need?' (Carpenter 2000: 142). This is a searching question which is relevant across a wide canvas of education in 2005.

In the debate about possible benefits private intervention in state education might bring, it is argued that private companies concentrate on achieving a sharper focus on the customers' needs. Indeed, private schools are often seen to be geared primarily to meeting families' wants and needs, boarding education, for example, whereas state schools are not. Also with state education, the perception is that a 'status quo' is on offer, the basic bland National Curriculum entitlement is what you get and even then only if you are lucky. The assumption is that there is more to be had from somewhere else, if one can afford to pay for it in some way.

Where partnership arrangements with parents exist, they are often primarily associated with vulnerable groups. Sometimes, they are regarded as required because the education offered is 'a deficit model' and so schools and groups of parents are needed to mobilize their resources to make up for deficiencies. Strategically, state education has not embraced the emotional and the practical support that lies within the full range of the parent population.

One of the reasons why PPS have not been more effective in empowering parents is to do with the original limitations of their remit. Initially, due to the conditions of the funding, the partnerships were associated with just the 2 per cent of parents whose children had statements of SEN; statutory entitlements of additional provision beyond that received for every child. Where partnerships broadened their remits, as they were free to do, they rarely touched beyond the 20 per cent of the wider group of parents whose children had SEN, but without statutory statements.

Some parent partnerships did broaden their roles beyond serving just the parents of children's SEN; serious attempts were made to do this in Walsall. The Suffolk Parent Partnership model is a good example. This partnership emphasizes working more widely with primary and secondary schools and across a network of professional groups.

> It capitalises upon its position within the LEA to work strategically to assist...in supporting school improvement. The approach is inclusive. It is based on developing practice in schools for working with the whole parent body rather than focusing on issues for parents of children with special needs.... An inclusive approach to Parent Partnership...has a universality which can place it at the centre of the debate on the development of an education system fit for the twenty-first century.
>
> (Leming 2002: 73)

Partnership activity of this sort may contribute to securing more schools which meet the legitimate expectations of parents, LEAs and the government. However, an acceptance of the responsibility that all schools are there to educate all the pupils who are able to attend is not an easily won principle.

There is little to indicate that those involved in the process of privatizing state education have great enthusiasm for practical inclusive policies which bring children whose needs make them more expensive to teach.

Parental choice

Aspiring parents and aspiring schools understandably want what they see as best for their own particular situations. Parents do not see their community's social needs as the most important or salient factor at a point in time when their own child's education is on the line. They see state education as existing to provide, from direct taxation, the means of having a good school for their child to attend so they in turn can gain, amongst many other things, the skills needed for personal success in later life (Profile exhibit 7.1).

Profile exhibit 7.1 Wanting and gaining the best for your own children's education and for the community

I certainly wanted the best education available for my own four sons and for my grandchildren. The question as to what is the best is not easily answered unless a stereotypical view, predicated on a singular prejudice, is the basis for the judgement.

Education is not just about schooling. Schooling is only the formal, statutory part of the process. So long as government policy promotes the idea that parents and children are consumers of education, rather than key participants in it, and that they must have other champions to defend their cause against the evils of the local authorities and the schools themselves, then things will not fundamentally improve.

Transformation of secondary education will only come about when parents and pupils are much more intrinsically involved in learning than they are now. From my experience of helping in both primary and secondary schools, over many years, it is patently clear that private sponsorship money is not the key to success. Rather, success comes from genuine interest on the part of the community; the kind of interest that values the work of its schools and hold them in high esteem and does something about it, when things are not as they should be. Real participation is what matters, not those trite notions about private sector service being universally superior.

I have lived for most of my life in Bury in Lancashire, England. My children and grandchildren were born and raised here. Although both I and my late husband have never been involved in education professionally, we have been active in our local schools in voluntary capacities during the period whilst our own children proceeded through the various stages of schooling and since, for over 25 years in fact.

Bury is a relatively small LEA, it is a metropolitan borough and is located in an urban area amongst other LEAs, which together offer a wide range of schools. Both Bury Grammar School and Bolton School are nearby and have very good reputations as selective private schools with excellent academic records of performance. When my children went through the transition from primary to secondary school, it was possible for a few children to gain an 'assisted' place at these fee-paying schools. This meant that the local authority would pay the school fees providing the pupil passed the entrance examination convincingly enough. Pupils with less convincing passes were offered fee-paying places. The state primary schools would enter their highest-performing children in the entrance examinations as a matter of routine. My eldest son was not considered able enough to be entered in these examinations but he still had to sit his 11-plus which he failed and so attended the local secondary modern school.

The following year, mainstream education became comprehensive in the borough so my second son, although having no 11-plus to sit, was entered by the school for both the private schools entrance examinations. At the time, we were happy for him to be entered and actually felt quite proud that he did well enough to be offered a place at Bolton School. After all, my husband and I had been the products of the selective system in Manchester a generation before and, we had been happy enough emerging from the different strands of 'technical' and 'grammar' schools as we had, although on reflection, the segregation seemed artificial and quite unnecessary. Traditions such as selection tests at the age of 11 in working class areas like Bury and in many other more middle class areas die hard!

Many people thought us unwise when we turned down the place offered at Bolton School and decided to send him to the same local, newly formed comprehensive as attended by his elder brother. Like the primary school they had attended, the comprehensive seemed very good. Staff were approachable and worked hard in establishing a healthy and a productive working relationship with the classes and the pupils. Subsequently, I requested that my two younger boys were not entered for the private schools' examinations.

My four boys achieved different outcomes from this same secondary school, though their attitudes and their approaches to school life and learning were quite individual. All have done well in their different ways. Between them they each achieved 4 good A level General Certificate of Education (GCEs), and then went on separately to get an Higher National Certificate (HNC), a first-class honours degree in computation from a leading university and an MBA. They could not have done better academically even if they had gone to Bolton School.

I do not see the need for the hype about private schools, private sponsors of state schools, independent specialist secondary schools and fancy academies. Local people should be the sponsors of their schools. I have paid £1 a month to our local comprehensive school since before 1980 when my eldest started and continue to pay to this day, even though it is 16 years since my youngest left. My grand-children are now in the same route.

The privatization issues seem to distract attention away from achieving what parents actually want from their local schools. In an urban area like Bury, it is possible to create choice across a range of different specialist schools but it is doubtful that a particular specialism would really be seen as at all relevant and certainly not the deciding factor in the choice of a school. In England, we are notorious for forcing our children to specialize their educational interests too early, anyway.

What advantage can there be in creating specialist schools for children aged from 11, apart from pampering to political rhetoric? The claims made that achievement is higher in specialist schools than in other schools are based on very slender indicators, the measures of greater success at best are only marginal. What matters much more than the so-called specialisms and independent status that is preened is the nature of the learning ethos which surrounds the pupils' lives at home, at school, at work and at play.

Pupils do well at school when they have supportive parents and teachers and when there is an easy and a ready dialogue between them. Parents and teachers are part of an educational group within the wider community. May be, as a family we have been particularly lucky in the schools our children have attended, but I doubt it. Most schools do well where parents are supportive and where parents are encouraged to help other parents understand what a particular school is about and what it is trying to achieve.

I have little confidence in those aspects of the state education system which seem based on trying to gain some advantage over others through artificial means of pupil selection, especially where this is based on the financial ability of the community to sponsor the school or on the inflated income of the parents which gives them an easy ability to pay high fees.

Perhaps the *Five Year Strategy for Children and Learners* will achieve a better start in life for every child by 2010 with more integrated services focused on the needs of parents and children. However, I see little harm in re-distributing some of the resources currently being used on feasibility studies and in the strategic privatization processes of tendering and bidding and instead, redirecting this money to those agencies in local communities and to schools and to voluntary groups who can actually engage learners at a variety of levels and really improve the quality of life.

Source: Margaret Benn, Former officer or member of the parent/teacher/ friends associations at Greenhill Primary School, Tottington High School and Peel Sixth Form College, Bury, Lancashire.

Parents know what an adequate school looks like for their children and how it should be in the community. They know from a simple range of indicators like 'no fighting on the bus' to 'high levels of success for pupils in gaining useful academic and vocational qualifications'. They also know that the quality of the relationships which exist between the groups of pupils who attend and the staff who are employed, are the vital ingredients. They know that the values which form the life and behaviour of the school are paramount. A new building may help, it will certainly make for extra motivation, but new or old, the building has to be clean and of fair fabric. Modern ICT facilities are important, clarity over expectations about routines and dress codes matter as does a curriculum which is well taught and from which their children will learn. These expectations are standard. If many of these things feature in the local school, then exercising choice is a low priority.

Parents do not base much on the inspirational or the visionary speeches by the head on new parents' night (though they need to draw some confidence), the fact that the school is a category of specialist school or is an academy, the size of the school's trust fund or the degree to which it is independent. But the cant and dogma about these things leads them to think that they should.

More choice is being exercised. As parents see the disproportionate investment in some schools over others, it is clear which schools they will favour. Walsall Academy had its admission applications increase ten-fold over the school it replaced within a year. When the building, the facilities and the resource levels are so visibly superior then the attraction is obvious. The challenge will be in ensuring that the investment and the glamour in new schools in 2005 still have their shine in 2030 and that a gleaming system of schools is open to all and not just to some.

Choice and school availability

Schools have some choice too, although this is usually exercised covertly. More than a few schools see those children of interested parents and from stimulating homes as potentially higher contributors to the aggregation of their exam results and league table scores and therefore to a higher ranking over other schools. Some successful schools do not necessarily want to expand because they know that might mean having to import the troubles of other schools.

Most schools also know that to try to expand beyond the capacity of available space and infrastructure is to embark on a route that can easily damage a finely tuned school ethos which the school needs to maintain in order to remain successful. Political ideas that choice and school availability can be improved for parents simply by expanding the most successful schools fail to recognize the level of reluctance to do this by many successful schools. Claims that such action is realistic and that real choice exists are, in many situations, simply illusions. The sensible way to create proper educational choice is by ensuring that abroad and domestically, relevant curriculum is available within the schools themselves.

Proving rapid success, showing excellence in fact, are high priorities for schools in new categories carrying high 'political' profiles. Consequently waiting for, or engineering, a better cohort of pupils may well be more attractive than following the more egalitarian approach of accepting those local families who merely want a place because they live close by.

These behaviours impact at both ends of the market relationship, schools and parents, where some schools attempt to seek out pupils who are easy to teach and perform well, whilst some parents seek high status schools and the good academic or vocational results associated with them.

Giving parents the freedom to choose their children's school is a fundamental principle of market forces. It makes good sense because parents know what they want and the exercise of preference has an impact on improving those desired features and on raising standards. But the downside of the current situation is serious. Exercising preference under these conditions can cause exclusion to those who are not granted their choice. Good pupils and good teachers are not evenly spread across schools, so the schools which are preferred, those that are oversubscribed, have to determine who should and who should not be admitted.

It is the behaviours around how the admissions criteria are applied that are contentious. Admissions criteria are subject, in more than a few cases, to manipulation by both schools and by parents. The distance a family lives from school is the most commonly used criterion for allocating places, so parents with the wherewithall to buy a house and have an address closest to the school of their choice have the best chance of getting their children in. Once the eldest child has a place then the 'sibling link' criterion will usually trump all, younger brothers and younger sisters will have no trouble in getting places. Socially adept and well-informed parents are usually better placed than most to respond to admissions criteria, for example, for admission to faith schools where their family's participation in the faith community might be heightened around crucial times. Similarly where there are grammar schools, where selection is by ability, it is the socially advantaged parents who benefit most. 'In grammar schools 2 per cent of children are eligible for free school meals compared to 16 per cent elsewhere' (Tulloch 2004: 30). Wealthier parents are able to increase their range of choice, not only by their ability to pay fees to private schools but also by their manoeuvrability within the state system's arrangement for admissions. Professor Tim Brighouse, the Government-appointed adviser for London schools, for example, feels that a common admissions system across London would make things far better. 'Until somebody tackles admissions criteria it will remain the case that schools choose children rather than children choose schools' (Brighouse 2004: 15).

Manoeuvres and covert selection on social grounds could be overcome at a stroke. An alternative has been widely publicized but so far has failed to capture political appeal. Places at oversubscribed schools could be allocated by using a simple ballot system. All those wishing to attend a particular oversubscribed school could simply be entered in a ballot which would, by random selection, produce a fair outcome seen not to be influenced by the parents' or the schools' ability to manipulate the admissions system. Perhaps, producing such a random curve of normal distribution is too risky within contemporary ideas and definition of freedom and democracy.

Levelling the playing field and putting admissions on an equal basis in some way would clarify this fraught issue. It would also mean that other issues to be faced, such as how private providers might offer new types of schools and how the government's ambition to promote collaboration between schools (schools which are often heavily divided), might be approached with less complication. Making school admissions a transparent and fair exercise would relieve both schools and parents from accusations of vested interest. It would place them, as the agents of supply and demand, partners and consumers, in a position where there would be tangible advantage for both to work for an overall improvement across the whole system rather than continue to pursue sectional, local and personal agendas.

Informing choices

The advantages and disadvantages of Ofsted providing unbiased objective information about schools and LEAs are discussed in Chapter 4. Ofsted is adept at giving summary evaluations in its reports on schools, including attainment and achievement of pupils, by using both qualitative and quantitative indicators. Whether Ofsted reporting is a more valid and reliable method of giving parents and LEAs information about the performance of private sector firms, than using typical monitoring against contractual targets is open to debate. Here, we look briefly at other sources of information, which are used to inform league tables and other such measures, which in turn influence the judgements by Ofsted.

Head teachers, governors and teachers generally do a good job of informing parents about their schools, levels of bias are kept within ethical proportions. Open days and evening meetings for parents to visit schools and meet staff and students are commonplace. Brochures spell out aims, have charts showing the structure of staffing and describe approaches to teaching and learning, the nature of the curriculum, the expectations on pupils and students, the home–school policies and, often, include a paragraph on how the school is judged to be doing. Strengths and particular qualities are usually emphasized with maybe a quotation or two from the most recent Ofsted report.

Only a few schools make reference to their position in league tables. Even those that are high in the tables are usually cautious. Why? For two reasons:

1   Since the educational community tends rightly not to value league table positions as particularly significant indicators in real educational terms.
2   Once used, a subsequent drop in position in the following years will suggest quantifiable decline, which may not be truly the case in terms of the school's actual performance.

The relative performance of similar schools is an important benchmark to use as one factor in evaluation processes. However, to rank scores (be they 'raw scores' national averages or 'added value') in a public league table and then attempt to use the position attained as an indicator of how a school is performing overall is unreliable. To go on to use this as a means of choosing a place for a pupil is to base the selection on a very narrow set of measures indeed.

There is also the annual cry that the statutory assessment tests (upon which the league tables are constructed) are not conducted fairly. The claims are usually about LEAs and the DfES turning a blind eye to 'malpractice' because everyone wants scores to go up in order to keep political egos satisfied. The accusations usually include those presented by the anonymous primary school teacher writing in *The Guardian* newspaper (2004: 8):

• subjective interpretations of marking criteria that can be so ambiguous as to allow a self-serving marker to push the grades up...
• removing pupils with SEN from the classroom during exam time and completing the tests with those children behind closed doors, giving them the answers...
• delaying submission of completed papers to allow pupils to correct their answers well after the original test day...
• in order for teachers to get their periodic performance-related rise they have to meet certain targets that include a percentage of children reaching a specified level and so teachers inflate grades where they can so as not to lose out or appear to come across as an underachiever.

Nevertheless, successive governments continue to publicize comparative league tables and by so doing emphasize the importance of them as indicators of school performance, no matter how false they may be. Politically, it is difficult for any government to reduce the profile these tables have in the educational culture, simply because such an act would be deemed as 'going soft on standards' and would be leapt upon as such by their opposition. Accountability is an important principle that has to be retained but the league table contribution is an over-rated and an unreliable component. The problem is one created by politics and political returns becoming too close to the operation of schools. Few politicians want to be seen to align themselves with a school that does not appear to be doing well, even if the reasons are more to do with the outside environmental issues and not within the school itself.

Removing annual league tables from publication would not seriously dent the accountability of schools and the trust of the public in the education system; it would more likely restore some public confidence in the government's regard for parents' own abilities to seek out better quality information on schools in their localities.

The reliability of league tables and the testing arrangements which provide the scores for them, is beyond the scope of this commentary. However, there are real questions about their true worth. These questions are especially significant with the role of the private sector increasing and with measurement against such targets so central in contractual specifications and to the private companies' modus operandi.

There is a parallel between school league table ranking and measuring for contract compliance. League tables of schools are often very misleading even where there is no malpractice. A good example is the position a school can find itself in due to the conflict between its appropriate inclusion of pupils with special learning needs and the consequent dip in their league table position based on the lower-test score aggregation. The league table construction and publication do not show a school's, or an LEA's, success with pupils' achievements at target levels appropriately set below national expectations and national averages, yet these by definition represent aspects of realistic achievement for a significant proportion of the population. The parallel is that as most private sector contracts are based upon performance indicators of the quantitative type, then this type of failure of accountability to parents by league table measures is likely to be duplicated in the contractual measures placed on private providers.

Judgements as to whether contract specification and targets have been reached are made around measurable performance at system level. Yet, the product of much of education is about the finer nuance of need. Although not impossible, this is certainly more difficult to quantify in contractual terms in the field of education than it is in other spheres. Depending on the circumstances, success relies to a greater or a lesser degree on professional trust and integrity at detailed levels of delivery and it is important that this is cultivated and controlled. No doubt, this is achievable in a privatized world, but the level of sophistication in measuring, monitoring, evaluating and reporting will have to be considerably more refined than it is now to bring it about.

False ceilings and mean language

Many adjustments have been made in the way measures of schools' performance are taken and in the composition of the school performance tables. One development, thought to be positive, was the introduction in 2003 of 'value-added' indicators. These were brought in to demonstrate the degree of progress in pupils' learning, rather than presenting just the pupils' raw positions in tests. Are these value-added indicators an improvement, are they fair? Many teachers and head teachers think not.

As an example, let us take the performance of pupils at age 7 and 11 in National Curriculum tests in English and maths. The expected levels for these two age groups are level 2 and level 4 respectively. An able 7-year-old scoring an above average level 3 who then scores an above average level 5 at 11 would be classed as making satisfactory progress, the school would have 'added the value' expected, satisfactory. Yet, the 'ceiling' of level 5 in the tests for 11-year olds means that the child can do no better by that National Curriculum measure. In practice, it is likely that the school will have enriched and broadened the child's education immensely, immeasurably one might say, by the experiences provided and the teaching and the learning engagements over the four years; but the measure used to hold the school to account will not recognize that. With the majority of children in a year group performing in this way, the best value-added judgement available to a school would be 'satisfactory', whereas the education provided could actually be very good, even excellent.

To avoid this happening, a school might be tempted to depress scores at seven, either by complacent teaching or by applying over stringent testing conditions, so as to give head room for more value-added results at 11 years of age. The reverse, that is of falsely inflating performance at 7 (for whatever reason), could result in the school showing unsatisfactory value-added progress by 11. All ways the school appears the loser, how does it show its work and its fair and honest endeavour as good?

There are few 'false ceilings' for the rolling programme of new specialist schools and particularly academies which are being established in areas of so-called failing performance. With new curriculum arrangements for 14–19-year olds and changes planned in the examination system for 16- and 18-year olds over 2005–2010, there seems little chance that measures will show anything other than huge 'value-added'. That will be great providing it is real.

The arguments in these scenarios are well rehearsed and most state schools, subjected to statutory measures and controls, seem to have become resigned to their fate and generally take all that is dealt in their stride. Challenging the injustice is seen as not worth the hassle. All this does little to build trust and integrity across the teaching profession, the governors and the parents; the 'agents of managerialism' are viewed with some suspicion. But many parents, governors and teachers find confidence in joining the powerful managerial clan, who would not?

Information rich–knowledge poor

The phrase 'data rich–information poor' was used frequently to describe the situation where lots of monitoring of teaching and learning had occurred but with a consequent lack of useful interpretation. The response to this has been an explosion of interpretative reports which attempt to pull meaning from data. A new stage has been reached where we are 'information rich–knowledge poor'.

The transfer of information into useable knowledge to determine better ways of doing things, to inform policy, including the gathering, the measuring and the presenting of information about school performance is not considered in overview. One policy initiative washes towards another. Few clear and coherent educational policies are formed and shaped from what is truly known. Those that are tend to be lost behind sound bytes such as 'diversity', 'innovation, 'excellence' and 'partnership', all worthy ideas in themselves but adrift in a sea of misinformation and free market confusion. With lack of validity in information, lack of coherence in policy development follows. The watery chasms which open are usually left to schools to bridge and weaknesses in those bridges are reported as new information about failure of schools. Politically the twist is clever, for those in education it is not.

Beyond the headlines about new curriculum for 5–14-year olds which focuses on excellence and enjoyment, and the need for reform of the curriculum and the examination system for the 14–19 range, what does the information actually tell us? What is our collective knowledge about the best ways of addressing some of these specific issues and those in the Government's *Five Year Strategy for Children and Learners* (DfES 2004a)? We know lots of success stories, for example, that primary school children have improved their performance considerably in reading and mathematics, and that standards in GCSE and A Level are rising. However, what is the state of our knowledge on what to do about some of the recurring problems?

We know that:

• comparatively high numbers of young people do not continue at school or college beyond 16 years of age;
• many pupils, boys particularly aged 13 and 14 become disinterested in what is happening at school and disengage;
• the very brightest pupils are not stretched enough;
• course work is often too onerous and, along with external examinations, the marking of it can be unreliable;

- employers feel that young people entering work lack basic skills in arithmetic and communication;
- academic subjects retain higher status over vocational qualifications.

Does this knowledge stack up and shape into the policies that are informing what is to be done in the future? It seems not. If pupils are doing well at 11 years of age then how come they lack the basics in arithmetic and communication at 16 years of age? What goes wrong at secondary school? What happens between 11 and 13 year age group? Is there too little 'excellence and enjoyment' in the curriculum at this stage perhaps? Is there still more of the same diet of literacy and numeracy when different applications might be more appropriate to meet learning needs? Are the schools and the education services which have been privatized actually doing things differently and making specific improvements in these areas, for example, for the 11–13-year olds?

It is worth returning to the Profile exhibit 2.1 by Trevor Scholey in Chapter 2, to reflect on what the needs of this 11–13 age range might actually be. Also, it is worth noting the unconventional developments in secondary schools in Cuba where it is reported that 'learning and behaviour had improved in secondary schools where each class was now taught by one teacher for nearly every subject. Teachers had suggested the change and the Cuban Government had agreed' (National Union of Teachers 2004: 11). This is the absolute anathema to those in England and the USA, who preach the subject specialist/subject knowledge mantra, but if the notion of 'privileging the academic' is shifted to 'privileging inclusion' then such a move may have some merit.

Having a curriculum (and an approach to it) which is relevant and purposeful to pupils is probably the key to improvement and having an appropriate academic and vocational balance is at the heart of it. Measuring relevance is sophisticated and subtle. With more investment in secondary schools than ever before and with the latest technologies installed, boys' maturation between 11–13 years of age should not present the levels of disengagement that are occurring. To continue the emphasis on getting pupils scoring on academic measures and then publishing results will not help to break the cycle of problems.

Shortcomings in the information used by parents to make choices about schools, privatized or otherwise, not only relate to the measures used to gain the information presented. The nature of the information gathered is about the status quo. Inadequacies of the system in which schools are placed, or within the systems of an individual school which are not chosen for measurement, bypass scrutiny. What is being done to address such problems of inadequacy at the levels of system and schools? How are government, LEAs, schools and the private sector responding?

8 State schools in a changing culture of privatization

> If a man does not keep pace with his companions, perhaps it is because he hears a different drummer. Let him step to the music which he hears, however measured or far away.
>
> (Henry David Thoreau 1817–1862)

Culture change is occurring across the education system as a whole, in schools themselves and in the organizations in which they exist. This chapter is about the change towards privatized influences on schools rather than the systems that operate around them. The emphasis on culture change in 2005 is very much on secondary rather than primary schools. The aim is to get secondary schools to work together more effectively.

Memories of the highly competitive GM schools of the early 1990s, still loom large as examples of how it was thought direct competition between schools was the market-driven way to create rapid improvement in them. It was not! To go into the detail of what is now history is not relevant here, but these schools often perpetuated many of the difficulties described on these pages so far. This succinct quotation catches the essence of that history 'Grant maintained schools have control of admissions and are usually elite schools' (Lauder and Hughes 1999: 132). Although these schools are now history, the principle that was behind their GM schools now forms the bedrock for the expansion of 'foundation status' for schools in 2005.

The concept of 2005 is somewhat different however. The government's five-year education strategy includes some old ideas and some new freedoms. The major feature is the encouragement for schools to work together in foundation partnerships. Oversubscribed schools will, however, be free to expand, a concept at the heart of the GM ethos. It is not a concept that brought new insight to the problems faced by the schools in the communities with the most difficult circumstances in the last decade, nor is it likely to now. Furthermore, it does not sit comfortably with the ideas to establish closer working partnerships between schools. The new ideas and freedoms do represent better possibilities that these old ones around competition and expansion are forcing closure on the less popular. There is freedom to extend school provision in different ways, for example, by offering services beyond education. If taken forward dynamically and proper links are established between groups of schools and their communities, then there will be opportunity to heighten achievement as a part of inclusion for all.

Independent status and foundation partnerships

Most crucially though is the drive for different sorts of schools to work together in foundation partnerships, jointly taking responsibility for services currently provided by LEAs, such as school improvement, provision for excluded pupils and for pupils with SEN. It is intended that the different sorts of schools involved will be drawn from across the system, including independent schools. In taking on these roles, foundation partnerships would step into not only exercising those functions of LEAs but also, in the case of school improvement services, to those seen as particularly attractive to the private sector commercial companies. The strategy is curious in that it creates substantial additional challenges for secondary schools, on top of those they already face. On the one hand, this may stimulate new solutions being found to old problems, but on the other, and this is more likely, it may divert schools away from improving their core business of actually educating students.

The manner in which these foundation partnerships actually develop their ways of working will be critical.

- Will membership of a partnership be compulsory for all state and all independent schools?
- Will funding flow through the partnership rather than through the LEA, LSC or school?
- Will the partnerships include specially commissioned private sector companies and the LSCs?
- Will this bring a more collaborative approach to organizing the 14–19 curriculum as opposed to the 16–19 curriculum as seen so far?

The real purposes of such collaborations are to improve things, for example:

- the relevance of the educational reasons for students staying on;
- to switch those disengaged 13-year-old boys back into school life with some excitement and interest;
- to give employers skilled young people able to handle numerical and communication demands with competence and pleasure.

Such partnerships may even be able to extend the challenge for the academically and vocationally talented, and in so doing break the prejudice that vocational programmes are a second class bolt hole for the less academic and instead create recognition of their importance to social and economic regeneration and prosperity.

In whatever ways these new found partnerships develop, the LEAs' role will decrease. It will decrease in support for secondary schools directly and shift towards commissioning work for the foundation partnerships and primary schools. As LEAs become the champions of pupils and parents over educational quality and achievement outcomes, this activity will replace their historical functions and entanglement in provision.

New and wider avenues of access will open for private sector companies. However, whilst successful secondary schools enjoy the opportunities brought by their amended sets of autonomy and partnership responsibilities, corresponding threats to achieving clarity over strategic direction and joined-up policy and practice across communities will emerge, unless certain competitive cultural traits recede into the background rather more than they have, by 2005. Some schools struggle outside the new drive for academies and specialist schools despite their enthusiasm for the schemes or something like them.

Inventing new categories of schools

Inventing new categories of schools is not an original activity; it is a common ploy with its recent origins in the late 1980s. The tactic of 'if in doubt change the name' has a tradition that goes back further. The popular political practice of inventing new categories of schools is outlined in the historical perspective in Chapter 2.

The new categories seen in 2005 are hybrids of those schools of the City Technology Trust formed in 1987. Shifts in political and educational orientation along the way have brought independent specialist schools and the associated academies. The precise nature of the private sector's involvement with these two types of newly invented schools (academies and Independent specialist schools) is the focus of much interest. The halo around them is about new aspirations.

The government's aim is also to have closer relationships between private schools and state sector schools and new arrangements for sharing the provision of education across groups of schools through foundation partnerships and federations.

Academies

Academies are central to education policy development in England, there are to be 200 by 2010, yet there are no plans to develop them in Wales. This stark difference in policy raises questions in itself.

Academies superseded CTCs and City Colleges for the Technology of the Arts (which derived from 1988 legislation) and are a name change of City Academies (derived from 1996 legislation). The broad concepts around these types of schools are favoured by the major political parties in the UK, but not by one of the main teaching unions. Academies are supposed to bring new investment and new solutions to problems in secondary schools and break the cycle of underachievement in areas of social disadvantage. They are indeed located in England's most disadvantaged areas, in the north-east in Gateshead and Middlesbrough, the West Midlands, central Manchester, Bristol, Nottingham and London. The intention is that they will reinvigorate and in many cases replace, schools which have failed pupils for generations. If this intention is to become a reality and academies are to be able to provide effective solutions to intractable educational difficulties, then they will still need time to bring about real transformation (Profile exhibit 8.1).

Profile exhibit 8.1 Tackling obstinate challenges

I write as a head teacher, facing some longstanding intractable difficulties in a large-split-site secondary school just inside the ring road round the City of Leicester. The DfES is telling me that we are probably the lowest performing school in the country. Those people who know the school and its history say it could also be the most difficult, given the combination of circumstances that prevail. We are a local community school.

Serious reservations exist about the control of state education moving away from democratically elected local bodies. However, the realities to be faced in bringing about major improvement to schools which are consistently underperforming because of layer upon layer of problems, need energy and resources drawn from deep and wide sources beyond the scope of traditional LEA networks.

I am in favour of the drive to extend academies. The academy route is probably the only realistic and pragmatic way of turning this school around and setting it on a different course with a chance of sustained success. Academies have no track record as yet. There is no data base to show trends over time of either their own success or the impact they may be having on other schools. But the early signs are positive. Academies are popular in their communities with the parents and the children, and young people who are able to attend them. The early signs are that they are having a positive impact on their performance, but most importantly they are giving self-esteem, pride and aspirations to the pupils and their parents.

If the government gave this school £20 million with no private sponsorship strings attached, then could as much be achieved as with £22 million and privately sponsored school governance? It is doubtful. Even if savings of £2 million were made (starting, for example with the fees to signature architects) to equal out the cash investment, it would be the loss of the potential influx of skills and network connections that this community would miss. The potential importance of a different source of human resource should not be under-estimated. The cash sponsorship is relatively trivial, anyway, in the scale of things.

Academies are fundamentally state-funded independent schools. They are resided over by charitable trusts set up for the sole purpose of establishing and maintaining the academies. They provide a fantastic opportunity to rethink the nature of the school from the ground up, challenged in so doing by influential perspectives from outside education and focused on meeting the specific needs of the communities they serve. Thus, they can bring together the best characteristics of the private sector and the state provision.

Bringing together the traditional or perhaps the stereotyped characteristics of state provision in education with private sector, business practice may look, in simple terms, like this:

State school characteristics	Private sector characteristics
People focused	Outcome focused
Process orientated	Product orientated
More limited in ambition	Often very high in ambition
Tolerant of time-scales	Intolerant of time-scales
Low in presentation and profile	High in presentation and profile
Driven by perceived professional wisdom and understanding	Driven by financial considerations, consumers and markets
Slow to respond to external forces	Quick to respond especially, when it impacts upon profits
Lacking in strong sense of control of own destiny	Determined to influence rather than be controlled by events

The listing of these paired characteristics illustrates possible adjustment in their balance; no hard and fast classification is intended.

Like most people working in schools, as a product of an entire career in state education, I feel better able to tackle the causes of problems than those who have harboured their lives in private schools. But most people in the private sector of the community at large share the egalitarian principles of state education. They have grown up through that route and have made their way in the enterprise of the private market within our democracy. In education, we confuse too easily 'private' with 'private school' and then mix in our minds the traditions that go with them. The current efforts by the Secretary of State to draw the state and the private school sectors closer together may not help clarify this. Academies and schools in difficulties need help from the real commercial world not just private schools.

Privatization is likely to provide only part of the solution not the whole solution. Any presentation of it as the solution is more likely to undermine its contribution and its credibility rather than support and sustain it.

Like all 'labels', new titles for schools unhelpfully hide subtleties and seem designed to inspire or to trigger a response more likely to come from dogma or from prejudiced belief than from fair observation or from eventual analysis. Academies and what they are about are, it seems, often deliberately misunderstood. Misunderstanding stems from ignorance. The press for academies so far seems to owe more to the writers' and the reporters' own philosophical positions or beliefs about how education should or should not be, rather than about objective reporting of initial observations.

More responsible and less sensational reporting would reduce unhelpful polarization.

Ignorance stems also from fear. Where education has been difficult, overdue intervention has been coupled with fear. The language of inspection and intervention is punitive even if helpful resources follow. Less punitive regimes of inspection and accountability in education would reduce fear and help find ways to restore achievement more quickly. The private sector both in education and in commerce and industry would not tolerate what has happened in practice under the name of accountability in state education. Accountability is necessary, it is an essential principle, but the manner in which these mechanisms are sometimes applied where difficulties are in the extreme are not compatible with maximizing the human potential for recovery.

The development of academies is, in my view, a positive use of private resources and the proper use of the freedoms to tackle the most obstinate and intractable educational challenges of underperformance. The three-year independent study which is currently underway, is a realistic way to establish the success of the blend of characteristics this kind of public and private partnership offers and 2008 will soon be round.

The problems faced today, however, will not wait until 2008 for solutions!

Source: Allen Andres, Head Teacher, New College, Leicester.

Academies are independent state schools usually established by private sector sponsors within charitable companies. The sponsor is required to contribute an initial capital sum, up to about 10 per cent of the total capital investment. For a new build that is typically about £2 million of the £20 million total, it is sometimes more, sometimes less. The remaining 90 per cent of capital and all future revenue costs are met by the government. It is the input of expertise and drive for improvement, which the private sector is thought to possess, which is the other important contribution from the private side. Personal and corporate energy, new ideas and insights and the ambition and determination to succeed are the widely reported qualities perceived to form the basis of this new expertise.

The curriculum in academies must be broad and balanced but it need not follow the National Curriculum. It should have an emphasis on at least one curriculum area, similar to the expectation on the curriculum in specialist schools discussed later. Pupils have to be of different abilities, although options to select 10 per cent on aptitudes are available and pupils should be mainly or wholly drawn from the area in which the school is situated.

By the end of 2004 there were only 12 academies opened in England, only a tiny proportion of secondary schools nationally, but with the government's declared intention to open 200 by 2010 this will represent almost seven per cent of secondary schools by that date and replace those schools which are struggling in difficult areas.

Publicly funded privately controlled concerns

There are two fundamental concerns here about:

1   the ease with which private sponsors, with no democratic mandate, can gain influence and direct control over state education;
2   the perception that this is a way for the private sector to buy into a state school very cheaply and then direct its subsequent expenditure of taxpayers' funds in ways which might favour its own private sector interests.

These concerns are more than theoretical. Certainly, local democratic controls are reduced but not those at national level. Academies are subject to funding agreements which give the Secretary of State the right to close the school if there were serious concerns about its management or performance. Where concerns have been expressed about payments by schools to their sponsors and associates (for services rendered), these have to date been relatively insignificant amounts paid out have been small. An academy in the north-east of England paid a total of almost £300,000 to a range of sponsor-related companies and an academy in London, likewise, paid out £180,000. Given the millions invested and the value of expertise provided in kind, these figures are small and, as claimed, could well represent good 'value for money' service purchases.

This issue though is serious as one of principle. These examples could be just the thin end of the wedge. With accountabilities directly to central government being more distant than to those locally, inaction can be less noticeable, especially as academies and independent specialist schools expand in numbers. Indeed, questions have already been raised over the proportion of the capital pledged and that actually paid by sponsors at the time of their schools opening. Two were reported to have paid amounts of 'less than £200,000 in projects with building costs of more than £25 million', (Mansell and Stewart 2004: 8). Also, there are tensions when private companies tender for large government contracts worth tens of millions of pounds a year and win them when senior executives in those same companies are personal sponsors of academies or specialist schools. Although stringent rules are observed in both the award of contracts through public-sector procurement processes and the receipt of sponsorship donations for schools, accusations of 'conflict of interest' are understandable.

There are other areas of contention:

- Independent state schools take properties and assets out of state ownership. Although there are safeguards to ensure that their use for educational purposes is maintained, the history of GM schools selling off playing fields sits uncomfortably in the equation.
- Although admissions criteria for academies are set in consultation with LEAs, there is a view that profiling the pupil intake so as to secure the required spread of ability across the school's population actually skews local admissions and further complicates attempts to achieve greater transparency in secondary school admission arrangements. The early attractiveness of academies means that they are well oversubscribed (two applicants for one place is often reported) and, with a 'profiled' interpretation of the admissions system, academies may be able to admit pupils across the range of ability but still avoid taking the weakest learners in the profile.
- Related to this is the perception that academies sponsored by church foundations may have implicit selection policies, when they promote their special Christian ethos. Church secondary schools outperform their secular neighbours by about 10 per cent in five good GCSE grades. It is argued that this is because the Church schools' intakes are comprised of pupils from church-going families (presumably of higher educational performance), though the charge of 'selection' tends to be disputed by these high-performing schools.
- Concerns arise around the educational philosophy of sponsors and the impact that can have on the curriculum of academies when they are not required to teach the National Curriculum. An example of this is where worries about 'creationist theories' being taught in one academy caused plans for another academy, to be opened in south Yorkshire and supported by that same sponsor, to be blocked. Nevertheless, plans are proceeding with this sponsor to open seven more academies elsewhere in the country.
- The rate at which pupils are being permanently excluded from academies is well above the national average. In one academy, in its attempts to clamp down on poor discipline and misbehaviour, the rate of permanent exclusions rose to over ten-fold the national average,

2.51 per cent compared to 0.23 per cent. Independence means, academies can act as they wish on exclusions by following their own funding agreement terms of reference, rather than established DfES guidance. Although it is sometimes argued that permanent exclusion is the tough school management action necessary to sort out the problems previously encountered in difficult areas, support for the same argument would be unlikely in the normal state secondary school sector. A school in this sector would find itself heavily penalized financially for permanently excluding pupils in these proportions.

- It is not only pupils who find themselves leaving academies before their allotted time. The turnover of school principals and senior members of staff working in the first wave of academies appeared unusually high during the early years of following opening. Four principals stepped down from only 12 academies. 'We are very concerned at the rate of turnover of academy heads and other members of their leadership teams. There is a misplaced expectation that these schools which may have been in difficulties for many years can be turned around over night. Ministers should be more patient' (Dunford 2004: 3). The unrealistic expectation described here about Ministers' understanding of turning around schools in difficulty has direct parallels with the situation described in Chapter 6 about expectations in turning around underperforming LEAs.
- There are anxieties about how different models for academies might develop and how autonomy might increase. Sponsors are known to have invested on the basis of academies being independent of LEAs and, increasingly, relatively independent of government. Arguably, sponsors feel they need more freedoms and flexibilities. The fear is that academies have scope to make the rules up as they go along.
- Flexibilities and uncertainties about future developments are in themselves a cause of concern. Given the interest, for example, of GEMS (described in Chapter 3) in sponsoring academies, one might envisage the possibility of Academies being developed on a GEMS star-rating system which offers graduated quality of education provision, determined by the level of financial sponsorship in the initial capital investment (another class of league table) or provision which is based on an open philosophy of really screening the intake, in order to maintain a certain level of behaviours.

It is not surprising that the policies for establishing academies are so regularly challenged. They are often seen as a perpetuation of the back door to choice, to private education for the middle classes. Having removed the last of the assisted places scheme in private education, this is seen as the new wheeze! Although the assisted places scheme was not popular, it was at least seen as transparent because it gave opportunity to pupils of high academic ability who won their place by examination, access to an academy may not be seen as so transparent.

Summaries of the concerns expressed around aspects of 'conflict of interest', therefore, are along these lines.

- Academies have only small financial contributions from private companies but these firms nevertheless want exclusive say in how they are run.
- They can select pupils, expel troublemakers and exclude pupils with SEN because they cost too much money to teach.
- There is a fear that academies will be set up by the rich, run by them and end up educating the rich at the taxpayers' expense.
- Academies represent crude elitism and profiteering.

Warnings such as these are well worth heeding. However, as the political commitment to seeing these schools expand is so entire, there is little doubt that they will be established in increasing numbers. It will be important to ensure that they do not regress to a system that confuses and divides people even more. I do not think this will happen in the longer term.

Given where these academies are located, their declared purpose and the nature of the companies that run them, then there is reason to be optimistic about the contribution they will make for all, especially if citizens are active in exercising their democratic influences at all the levels available to them. A profile of the Walsall Academy is published in the *Five Year Strategy for Children and Learners* (DfES 2004a), which gives a very positive view of its progress over its first year in existence. Profile exhibit 8.2 about Manchester Academy, though quite different in style and location, is similarly optimistic.

Profile exhibit 8.2 The Manchester Academy

The Manchester Academy is a new type of all-ability school that is making a difference for the local pupils of Moss Side in Manchester. Its private sponsors are the United Learning Trust (ULT) and Manchester Science Park (MSP). The ULT is a subsidiary of the Church Schools Company (CSCo) and shares with it the objective of managing schools which offer pupils an excellent education based on the Christian principles of tolerance and service. The Christian faith recognizes the value and the uniqueness of every human being and teaches love, respect, forgiveness and the need to work for peace and justice.

Whilst the Christian ethos is the starting point and the central focus for the ethos of the academy, we appreciate that we live in a multi-faith and multicultural community and the beliefs and the practices of other faiths and cultures will be valued and respected. Parents, students and staff of all faiths, and of none, will find our Academy a welcoming community. We welcome other faith leaders to participate in assemblies from time to time, especially on days when they celebrate their own important festivals.

I have been in state education for over 30 years and believe in it. I am supportive of the academies programme, not because it levers in a mere ten per cent of capital funding, but because the involvement of different parties brings a fresh and a more radical look at some of the previously intractable problems that have faced the state education sector in the most difficult areas of our inner cities for the last 20 years.

Academies are highly contextualized within their localities and need to be a pivotal point for regeneration which means having more and different partnerships than schools have ever had before. This Academy is already building strong partnerships with other primary and secondary schools in the Manchester area. It will play a leading role in the community and the school already hosts a number of community groups, such as the Jamaican History Group. Links with the business community are strong. The Academy aims to create an interest in entrepreneurship by showing that in the future, starting a business is well within the pupils' grasp.

Schemes such as 'Academy Patrons' have already established strong links with local businesses, such as MSP, which act as the first points of contact between the pupils and the science and technology and business parks. The pupils get a fast track into an understanding of the world of entrepreneurs, science and technology. In this way, pupils and students will be able to contribute directly to the continued regeneration of their own locality and city.

Manchester Academy serves the community. The students are not selected in terms of their ability or faith. Emphasis is placed on ensuring the success of each individual through mentoring and personal support.

Freedom from LEA control is not without responsibility. It is a freedom to use professional judgement without bureaucratic stifling, not that Manchester LEA stifles in anyway. Whilst things go well, the community support needed and received will facilitate progress, and the democratic influences will be achieved through the community at large rather than through the LEA specifically. Good collaborative projects have been established with other schools in the area.

The improvements in the operation of the school, as the new Academy, on this site since the previous school of Ducie High School are reported as transformational. Past pupils, including the author of this book, are impressed with developments so far. The aspirations for the school when it takes over its new-purpose-built accommodation in 2005 are immense.

Source: Kathy August, Principal, Manchester Academy.

Specialist schools

Like academies, specialist schools are variations on earlier school types. The Specialist Schools Programme was launched in 1994 when a small number of GM schools and VA schools started operating as technology colleges, a development under the City Technology Trust established in 1987 which became The Specialist Schools Trust in 2003, the lead advisory body for these schools. The Trusts aimed to support the transformation of secondary education in England by building and enabling a world-class network of innovative, high-performing secondary schools in partnership with business and the community. This mission expanded. With the publication of *A New Specialist Schools System: Transforming Secondary Education* (DfES 2003b), the government declared its aim to create a new specialist system where just about every school has its own specialist ethos and works with others to spread best practice and raise standards. This move was particularly important as it signalled the removal of the original restriction, that only about half of the schools would be able to achieve specialist school status and also lowered anxiety levels about being tagged 'bog standard', an unfortunate label that had become associated with those schools that would have had difficulty in qualifying to be 'specialist' for whatever reason.

There is some evidence that educational outcomes are slightly better in specialist schools than in schools that are not specialist. Raw scores from examinations are certainly higher but, given the slightly higher attainment by the pupils on entry to the specialist schools then the value-added gains are minimal in most. The research into whether the extra funding that these schools receive is having any likely impact on standards is the subject of much investigation and claim. 'In 2003, specialist schools averaged 56 per cent of pupils achieving 5 + A*–C grades at GCSE compared to 47 per cent for non-specialist schools. This 9-point positive performance gap was not a matter of a more selective intake, as closer scrutiny of the results revealed. In fact, the intake of pupils in 1998 when the 2003 GCSE pupils entered secondary school at age 11, was broadly similar to that of other comprehensive schools, when the results of pupils' KS 2 tests were examined' (Taylor and Ryan 2005: 77). This type of analysis suggests that specialist schools add more value, at least it seems so in this sample.

Slender evidence of better educational outcomes over other schools and the genealogy specialist schools share with the earlier CTC has stood them in good stead. Their expansion in numbers has been rapid and is expected to continue to exceed government targets. Of the 3,200 eligible secondary schools, 2,000 were specialist schools in 2004 and 3,000 are anticipated to be by 2006.

The Specialist Schools Programme helps schools to develop particular strengths and raise standards in their chosen specialism or specialisms in partnership with private sponsors. In addition, schools are expected to share expertise and become a resource for other schools and their local communities. The range of specialisms available has increased to 11 and it includes:

- technology
- arts
- languages
- sports
- business and enterprise
- engineering
- maths
- science
- humanities
- music
- community.

Specialist categories often have sub-classifications, for example, the arts specialism could be performing arts, the visual arts or the media arts. Some, but not all, of the school specialisms have provision for schools to select up to 10 per cent of pupils by aptitude in the relevant specialism, but fewer than 7 per cent of schools choose to take up the option where it exists. Sponsors came forward in large numbers; over 20 had donated in excess of £1 million each by 2000 and hundreds more had donated £50,000 or more.

Financial incentives

Satisfying the government's criteria to become a specialist school means that schools must set targets in line with the aims of the scheme, demonstrate at least reasonable standards of attainment in the specialist subjects and have well-conceived development plans for both school and community with targets and performance indicators for extended provision, increased take-up of courses and improved outcomes. Most significantly, they have to raise private sponsorship to the value of £50,000 (£100,000 until September 2000).

Once these criteria are met and specialist school status is achieved, then the financial rewards to the school from the taxpayers' contributions become considerably greater than that from the sponsorship. A specialist school usually receives, from government funding, a one-off capital grant of £100,000 and annual funding of about £130 per pupil for four years, the larger schools receiving more. So, for a private sector contribution of £50,000, a typical secondary specialist school of 1,000 pupils receives in the region of an extra £620,000 of government funding. As with academies, the question raised is about the amount of influence the private sector receives for what is considerably less than a 10 per cent investment in the state specialist school.

Given the availability of this extra funding, it is no surprise why schools actively seek specialist status, even where they feel that they do not really have a specialism to offer. 'Specialism' has little meaning in most areas. People do not care to have their one local secondary school designated a specialist school, what usually matters to them is that it offers a good all-round education, and that it does not lose out on its equitable share of resources for being just that. Being a good 'generalist' school will not bring the extra £620,000 unless it can present this as a specialism in community!

Public and private control, foundation status and specialisms

Specialist schools are to become independent specialist schools in the Government's *Five Year Strategy for Children and Learners* (DfES 2004a). Tensions over the public and private resource balance for academies apply to independent specialist schools too. With more of them being encouraged, by The Specialist School Trust, to gain 'foundation status' these schools are likely to become increasingly controversial as similarities in this status to those of the former 'grant maintained school culture' are re-introduced. As this trend continues and with the possibility of sponsors becoming the controlling majority on governing bodies, democratic balances in school governance will destabilize.

The rules governing sponsorship require that it must be given without any conditions which could result in a financial benefit for the sponsor or any other party and it must come from the private sector. The rules are not tightly observed. Sponsors often have their logos on school letterheads; some schools have actually refused sponsorship because of that particular expectation by the potential sponsor. In other situations, schools have used legacies to count as the private sector sponsorship donation, something of a stretch from the spirit of business sponsorship.

Many, but not all specialist schools (it depends on the specialism) are allowed to select 10 per cent of the pupils on their aptitude for the specialism, but few do. The majority of parents do not appear to choose a school because it has a particular specialism (though research evidence on this is thin). They choose because of an existing good reputation, positive ethos and successful examination performance. 'About one third of headteachers believed that specialist school designation had contributed significantly' to their schools being chosen (Ofsted 2001: 10). If the specialism happens to coincide with their child's interest and aptitudes then that might be seen as a bonus, if not then the school and the parents make little reference to it.

On one hand, if this is the case and schools do not select and the parents do not choose on the basis of the specialism, then the specialism as such becomes an irrelevance (Profile exhibit 8.3). This is perhaps just as well because if the specialisms were seen as real and significant, then parents could face a real dilemma in wanting a place for their child at a specialist

Profile exhibit 8.3 What's the point of a designated DfEE Arts College?

The community school where I was head of art achieved specialist Art College status in 1997, early in the Government's initiative though a decade after the start of City Colleges for the Arts and Technology. It was one of the first of its kind and has been very successful. The specialism is in the expressive arts (dance, drama and music) which is separate from the visual arts. Visual arts were my prime responsibility. The school is regularly oversubscribed as local parents want their children to attend.

I do not agree with the uneven distribution of resources to create specialist schools. Ever since the school achieved specialist status, it has been a constant muse to me as to what a specialist school is doing differently to any other school apart from focusing additional resources disproportionally on the area of the specialism. There can be no doubt that the facilities are superb and teacher deployment is lavish for the expressive arts at my school.

What *are* specialist schools actually supposed to be offering? Is it that parents can choose a place for their son or daughter because of a particular interest or talent they have within the specialist area? I contend that parents do not get a real choice of schools based on their children's aptitude or ability. At first hand I have seen no real evidence of that at Heathfield, nor at other specialist schools. Surely it defeats the purpose of having specialist schools if pupils with aptitudes in those specialisms cannot gain admission because the school takes its full quota from the local population.

Students at Heathfield choose an arts subject as a compulsory part of the core programme. If they attend the school without a particular aptitude in that area then why should the arts be a compulsory component for them? This limited choice occurs because the school has to demonstrate a commitment to the specialism and secure high take-up and success by the students in that specialist subject, in order to maintain the flow of additional government funding.

In an age of league tables and constant performance reviews for all, the pressure on the specialist department staff is heightened. They carry the normal anxieties of teachers and the added pressure to perform extra well in the specialist subject and secure especially good examination results. To achieve these results, the expectation is that students in dance, drama and music will make disproportionately high commitments to these subjects. Students commit themselves to weekend and after-school activities to such an extent that this can have a detrimental effect on their work in other subjects, for example, turning up to lessons under-prepared and not having met more realistic homework expectations. Consequently, their achievement in other subjects is easily compromised.

Do not get me wrong, good teaching and learning across the school achieved excellent value-added performances in most subjects; the school was 12th in the national league table for added-value at KS 3 and KS 4, in 2003. Also, the resources gained under the banner of expressive arts, made my teaching groups smaller in years 8 and 9, assisting in the achievement of good KS 3 results. However in KS 4, students who were adverse to public performance were forced to opt for visual arts as the more 'private endeavour', but really would have preferred not to have done art at all, but rather a subject more in-keeping with their particular interests and aptitude, an option usually available to them in non-specialist schools.

Source: Mary Harding, Head of Art 1998–2004, Heathfield Community School, DfEE designated Arts College.

school with a particular specialism that simply was not available in their area, music would be a good case in point in most places. It is difficult enough to create ordinary schools which parents feel are adequate. By complicating the scenario with quasi-choice options does not in itself help to improve things. The relevance and value of the specialism in itself is slender.

On the other hand, having a specialism does have a use in identifying a subject for the school to produce higher attainment targets in an area of teaching and learning where they have the best chances of doing well or showing improvement. So in this respect, and coupled to the extra funding, it is motivating. It is also helpful in giving a focus for attracting sponsorship, in creating a sense of diversity and encouraging sharing of expertise, so that schools feel that their contributions are distinct, supported by the real world and that they are not placed in a general competition with other schools.

Lessons learned from Education Action Zones (EAZs) and Excellence in Cities (EiCs)

Drawing private money and expertise into the running of state schools with a view to groups of schools cooperating and sharing good practice were key features of the EAZs. These were set up in England following bids from groups of schools in 1998. By 2000, there were 72 EAZs, each operating for a three or five year term. They were partnerships, usually formed between a group of schools, their LEA and other organizations such as businesses and higher-education institutions. They were, in theory, 'set up to tackle problems of underachievement and social exclusion, in disadvantaged areas by devising 'innovative methods and strategies that would involve disaffected pupils more fully in education and improve their academic performance' (Ofsted 2003b: 5).

EAZs were regarded as having some positive effects on schools in disadvantaged areas, but not comprehensively or consistently so. Overall EAZs were not deemed particularly successful; they were slow to become established and partnerships often proved unwieldy to manage. Raising private sector funding often proved difficult, the contributions from the business community sometimes being in kind rather than in cash. Expertise and resources on offer did not always meet the schools' needs, for example, consultants from the private sector who were made available to help in related benchmarking activities such as 'Investors in People' or the offer of office space in locations not ideal for the schools, did little to move the central educational objectives forward. Effort was spent on inventing new management systems for the EAZs and trying to create an innovative approach at this level rather than using existing systems and building upon their strengths. 'Directors expended time and energy raising funds, recruiting and retaining central teams was often problematic, and the early management of zones was often weak...Too few of these initiatives tackled the real barriers to pupils' achievement and progress or did so in a deliberate way' (ibid.: 69).

New provision needs to be knitted into the mainstream work of schools. This requires leadership in schools to be in a position to be able to focus innovative practices directly onto teaching, learning and pupil care. New initiatives work best, where they are integrated into the life of the school and the community and into their systems, to attempt to graft on to existing systems an initiative such as an EAZ is likely to cause confusion and duplication. It will be important to ensure that academies and independent specialist schools do not go the same way as EAZs.

EAZs were often viewed with some suspicion. It is the same over the Government's current motives. Could EAZs have perhaps become a future alternative to LEAs? Had partnerships of schools and business groups managed to raise funds and tackle the problems of achievement and social inclusion in disadvantaged areas successfully, then they may well have had a future. But they did not. Instead, the good work that had been achieved was brought into a parallel initiative called EiCs (also known in urban areas which were not cities as Excellence in Clusters). These EiCs were generally more effective and had planning, funding and structures which were simpler than in the EAZs. The emphasis in EiCs on making provision directly for pupils through schools' leadership and management is more straightforward and incisive than through the wider concepts involved with EAZs, which are frequently served to distract.

School leadership and management

As is so often the case, the success of large-scale system innovation is dependent upon the quality of interpretation at the local or institutional level. The success of initiatives in schools relies on the quality of the schools' leadership and management and on the breadth of their view as being a part of the wider community.

The NCSL is investing heavily in the training and development of not only head teachers, but also potential head teachers and middle managers in schools. The training involves work being undertaken on improving the strategic direction and development of schools. Although much of the focus of the training is on the leadership of schools as separate and individual units, there is a healthy emphasis on the vision which school leaders might develop more widely and on the nature of the underpinning values. 'The school's vision has to be well known and, as far as possible, shared by all who have a stake in the school's success' (NCSL 2003: 9). This NCSL programme guide illustrates the dangers of following a vision which is based upon a too narrowly conceived constituent group. Such a vision is likely to be resisted by others, especially by those who are not included and see themselves relegated to a merely passive role.

With the government's record of appearing to diminish local democratic influence in education and favouring what have proved so far to be rather meagre or unreliable contributions from the private sector, the risks of large parts of the state education sector feeling disempowered and reduced to a passive role are very real. If schools hold a vision which is too parochial, and whilst the Government presents a view that private provision is superior to state provision, then an assimilation of these views and resolution as to the best way forward will be difficult.

Schools must create a vision for their communities beyond their immediate school boundaries and cause that vision to be seen in their actions. Too often during the 1990s, head teachers were heard to say that they were only concerned about promoting their own school and that those other schools were not their business. What nonsense! Whilst understanding that the job of being the head teacher of a single school is difficult enough, there has to be recognition by head teachers and governing bodies of the place of their schools and their duties in the wider community. This, in turn, brings responsibilities to persuading others about community responsibility.

School leadership groups and governing bodies are presented with many difficult challenges; some are of a very high order. The success of initiatives in schools and across groups of schools will rely on the quality of their leadership and management and the impact of this on the teaching, the learning and the care provided for pupils. In creating a 'learning establishment' which extends beyond the confines of the traditional school, new ideas will have to be tested and given chance to embed. However, new ideas must also be integrated into the life of schools and within the best of the system features within which schools operate.

Transformation might be called for in secondary schools but this will not be achieved by attempts to weaken the basis of the democratic system in which they operate or by inadvertently diminishing trust in the systems themselves. Ownership of change is what is needed. Ownership is required by people who recognize that very different values and aspirations prevail, that democracy is about sustaining the interests of the minorities and that schools should reflect that in their attention to the needs of individuals. The citizens' belief that schools serve a social purpose as well as meeting the individual needs of pupils and the aspirations of their parents who send them, should not be relegated to a second division.

Private schools helping state schools

In 2004, efforts were made to see whether state schools and private schools could work more closely together. The Secretary of State's expressions are about breaking down old-fashioned barriers between the independent and the state sectors and removing the history of distrust.

State schools will need little help in the adoption of middle class school symbols such as school uniform, blazers and ties, and 'house style' pastoral arrangements. There are many more fundamental areas where help across the systems are needed. Collaboration on tackling the issues of under-achievement and poor behaviour could be very useful. Collaboration is a component in successful local education systems. Having state and private schools working together, adds to that component as does the drive for academies and private sponsorship for specialist schools. The suspicion that a middle-class elite will find ways of using new collaborative channels to benefit their own ends, at the expense of others, will need to be allayed convincingly very early on.

Approximately £6 million of taxpayers' money has been put into creating links between independent and state schools in 2004. Although head teachers seek to move the relationship to new and more cooperative levels, many report that the different circumstances faced by the two systems make real collaboration difficult. It is easy to see why.

9 Future standards
Leadership and partnership, compliance and participation

> It is a very grave mistake to think that the enjoyment of seeing and searching
> can be promoted by means of coercion and a sense of duty.
>
> (Albert Einstein 1879–1955)

Privatizing schemes are varied and cover pretty well the whole of the
education landscape. Schools and the systems that maintain and support
them comprise the subject of these schemes. Although clear indicators of
improvements to school buildings and claims of raised academic achievement in the passage to private sector involvement can be identified, there is
little to suggest that this is due to the private sector.

State schools are being placed in private control, sometimes for what is
seen as a token investment. With it comes the potential for profit made
from the business of the school. Alongside is a growing interest from
proprietors to extend their ownership of fully private independent schools,
whilst working in the sponsorship schemes of the state schools. Although
responses from the private sector in the 1990s were tentative and showed
the difficulties they envisaged in making a profit from running state schools,
the signs are now that things have changed. Large and medium-sized
companies are involved and interest is domestic and international. Schools
can themselves become the providers of educational services to other
schools. New interest has been invigorated. The government is enthusiastic
about bringing private and state school practices closer together.

The centralization of power over education to government has been
extreme. Themes of independence and autonomy now suggest some release
for those schools with new or recent funding agreements. Historic and philosophical differences between state and private schools are seen as capable of
being removed or certainly bridged. Privatizing education is part of the brave
new world, where the vision is for egalitarian and individualistic aspirations
to meet for the benefit of the individual and the state. Interwoven are the
differences perceived by particular social groups as to what education is
actually for and how they can get from it what they want and need. 'The
education market...becomes one of the most important loci of the class

struggle, which...gives rise to an inflation of academic qualifications' (Bourdieu and Boltanski 2000: 917). The relative balance between the marking of academic achievement and the measures of the quality of socially inclusive educational practices is the fulcrum of future standards in education.

At a preliminary review, it would appear that the privatization of schooling is associating itself with secondary rather than with primary education. The huge shifts planned for examination and curriculum reform at secondary level to 2010, coupled with a large-scale building programme to attain much improved building stock shapes the opportunity. But, it is at primary schooling where pupils learn the key transferable skills they will need for life. Primary schools will need to find a clear leadership role within the privatizing environment in order to secure their vital participation in the new and developing partnerships. The ambiguity of 'leadership' within a 'partnership' will need continued attention and management.

Modernization of public services forms the backdrop for the privatization of education support services. With government providing these large capital-funding schemes for new secondary schools, opportunities for contractors to link building design with new technologies for teaching and learning are being taken. High-level partnerships between commercial companies and government have been set up with the express purpose of coordinating large-scale contract procurement at local levels. School leadership has become linked to the privatizing philosophy, professional networks within political circles shape up to head the privatizing trends. Accountabilities remain central but still use measures that are not on the level. Different criteria and processes apply to schools and services in different parts of the system. Meanwhile, the privatized aspects of Ofsted school inspection recede as more of this work is taken back to the centre, signalling a move away from that particular privatizing trend of the 1990s.

From the commentaries and the profile exhibits presented, many potential benefits about privatization can be drawn, though cautiously. On balance, moves towards the privatization of state education are favoured; the strong political consensus for them closes other options. It is largely based on a pragmatic view. The characteristics for privatized education are set within powerful social and economic forces which prevail in many developed countries, most notably in England, the USA, Canada, Australia, New Zealand and parts of Europe, South America and the Middle East. Wheels have already turned, the cogs are in place and things are gearing up. Going private on a global scale is almost 'the only show in town'. The world is increasingly becoming a single community; whilst recognizing that people are all different; global education empowers people not only to see how they vary but also to see how they are the same.

Given these global trends and the political consensus for them, serious alternatives are not pragmatic. But the dangers and inequalities described throughout the pages of this book are very real. Checks and balances are needed at a range of levels. The most significant of these are through traditional local democratic arrangements. Securing ethical, educational leadership which invites broad democratic participation in attempts to continue to raise standards and to improve access to inclusive education is at the heart of the matter.

Democracy and education

Shifts towards a future with more private influences on education are inevitable simply because the use of the private sector satisfies such a broad political constituency. Throughout the chapters on forcing educational change, democracy and citizenship and in the case study of government intervention, questions are raised about the appropriateness of the match of attempts to improve education to the differing expectations of the various stakeholders.

What is expected of the democratic processes which operate at local and national levels? Trying to understand these expectations is particularly important for state education in England because responsibilities are carefully balanced between the individual, the school, the local council and the national government. What do we expect from democracy of this sort, what is the picture we have of it in our minds?

Richard Posner (2003) argues that democracy can be perceived in two distinct forms but that only one of these forms has any substance in reality:

- 'Democracy One' is where people are civic-minded and oriented towards the public good. It is a John Dewey type of understanding of democracy where public policy is shaped by public debate in which citizens and their elected representatives participate on relatively equal terms and with a sense of duty to be as public-spirited as possible. This democracy presents a consensus approach to forming policies and statutes that are in the collective interest. It is in this form, I would suggest, that most teachers and educators view democracy, local government influencing and interpreting the application of central legislation to meet local need.
- 'Democracy Two' is more about pragmatism than civic-mindedness. Posner argues that this democracy is viewed in mainly economic terms where a competition occurs amongst different groups with self-interests and where the constituent groups are not necessarily, particularly well informed. Rather than seeking consensus, a clash of interests is inevitable. It is the approach to democracy characterized by Joseph Schumpeter (the Austrian economist); where competition rather than consensus drives the debate. This is not the view of democracy most educationalists would claim.

However, it is 'Democracy Two' that Posner argues is the only realistic operative model. The other is too idealistic because it puts human nature on a falsely elevated plain; he argues, light-heartedly, that people by nature are self-serving and manipulative. Politicians and business leaders are better thought of as actors, salesmen and brokers than as public-spirited statesmen. He suggests that rational debate does not bridge differences or bring people together; people are brought together not by ideas or arguments but by interests and preferences. The USA and the UK are successful democracies because of the unsentimental acceptance of the competitive democratic model, particularly in the UK. With little proportional representation and a 'first past the post' election system in the UK, a large parliamentary majority means that the chances of 'Democracy One' being pursued are made more slender.

The government has a mandate to get on and govern. The system does little to encourage rational and public-spirited debate towards a consensus. 'Cabinet government' is reduced in favour of 'presidential practice'. Leadership in this situation can be felt to be from the front, heroic, strutting and striding. Particular leaders of industry, commerce and education, having drawn close and gained the ear of politicians, follow suit. To many of the electorate it might seem that efforts to restore elements of 'Democracy One' are well overdue, but the option to pursue this course through democratic means appears elusive.

Comparing these ideas to the contemporary political and educational scene in England since the late 1980s, then the characteristics of 'Democracy Two' certainly predominate. The strategic and tactical moves of those who led the original CTCs developments and the establishment of GM status, have kept a particular network of protagonists at the forefront of educational developments with successive governments since CTCs began in 1987. Whilst the notion of 'schools in competition' has been exchanged for 'schools in collaboration' in more recent years, the traits of 'Democracy Two' have firmed up considerably and notions of elitism linger. The huge expansion of specialist schools with competitive bidding and tightly prescribed target approaches to schooling already form the landscape in secondary education. The prospect of a change in political direction over privatization, at least at this relatively low level of sponsorship, is slight indeed. With the democratic system as it is, and with the economic direction and power of the majority of political parties facing towards privatization so squarely, then local democratic groups will find it more expedient to gain those apparent educational improvements that can be observed (like new buildings and improved school budgets), by addressing planning and implementation rather than seeking policy alternatives. It will be in ensuring proper democratic participation in local planning and implementation, where opportunity for participation will lie.

Dilemmas in shifting attitudes towards privatization

Tangible improvements, even if seen as partial and not for the system as a whole, certainly satisfy the observational scrutiny of many. Conclusive research and reliable analysis take time. Observable improvements through refurbished facilities and new school buildings coupled with the potential these bring for changes in school ethos, count for a lot in any community, whatever the democratic character. They count for a lot particularly in the short term and can last.

To participate in the type of competitive democracy which is prevalent and based on the rules of the private market, shifts have to be made in the values people hold and the behaviours and the language they use. For many teachers, governors and parents who hold a traditional, civic-minded welfare ethic, these shifts are difficult. They are especially difficult for those parents who not only prefer the civic-minded ethic over the competitive, but also have failed, as yet, to get a place at a decent school for their child. The necessary delay in bringing even building improvements to the most intractable problems, particularly in inner city schools, requires parents and communities to be trusting in their wait. Yet, the style of democracy encountered works against gaining that trust. Parents are cast in the role of entitled, impatient consumers not as participating citizens and understanding neighbours.

These shifts in values, behaviours and language are not from just 'old to new', 'ancient to modern' or 'outdated to fashionable'; they are about being forced to rethink and to change often long-held and fundamental commitments. Unless successful in the competition early on, the alternative is to lag behind and drop further back. This is felt to be punitive, being a loser in the market equation. 'Conflicts arise because the market functions as a system of rewards and punishments, a disciplinary frame-work, fostering particular cultural forms…and dispositions and marginalizing others' (Gewirtz 2002: 49). People do feel marginalized when they see themselves as having emerged through a social welfare system and then find there appears little value for that system and perhaps for them as individuals as products of that system. They feel this acutely when dealt injustice. For the winners the rewards are evident and worthwhile; but the winners are often the ones who have economic and social capital already and do not need to achieve the shifts described.

Many citizens, when considering entitlement to education, have difficulty with this whole competitive idea. They see those who become marginalized never buying back into the system again. They then become a problem. There are many examples of this, an obvious one being disenchanted boys who refuse school. The environment, however, as it is developing in England, is not a purely private market. Compensatory factors are built in.

Let us take the typical characteristics of how a private and a competitive education market might be seen. 'Within a market culture it is acceptable for there to be winners and losers, access to resources which is differentiated but unrelated to need, hierarchy, exclusivity, selectivity and for producers to utilize whatever tactics they can get away with to increase their market share and to maximize profit' (ibid.: 49, 50). This means that the motivation for both the private partnerships which provide education and for the parents and the pupils who consumer it, is self-interest. With self-interest as the motive, the principles upon which welfare state and comprehensive education was conceived are swept away. However unpalatable, this has to be recognized.

However, there is a major difference, a saving factor, in the privatizing conditions being developed for education in England. This factor is that the differentiation of resources is reversed. Resources are directed to the greatest need. In the developing model of academies, for example, resources are focused specifically on those areas with the most intractable educational problems. An element of discriminating positively for the poor is centrally retained.

Other features such as schools having subject specialisms or opportunity for limited pupil selection are largely irrelevant; the profile exhibits in Chapters 7 and 8 illustrate this. This approach achieves the appeal of apparent choice for the individual aspirations of the middle classes and, for the egalitarians wedded to the principle of more resources being directed to the most needy, a tangible strategy to do that.

These market conditions in education form a unique set. There are other controls on the education market. A free market would not impose aspects such as National Curriculum, testing devices, performance management and the agendas set for schools by government inspectors. Then, there is the new energy attracted by major investment to those areas of greatest need. Whether the market will be cost effective in the quality it achieves is not the issue right now. What matters in 2005 is whether people with fundamentally different motivations from those of the competitive market can find genuine ways to engage in what is a different basis for state education from that of the last 50 years. Quality will be compromised if they do not.

Ingenuity and enterprise in primary and secondary schools

Market-driven conditions and new relationships with the private sector effect secondary schools and LEAs most directly. The impact on primary schools is largely through their association in clusters with secondary schools and through the sources from which they draw their educational support services. As private companies extend their involvement in education then primary schools will be drawn fully into this new cultural form. Secondary schools, as well as educating pupils, are already often engaged in the sale of education products and services. Primary schools are likely to become increasingly involved in such commercial enterprise, both as providers for other schools and consumers. Primary schools may sell service to secondary schools as often, the practice in primary schools is held up for possible emulation in the lower years of secondary schools. Opportunities will open up in many directions for enterprising schools.

As LEAs lose their role in providing school improvement services directly, new openings might be taken by private companies, especially in the provision of online curriculum and assessment materials which have mass market potential and, therefore, safe thresholds for profit. Face-to-face training and continuous professional development is more likely to fall to the federations and the clusters of schools. 'Peer challengers' and 'school improvement partners' may be well placed to gauge the potential for profitable trading.

The cautionary consideration here is whether trading services should actually be the business of schools. For specialist schools with specialism in 'business and enterprise' it clearly is and given the prevailing culture, is the contemporary view for all schools. Schools and their pupils need to develop entrepreneurial cultures and enterprising attitudes. So it follows that these should be within the ethos of the whole school.

'The town's current entrepreneurs were united in arguing that the future success of Rotherham's economy depends on a new and stronger generation of entrepreneurs coming through. They want to see more young people ready to take risks, test new ideas and try to set up and grow their own businesses. And they are certain this inspiration must come from entrepreneurs rather than educationalists' (Ball *et al.* 2004: 8). If this should be done then the question remains as to how it should be done. Education and entrepreneurship will need to draw close and show a relationship. Certainly, enterprise should not be seen as something for a small elite which is beyond the ambition of those in state schools, an enterprise culture is based on a 'can do' confidence that should span all groups including those directly involved in education, teachers and pupils.

New ideas about how schools should be trading are somewhat different to the more traditional 'trading activities' with which most schools are familiar. When, for example, schools have been involved in school-centred initial teacher training (SCITT), or in sharing good practice, the benefits to education specifically were obvious. With new trading ambitions, and linked to sponsors who may press an aggressive profit motive, there are serious questions about whether schools' attention will be distracted from the central purpose of educating and caring for the pupils, and instead pursue the sale of professional development products as their new prime endeavour in demonstrating their enterprise capability. Both roles can be complementary, are not mutually exclusive and each can work to the advantage of the other.

The questions raised for schools about trading services are parallel to those they face about ensuring that students' work experience placements do not slip from good education into mundane free labour. Schools have to be mindful that education remains their mission and does not over time, slide beneath seductive entrepreneurial interests and rewards.

The tension in this for head teachers is not new. Most LEA advisers and inspectors and HMI enjoyed or tolerated a period in their former headships when they were 'used' in outreach work with other schools. Their decisions to leave their schools as head teachers and take up work in the advisory or inspection services were often taken so as not to compromise the important but different priorities of both the roles. Now, with more private opportunities firmly in the culture, head teachers and teachers are able to sell their services in the wider world of professional development whilst retaining substantive posts with their schools.

A new breed of 'executive principal' has emerged. These are successful head teachers who cultivate a roving portfolio of part-time advisory head-ships at other schools and other consultancy work. The deputy head teacher back at the 'host' school assumes those internal school responsibilities more usually taken by the head teacher. This 'executive role' enjoys high prestige. The income generated, or at least part of it, is usually ploughed back into the schools' budgets to cover any loss of teaching or management resource. Clearly, many gains from the travels of the executive principal are also accrued for the benefit of the 'host' school. Investments can also be made in other schools. In the case of Thomas Telford School's non-profit com-pany, some of the surplus income generated (from sales of curriculum materials and consultancy fees) was given to schools in neighbouring com-munities which were unable to raise the £50,000 necessary for specialist school sponsorship from their business sectors. In this way, a network or federation of schools is possible under a new form of patronage from spon-soring schools, rather than from the business and the commercial worlds.

Schools' sales of online courses for ICT examinations are not unusual. The majority of the products cost the schools wishing to buy them approx-imately £3,000 per course per year. Reaction about the quality of the courses are predictably mixed, some teachers feel that the online approach is uninspiring, especially for the less academic pupils, whereas others report that the pupils absolutely love the skills-based nature of them. The response to examination courses was ever thus! Schools producing such materials become the direct competitor of the ICT 'textbook' publishers.

Local schools and federation of local schools will need to employ any 'special market' conditions they can create so they might achieve maximum wins for their pupils and, through new collaboration in these conditions, collectively trying to ensure no losers. Difficulties will lie in the different dispositions across the federations and communities of schools. With the legacy of autonomous self-seeking school competition in the 1990s still very much a part of recent history and in the forefront of memories, attitudes which make collaboration possible may not be as well developed as is sometimes thought or claimed.

Is it possible to have privatization with no losers? If the supply of places at decent schools, and the availability of good educational services matches demand then, there seems to be a chance that it is. English democracy is based upon market trading; it is part of the heritage, a national strength. In his book, *The Wealth of Nations* in 1776, Adam Smith argued that parents 'ought to pay at least some of the cost of their children's education directly to the school. If the state were to foot the entire bill, he suggested, the teacher would soon learn to neglect his business' (Smith 1937 in Gewirtz 2002: 8).

Adam Smith appears to have been not over-trusting of teachers, accountability clearly had a hold in education in 1776!

The triangle around reward, punishment and social inclusion is difficult to construct. There is a reflex angle in the trio, which is hard to flip in order to make it fit in. Difficult as this construction may be, profit is needed for schools to produce the wealth to achieve social inclusion.

As the Chancellor of the Exchequer puts it 'With innovation and competition the driving forces of the new economy, the winners will be those who can demonstrate their ingenuity, flexibility and resourcefulness in enterprising and entrepreneurial ways... Crucial to our success will be our ability to embed a culture of enterprise right cross the country, stretching from the classroom to the boardroom (with) opportunities opened up beyond the few to the many, where what matters is not where you come from but what you aspire to' (Brown 2004 in Balls *et al.* 2004: 5). Maintaining local democratic control for education within this free market will be very important to this success and may be made possible in different ways, perhaps as LEAs become the 'champions of parents and pupils'.

Managerial supremacy, trust and professionalism

Privatization utilizes the characteristics of competition, market forces and managerialism. It also uses the qualities of professionalism and trust, but these do not distinguish the process. Managerialism dominates. Yet a recurring theme throughout the commentary in this book emphasizes the importance of trust and professionalism for the providers and the users of education. They are just as important for pupils and parents as they are for teachers and governors. Any perceived lack of these qualities jeopardizes the effectiveness of the education process.

Those involved in the education system link these qualities with the importance of the individual's contribution in schools and the need to attend to the detail of interactions in leadership and in management, and in teaching and in learning. The two profile exhibits in Chapter 1, in their different ways, spell out the need to attend to this detail in specific professional ways rather than rely on a managerial compliance as the key path to improvement.

Compliance undermines as much as it builds trust. It certainly reduces initiative. The idea of 'leaving your brains at the door when you go into work' has been used by many business leaders when criticizing the basis of 'time and motion' and 'systems-based' compliance. The universal acceptance of managerialism with its focus on systems, targets, measurement, ranking and audit is seriously questioned by many teachers in England. There is a persistent call to end many managerial features such as, for example, government led target setting and national tests. This call is still a central proposal put forward by one of the major teaching unions in England and Wales (National Union of Teachers 2004). In Wales, the testing regime has been heavily reduced. Similar views are held in many different parts of the world. Highly reliable schools can be achieved through the application of professional standards not contained within national systems of compliance. Private schools promote the view that this is achieved as a matter of their normal course.

National moderation of some standards is vital. Education credentials, for example, examination qualifications, must be known to have high reliability. Results have to be fair and dependable. Accountability is essential and it should not be undermined. However, nor should it be the be-all and end-all of education. Alternatives to national testing resulting in league table rankings and the pursuit of nationally imposed targets are proposed and could be adopted. But, apart from adjustments to the testing of 7-year olds, few changes are seen in England.

The inspection and audit regimes described in Chapters 4 and 6 are typical examples of revered accountability, where managerial power tends to create its own version of interpreted truth. The debate about the relationship between truth and power is relevant in education. Those who dismiss or criticize teachers' calls for more trust and less managerial accountability, seemingly do so with little understanding of why it is important.

An example of this is reported from New Zealand by Keith Ballard (2003). He refers to a speech made by the Chief Education Review Officer for New Zealand (Aitkin 2000) where she claimed 'there is "international approval" of New Public Management and refers to the "dog in a manger" grievances of those who lament a loss of "relationships of trust" ' (Ballard 2003: 23). By contrast he draws attention to a Ministry of Social Policy report on the government's relationships with community groups which concludes, 'a decade of . . . state reform has left many in Kiwi (Maori) and community organizations mistrustful of government . . . One respondent to this study said, "We have learnt not to trust" ' (Wilson 2001: 10, 16). The language of 'New Public Management' and 'reform' is parallel to that used in the debate in England about education since 1988. Society cannot afford to let its members learn not to trust. It must be active in seeking ways of building trust and teaching the corresponding responsibilities.

Democracy is about the majority having its interests represented, but it is also about protecting those interests of minorities which do not damage the rights and freedoms of others. There is a fundamental basis of trust in that. Some elements of 'Democracy One' have to be retrieved, but trust is needed even in the cynical and the realist world of 'Democracy Two'.

Managerial success: evidence and hunches

Assumptions in the market and in privatizing culture are that the structures which form managerialism secure more success and greater reliability than the qualities of professionalism which lack defined performance outcomes and associated reliability. Also, managerialism is strong on the view in education that without intrusive devices of accountability to check standards, poor teaching and low standards would not be tackled and poor quality leadership will become entrenched.

The view often expressed is that before Ofsted inspection began in 1992, the lack of a systematic regulatory function allowed schools to continue with poor practice and underachievement. Most would probably agree that the drive for improvement in schools through the managerial approaches of Ofsted has been successful. However, there is little against which to measure its relative success over possible alternatives. Once established, successive governments have been reluctant to let it go or change the focus or process. The managerial model creates its own truth, its own worth and its own place in the priorities.

The Ofsted spend on inspection alone of 0.41 per cent of the government funding for schools of almost £20 billion in one of it mid-term years, 1998–1999 (Matthews and Sammons 2004: 141), means that approximately £100 million (more if the additional costs for school improvement and thematic inspection are included) were spent on that particular managerial model of inspection and accountability. Leaving all the other accountability costs out of the equation, the potential of an annual resource of this size, invested in other schemes, makes for some impressive possibilities. Since 1999, for example, even at today's prices, the cost is equivalent to 25 extra academies or 250 extra primary schools, and that is just from inspection without touching all the other accountability devices. Once a managerial model is running its place in the priorities is self-perpetuating. It is the nature of it.

The point is that despite all, much of what is happening in the privatization moves is based upon assumption. Where measures are applied to new managerial operations, results are often presented without reciprocal measures on their impact elsewhere. Indeed one of the issues about the pursuit and expansion of academies is that the belief in their potential success is based on wishful thinking. It will be three or four years from now, a new decade almost, before any objective analysis of their performance is available. Nevertheless, the hunch, the political hunch in this case (a trait, incidentally, of professionalism and parenthood rather than managerialism) suggests that academies will be good schools for all across their communities. It is a hunch that is being followed and which in turn implies a request for trust.

Other more dramatic examples can be found where political hunches inform costly policy and action. National managerialism is a blunt and an unresponsive attitude for capturing creative ideas and taking up local options. This managerial mindset causes the creation of such things as the DfES Innovation Unit, the managerialist approach to creativity. If people are trusted to try things out and do things differently then innovation is more likely to come from this route than from a government unit assigned to bring it about.

Quasi-scientific assessment, evaluation and analysis therefore have to be tempered with professional judgement. Such judgement consists of degrees of knowledge drawn from past experience; and within it there is need for initial observation which, if applied within relationships of trust, gives helpful pointers to the way forward and to predictors of success. Intolerance of timescales and demands for immediate results might sound like no-nonsense and incisive managerial leadership, but some tolerances are necessary for real improvement to occur and for it to be sustained. Ballard argues this also:

> What I find particularly interesting about the New Right assertion that it has a scientific basis for its practices (and that teachers do not) is that empirical research on the market school system in New Zealand shows it to be in serious trouble. Schools have become increasingly divided along socio-economic and ethnic lines, there is increasing inequality of resources and there is a related decline in student performance in those schools that are the market losers in this competitive system. Although such evidence is there, Aitkin (2000) referred to those opposing the New Right marketisation of education as 'inhabitants of old and outmoded educational ditches' whose 'essentially industrial agencies' (teacher unions) 'speak for and on behalf of a well cloned body of teachers and school principals'.
>
> (Ballard 2003: 23, 24)

There are parallels here with England. The tone of the quotes from the Chief Education Review Officer of New Zealand is reminiscent of that of the HMCI in the early days of Ofsted in England.

Further criticisms of schools in New Zealand, similar to those made about schools in England reported by Ballard, include assertions that schools are centres of complacency and that teachers are too easily satisfied with their own work. Claims that companies have been more powerful as instruments of public education than schools in the past 50 years, show strong orientation towards the market. This brings different global attitudes to protecting corporate capital. Governments 'need to establish new conditions for accumulation' (Robinson 1996: 51). 'Teachers therefore serve the ideology and structures of globalised capital, their professionalism as autonomous agents who care for children replaced by the depersonalized authority of the manager of learning outcomes' (Ballard 2003: 24). Parallels can be drawn in England where the over-riding privatized and corporate interests are prominent. The services which schools used to receive were highly personal, now they are decreasingly personal. The warning here is about similar creeping depersonalized roles for teachers with their pupils.

Managerialism cannot claim unmitigating success despite those who profess it. Holding a belief, having faith without evidence of proof are in the repertoire of politicians, leaders, managerialists, teachers, parents, children and consumers. A commitment to the use of rigorous analysis of data and research where it is available, coupled to sound managerial structures of efficiency, effectiveness and economy, will also be crucially necessary if all sides are to be served well. The champions of measurement will not lose their place but central politicians need to make room for the unproven ideas of others as well as for those of their own.

Fostering leadership and participation

Ideas such as 'leading from the middle', 'earned leadership' and 'leadership through interpersonal processes' form the basis of contemporary debate about leadership in education. Disempowerment of those working in education and 'who are cast increasingly in the role of "implementers"' (Wilkins 2004: 7) is easily identified. Amongst managerial evidence, anecdotal reporting can also be found. Any depersonalizing of the teacher's role should be recognized and curtailed. The concept of teacher as 'a teacher of pupils' rather than as 'a manager of learning resources' is important. Whilst teachers do manager resources, privatization should not dilute the quality of the leader–follower aspect of participation for both in this relationship.

In 'remodelling the workforce' in schools in England, much debate has been around the role of learning support assistants (LSAs) as they move towards becoming better trained TAs and higher-level teaching assistants (HLTAs). Should they be called 'teaching' assistants or 'teachers' assistants? There is an important difference. Given a privatized educational world, it is not difficult to see how the main expenditure on employing qualified teachers could be swiftly reduced by employing, instead of teachers, less qualified but adequately trained HLTA to teach from centrally prepared learning resources. The option for such savings would be highly attractive to those 'for-profit' schools. However, it would be difficult to see how such a move would aid innovation and raise the quality of education for the population. Education is a powerful force in securing equal life chances and as such deserves the recognition of the professionalism upon which it has been based for centuries.

Serious debate is needed about the relative and the comparative roles of private and public participants in the governance and leadership of education in England. The influence of 'local' LEA advisers and inspectors will diminish, as the role of LEAs change and many of these jobs become redundant. This group will not exist in sufficient size to help lead reform. Also, the NCSL, staffed essentially by ex-LEA personnel, does not explicitly face the governance part of the agenda, and as it too becomes a part of the traded market environment, will find its own different challenges to occupy its talent. Governance and leadership influences will have new sources and these look like being independent secondary specialist schools with foundation status.

Teachers and head teachers roles in leading reform beyond their own schools will increase. Certain conditions are necessary for this. 'If teachers are to have the confidence and capacity to lead reform, they must be given a stronger sense of belonging to a nationwide, lifelong profession, and less sense of being technical operatives hired to meet the short term needs of their current institution' (ibid.: 14).

Experiences from the late 1990s of foundation status schools bring evidence of staff often being subsumed within their own schools. Those ASTs in some foundation schools, spring to mind, who made their so-called 'wider contributions' within their own schools rather than, as was intended, in other schools in greater need. Trust and new commitment will be needed to overcome the danger of this repeating itself in the newly independent specialist schools of the future.

New associations in the leadership of education and issues about the respective relationships between leaders and followers are developing. Whilst the Specialist Schools Trust and one of the major professional associations for secondary headteachers (SHA), combine on some important projects about personalized learning for pupils and the use of information technology, the loci of influence on education governance moves heftily to that partnership along with government and away from other stakeholders. Making locally and democratically held views on secondary education impact on the thinking of such a powerful group will be difficult, should the views be at variance to those of this trio.

Individual schools governing bodies operating in clusters and federations will find new and very different challenges in community education governance, as will other stakeholders wishing to make a leadership contribution from their respective positions. The relationship between the NUT and the Government has room for partnership improvement, especially for the membership not associated with the Specialist School Trust. The roles of LEAs, their redundant education advisory staff, privatized-contract inspectors and consultants who find themselves with less-contracted work due to government adjustments in market demand will all seek new relationships. If standards are to rise in academic and vocational performance and in achieving a socially inclusive society, then these relationship will need some grooming. The two profile exhibits in Chapter 5 written by the professional association representatives for head teachers and advisers, inspectors and consultants draw out the strands that will be required. Trust as well as competitive market principles will have to feature.

Fostering leadership for choice and inclusion

A broad base for leadership in education is necessary. To leave out the contributions of significant stakeholders is counter-productive, especially in the longer term. It certainly inhibits genuine steps towards economic regeneration and social inclusion. The move to the values of the privatized market and its partnership associations, as described throughout, is narrowing that base. The strategic management and the leadership responsibilities which were with LEAs will increasingly be influenced by private and independent school groups. Local stakeholders may not find places on school governing bodies. As independent sponsors call for greater freedoms and get them, local democratic influence will reduce and with it so the capacity of central government to mobilize resources when things in schools flounder.

Influences are likely to continue to lean heavily towards the measures of academic success as the important indicators of performance. 'The English education system is…increasingly being driven in the direction of "privileging the academic" ' (Bagley *et al.* 2001: 305). The dominant output feature in the contracts in the privatized market environment is academic achievement measured by public examination results. This causes time and resources that impinge upon or distract from that direct pursuit to be relegated to a lower priority. Hence 'the personal, social and pastoral aspect of schooling is a subsidiary element in discourse on what it is to be a successful school' (ibid.).

Academic success and success in personal, social and citizenship aspects often go hand in hand. Schools that are good at improving examination results for the majority of pupils are also likely to be good at meeting the needs of pupils with SEN, have good community links which involve parents and which in turn improve the richness and range of extra curricular activities. But then others, schools that overly 'cram' for the tests, are not likely to be good at those things, they focus on 'privileging the academic' at the expense of social goals.

The core business of education will need redefinition with entitlement for inclusive education promoted rather more completely for the new privatized, yet collaborative environment. Keeping and building new levels of trust across this changing educational community will be a very real issue for the future, especially given some of the closed community traditions and the covert admission practices described in Chapters 2 and 8. Privatization must be seen not to become a wider back door to choice for some and only an illusion of choice for others. The common good is a bigger aspiration. For pupils to do well, markets, charitable contributions and professional efforts will all require a political climate which regards people as neighbours and citizens first, and consumers and competitors second.

Strategic leadership in Local Education Partnerships (LEPs)

Partnership implies a consensual relationship rather than one involving a strong pairing of leaders with followers, although such a leader and a follower relationship can be an effective partnership. LEPs give an opportunity for innovation and for ideas to be born from all sides. Scope exists for LEPs to operate in fundamental aspects of education policy, even though their remit sits beside the 'BSF' programme and as such tends to be associated primarily with new school builds and refurbishment.

It is in the area of policy development that most openings could arise for creative partnership working, real participation and subsequent acceptable compliance to a wide variety management plans. These things need to follow properly constituted democratic consideration of direction and purpose. It is this direction that I suggest holds the most hope for the privatizing future. It seems possible that these partnerships will combine different arrangements of stakeholder groups, including the democratically elected and those public and private sector people with new vision of what will work best in the future, based on the extension of knowledge of what has worked well or not before. New policy direction, planning and implementation with different measures of accountability could dawn. Whilst wholly new solutions are required, respect for the educational inheritance of different groups will be necessary. Trust in each other through the adventures will need to be built.

Gaining trust now is perhaps the greatest challenge. So often with new strategies in education, their appearance is not the reality. Take, for example, the apparent devolvement of power to schools in England and Wales following the 1988 Education Act. Whilst this appeared to give individual schools, governing bodies, head teachers, parents and communities much greater control and influence over their responsibilities to run their schools, what actually occurred was an uncompromising increase in the Government's own central capacity to steer the most important aspects of school life from a distance. What happened was the reverse of what was said to happen. As influence was taken to the centre, schools and LEAs lost the meaningful autonomy that they had previously and with it the power to innovate. Schools received operational responsibilities in this devolvement, not power over aspects of education that matter most.

Schools have had opportunity to earn back some of their original autonomy by demonstrating high compliance. But in order to create the space for these freedoms to be exercised, the Government has had to loosen the legislative framework around the schools. This was done through the 1990s by inventing new school categories which brought varying degrees of remission, leading to the independent specialist foundation status proposed for 2005. In some ways, this is consistent with the principle of government intervention in reverse proportion to success, now that some success is claimed for some schools, and for LEAs. For specialist schools and academies in particular, the boundaries for autonomy are redrawn. It is these schools which, having complied to the centrally determined culture and set of target parameters, are released with new private sector allegiances, to the freedoms of trade and innovation. Is it these schools, well clear of local democratic influences that should be aligning with the venture partners in the preliminary LEPs?

So what is the destiny of the movement to privatize, perhaps through the LEPs with their range of democratically elected, visionary and talented local and international stakeholders? Trusting that they are to be genuine partnerships between authorities and private venture capitalists, then their joint contribution to strategic leadership of education in the realm of broad public service could be hugely significant. The need for new creative strategies to bring success in the double harness of educational achievement and social inclusion is immense. The question is whether there will be space for such strategic movement, given the parameters that will be set for the new autonomies for schools.

Who are likely to be the most appropriate and the most innovative education partners to link with the private company innovators? If it is the federations and new groupings of independent schools, then the quality and impact of their contributions to the system as a whole will matter more than their own individual positions in the league table. Properly managed, that approach could produce wins for the individual school and the wider community of schools and learners.

LEPs have the potential to tackle the ways in which education addresses its need to globalize. The media and communications industry will need to win contracts to work in venture schemes, which allow for some open 'blue sky' opportunities to be developed with real stakeholders. The warning here is that, the well-established central tendency of knowing what is required from thinking 'within the managerial box' before the question is even considered is likely to stifle both the vision and the path to achieve it. There will be a need for imagination as well as trust. Open-mindedness beyond the limited tolerances presently displayed by those holding the strings of central policy will be needed.

For progress on a global front, some national practices will have to be laid to one side. It is difficult to see how that might occur given the rigidity of thinking, for example, towards the maintenance of the current accountability frameworks. To maximize the local education resources alongside those available globally, and create a new style of learning establishment, will call for thinking beyond the level of irrelevances. Tangible aspirations should be achievable. How, for example, can primary age pupils be given fresh and ambitious opportunities in music, which are built upon at later stages in secondary schools? It is doubtful that this will be achieved through a few more specialist schools for music. The aspiration should be bigger than that. Given the mass popular interest in music it is astonishing that strategically the education system does so badly in providing this subject for pupils in relevant ways. There are many examples where the horizons are low and the system allows little more than a perpetuation of that level of aspiration.

LEPs may provide a different and welcome means of finding the best routes to the energy, knowledge, skills and investment needed, to meet the challenges to be faced and provide educational solutions to some of the most difficult problems. With open-mindedness, combinations of voluntary, public and private sector contributions will stand the best chances of transforming education from the grooves in which it finds itself.

Education is still hampered by the statement of the Prime Minister in the 1980s, the sentiment expressed that there was no such thing as society; it was the family that is the nuclear unit. The family is important in the society schools help shape. There is a bigger role to be taken than currently exists for the family in shaping the vision for education. Democratic representatives recognize this. As the quote from William Blake suggests at the beginning of this book, system change and pleas of general good tempt hypocritical flattery. It is the bringing of not 'the devil in the detail' but the 'pragmatism of the details of local solutions' to the global organization of education that matters. The challenge is to ensure that the aggregation of these details leans towards fairness, justice and prosperity and that increasingly it continues to bend that way, both internationally and across the sectors.

As we started with some words from Blake let's finish that way:

Everything that lives, lives not alone, nor for itself.
(William Blake 1757–1827)

Glossary

This glossary explains words and terms used in the text of the book and those commonly used when discussing education and its development and privatization in England (rather than in the UK as a whole) and makes regular reference to terms used in the USA. These may have a different emphasis of meaning where they are used in other education systems.

Academies (*formerly City Academies*) Independent but state 'all-ability' secondary schools run by private companies or charities and based on the model of CTCs. These schools attempt to offer innovative solutions for schools facing challenging problems in particularly socially disadvantaged areas. A proportion of pupils may be selected by aptitude but it is often claimed that they are not; a system of banding pupils is intended to create a school population that reflects the cross-section of ability of the applicants for admission. Governors choose the teachers and teaching assistants who can be paid outside national pay conditions. The DfES provides at least 80 per cent of the initial capital costs, often more, and sponsors the rest. As these schools cost almost twice that of other state schools there is political and professional debate about their value for money in educational investment. Cf. *CTC* and *Magnet schools*.

Accountability The explicit and transparent demonstration of the proper, efficient and effective use of resources for the purposes for which they were acquired through a system of checks, external scrutiny and publication. The use of the term is central in education at both political and professional levels. LEAs and schools undergo extensive scrutiny of various forms, including inspection.

Administration Education administration usually refers to the act of carrying out the routine business of the management's requirements, for example, maintaining registrations and preparing, holding and retrieving papers for policy consideration, ensuring communication and keeping systems operational. It is about keeping the processes and pathways of management well maintained and tidy. Cf. *Leadership*, *Management* and *Governance*.

Admissions   See *School admissions.*

Advanced skills teacher (AST)   A grade for skilled teachers introduced by the DfEE in 1998 in order to encourage good teachers to seek promotion by continuing teaching and sharing their good practice rather than through the usual channels of promotion towards headship with corresponding movement away from teaching in the classroom. ASTs are required to share their expertise with teachers in other schools (for 20 per cent of their time) as well as their own (80 per cent).

Advisers   In this context, professional educators employed by LEAs or government departments, often formerly head teachers or senior staff from schools. Their roles are various but include providing help to schools and LEAs in, for instance, supporting and monitoring curriculum, target setting, checking school self-evaluation, giving advice to governors and assisting with interviewing for new head teachers and staff. Cf. *HMI* and *LEA inspectors.*

American education   Public (state) schooling in the USA is primarily the responsibility of the 50 individual states and is organized within each state into relatively small school districts run by school boards. These boards often exercise considerable power and independence. The organization and delivery of education has little to do with the Federal Government although national and nationwide market-driven reforms such as 'No Child Left Behind' have parallels with the inclusion agenda and privatizing trends in England. School districts across the USA are numerous and varied, usually employ their own teams of superintendents, advisers and administrators and often have only a few schools under their jurisdiction, hence unit costs are high comparatively. Two-tier and three-tier school systems proliferate. Diversity therefore is the over-riding characteristic in the organization of American education nationally, not centralized policy-making and economies of scale. Where privatization is possible and promoted on a large scale and across states, then opportunity exists for private companies to bring the perceived advantages of corporate efficiencies and standardized organizational frameworks, for example, private companies such as Edison Schools and Platform Learning. Cf. *English education* and *Governance.*

Appropriate authority   The schools' governing bodies are usually the appropriate authorities responsible for the school. The appropriate authority for maintained schools whose governing bodies do not have delegated budgets is the LEA. The proprietors of independent state schools such as CTCs and Academies are the appropriate authorities approved by the Secretary of State and are usually the schools governing bodies, which are often constituted differently to other state schools.

Arts mark   See *Quality standards.*

Assisted places scheme   A scheme designed to help families financially which were unable to afford the fees for their child to attend an independent school but where their child had won a place usually based on high attainment. The Labour Government abolished the funding for this scheme in 1997, as it was criticized by advocates of state comprehensive education.

Audit Commission (AC)   Established by the Government in 1982, this independent body examines the financing and operation of public services, and since 1997 (working with Ofsted) including LEAs, encouraging greater efficiencies and effectiveness.

Basic Skills Quality Mark (BSQM)   See *Quality standards*.

Borderline   Marks just below or just above cut-off point. Examiners usually scrutinize these marks very carefully. Pupils attaining these marks are also known as borderline.

British Standard   See *Quality standards*.

Business Excellence Model   See *Quality standards*.

Butler Act (1944 Education Act)   This Act, named after R. A. Butler who planned it, brought important changes which were to affect schools after the Second World War. Education would become organized into primary, secondary and further education with pupils educated according to their age, ability and aptitude. LEAs introduced the tripartite system of grammar, technical and secondary modern schools as the usual interpretation of the new legislation in practice. The school leaving age was raised from 14 to 15 and then to 16. RE was made the only compulsory subject in all schools. The School Board was replaced by a Ministry of Education which ensured that LEAs carried out the duty of providing schools locally. The 1944 Act was not superseded until the ERA and the Education Acts (1996) and (1998).

Charter Mark   See *Quality standards*.

Charter schools   Primary and secondary independent state schools operating in about 40 states in the USA. They are usually set up by private companies (e.g. Edison Schools) or by church-affiliated groups under an agreement with the state or local school board. The organizers agree a performance contract (a charter) for the newly established school for a 3–5-year period, which sets out the aims and objectives of the school, the curriculum, the pupils to be admitted and the assessment methods which will be used to measure the school's level of success at the end of the contract period. For this the organizer receives state funding equivalent to the total state school budget per pupil, can operate the school autonomously and for profit, and free from the state regulations that apply to education provided in other state schools. Renewal of the charter is dependent upon successful delivery of the original contract specification. Issues about the interpretation of educational measures of success and access make the charter school movement contentious, although in 2004 there are almost 3,000 charter schools operating across America. Cf. *Academies, American education, CTC, Faith schools, Magnet schools* and *Specialist schools*.

Chief Education Officer (CEO) The CEO, sometimes known as the Director of Education, is the LEA's principal officer and reports on a range of educational matters to the education committee or executive cabinet of the local council and carries out its policies in relation to education and often other children's services and community matters. The CEO ensures that all statutory education requirements are met.

Church schools A commonly used term in England to describe faith schools with an historic Christian denominational background, usually Church of England and Roman Catholic. These schools may be independent and controlled by a minority religious group, but the majority in England are set within the broad provision of the state, being funded and often controlled by the LEA. Levels of funding and control depend on whether a school is designated foundation, voluntary-aided or voluntary-controlled. Cf. *Dual system*, *Faith schools*, *VA schools* and *VC schools*.

City Academies See *Academies*.

City Technology College (CTC) Stimulated by interest in magnet schools in the USA, these schools were established under the 1988 Education Reform Act as independent schools funded essentially by Government funding, although it was originally intended that they should be financed by industry and be an alternative to LEA schools, but sufficient private funding was not forthcoming. Only 15 of these schools were set up. They were the forerunners to City Academies (subsequently Academies) and continue to enjoy high status. Cf. *Academies*, *Magnet schools* and *Specialist schools*.

Class 1. A group of pupils registered as a unit within a school and often taught as a group, usually between 20 and 35 normally of the similar age group. Some classes are mixed-age classes, usually in small schools that have an insufficient budget to sustain smaller groups of pupils in class groups of just a single age group. A class may, therefore consist of a range of abilities. Class size is particularly relevant in the debate about privatization as it is a major determinant of cost/pricing. It is often a small class size that parents consider to be the most important factor when purchasing private education, even if the dynamics of learning are not necessarily helped below a certain critical number of pupils in the class.

2. The term used to describe the social and economic ranking of people or order in society, often used in England to identify client groups when private or selective education is discussed, for example, lower and working class, middle class and upper class. Also used is professional class, and less often, moneyed class, celebrity class and aristocratic class.

Classroom assistant See *TAs*.

Community schools The term used to denote a school which remained within its LEA at the time when others were 'opting out'. It has a wider use where local people are encouraged to be involved in education and where schools make particular effort to organize activities during the day and evening systematically. Schools can increase their income by the use of the school's facilities in this way. Cf. *Extended schools.*

Comprehensive performance assessment (CPA)   A component in the Government's performance framework for securing and monitoring improvements in local authorities including targets for education. Cf. *Performance indicators.*

Comprehensive school   A school defined as 'one which is intended to cater for the secondary education of all children in a given area'. It was felt that the tripartite system of the 1944 Act had not succeeded in bringing the best education to all groups of pupils and so comprehensive schools were established in the 1960s and 1970s.

Compulsory competitive tendering (CCT)   A system popularly developed during the 1990s in England to attempt to gain better value for money from services (such as school meals and cleaning and maintenance) from private firms competing over price and quality; services previously provided by the LEA. CCT followed requirements in the 1988 Government Act and the 1992 Local Government Act when the list of affected services was extended and where LEAs were required to ensure that fairness was observed.

Contract schools   Where private or voluntary sponsors take responsibility for schools which are perhaps failing or are in difficulty, often for a fixed period of 5–7 years, which may be renewed. They are normally subject to national policies on admissions.

Delegation   Entrusting another with the authority to act as an agent, for example, as an LEA entrusts a budget to a school governing body for appropriate expenditure, or a head teacher would be likely to entrust a deputy with leadership and management responsibility. Effective leadership and management in schools are often associated with careful delegation and less reliance on narrow hierarchical control.

Department for Culture, Media and Sport (DCMS)   The Government department responsible for the promotion of these activities and consequently involved in joint initiatives with the DfES.

Department for Education and Skills (DfES)   The Government department responsible for education and formed in 2001 when some employment responsibilities were removed from the DfEE and aspects of education and training were retained in the new DfES. These name changes and those of the Department of Education (DfE), the Department for Education and Science (DES) and others reflect shifts in emphasis and classification.

Department of Transport, Local Government and the Regions (DTLR) The Government Department responsible for local government and therefore issues that affect LEAs, notably local government finance. This department changed to become the Office of the Deputy Prime Minister (ODPM) in 2003.

Devolution The handing over of authority from a central body to a constituent part, for example, from central government to regional government, or from an LEA to a school governing body. Cf. *Delegation.*

Direct grant school Established in 1926, a selective secondary school receiving a Government grant. A certain number of pupils had to be taken from state primary schools paid for by LEAs or the schools' governors. These schools became either maintained or independent after September 1976 when direct grant schools ceased to operate.

Director of Education The principal officer in an LEA, usually including the role of the CEO and often other education, social, community and cultural responsibilities, especially with regard to services for children. Cf. *CEO.*

Dual system The 1870 Education Act established the existence of state schools along side church schools; the dual system. The 1902 Act allowed funding from local taxes to go to church schools, in return for LEAs nominating school managers and supervising non-religious aspects of the curriculum. New financial arrangements were agreed following the 1944 Act when voluntary schools were divided into aided, controlled or special categories. The category depended on the agreement made with the local authority. In 1959 and 1967, building grants for church schools were allowed. Cf. *Church schools, Faith schools, VA schools* and *VC schools.*

Educare A flexible system of childcare provision and education, proposed in 2004, for three and four-year olds that would give parents choice about when and how it could be used. Cf. *Wrap-around care, Extended day* and *Sure start.*

Education Action Zones (EAZ) Nationwide 73 EAZs had been set up since 1998. Due to a lack of commercial interest, low levels of financial sponsorship from the private sector and few zones meeting their educational targets, the scheme was generally viewed as less than successful. A number of the smaller EAZs were incorporated into the EiC programme. Cf. *EiC.*

Education Reform Act (1988) (ERA) A very significant education act as it fundamentally altered the basis of the education in England and Wales from the system followed under the broad legislation of the 1944 (Butler) Act to a tightly prescribed and centralized system with the National Curriculum, national testing, open accountability and LMS which brought a changing role for LEAs. In many respects this legislation began the trend of privatizing state education in England. Cf. *Butler Act 1944* and *School Standards and Framework Act 1998.*

Eleven plus examination A test for selection at age 11 to secondary schools set by the LEA.

English education In England, education is the responsibility of the DfES headed by the Secretary of State for Education, who is a member of the

Government's ruling Cabinet. Over 90 per cent of pupils attend state schools with less than 10 per cent attending private independent schools. However, the distinction between the two systems has become blurred with certain categories of state-funded schools becoming independent, for example CTCs and academies. Prior to 2000, the political unit for education was England and Wales, but since devolution distinctive differences have occurred in the way state schools and the education systems have developed in these two countries, especially in relation to privatization and in the systems of accountability. English education policy for state schools in 2004 is set out in a five-year strategy and is about raising standards, promoting inclusion and developing a new relationship with schools based on 'intelligent' accountability through effective school self-evaluation. Strands of policies appear to lack coherence as schools are encouraged to work in partnership across the state and the private school divide whilst, at the same time, are led towards seeking independence and becoming their own admissions authorities. Cf. *American education, Governance* and *School admissions.*

Excellence in Cities (EiC)   This scheme was launched in March 1999 to raise standards in schools in large cities. Extra resources were provided by government directly, rather than from private industry, for gifted and talented pupils, learning mentors, Learning Support Units. Allocation of resources was based on need rather than by making bids. By September 2001, 48 LEAs and 1,000 secondary schools were members of the scheme. From that date also, the programme was extended outside large cities through EiCS Clusters and has included aspects of the work from the discontinued EAZs. Cf. *EAZs.*

Extended day   Provision where schools regularly stay open after school hours for extra-curricular activities or childcare or make provision for homework to be done at school. Cf. *Educare, Extended schools, Out-of-school activities, Sure start* and *Wrap-around care.*

Extended schools   Schools that provide community facilities and educational and childcare provision beyond that usually expected of a conventional school. Extended schools would offer such things as an extended day, would have provision along the lines of sure start or educare and would be likely to seek to be part of a Children's Centre initiative where the school provides education alongside local 'one-stop' support for childcare, health, employment and parenting. Cf. *Educare, Extended day, Out-of-school activities, Sure start* and *Wrap-around care.*

Extra-curricular activities   See *Out-of-school activities.*

Failing schools   As a technical term, originally secondary schools in England where less than 15 per cent of pupils gain five subjects at grade C or better at GCSE. In 2004, the minimum target was raised to 20 per cent and 35 per cent for 2006. A failing primary school is usually regarded as one that does not respond adequately after being placed as in need of 'special measures' following inspection.

Faith schools Usually schools of different Christian denominations and sects in England and the USA, in England mainly state supported Church of England and Roman Catholic schools, but include schools operated by members of other faiths mainly for their faith communities. These include schools for Jewish, Sikh and Muslim communities. Overall the number of faith schools has been fairly constant in England over the decade 1995–2005. In the USA, faith schools are independent schools and there has been a significant increase in the number of non-sectarian charter schools formed by religious groups. In England, new faith state schools, whilst determining their own admissions criteria, are expected to take account of the pattern of school admissions across the community and must show a willingness to work in partnership with other secular and religious schools in that area. However the registration of privately operated independent faith schools, either through Ofsted or the Independent Schools Inspectorate's Council, is controversial because independent schools do not have to follow the National Curriculum and therefore can become registered whilst pursuing a limited curriculum which would not be deemed acceptable by Ofsted in a state school. Cf. *Charter schools, Church schools, Dual system, VA schools* and *VC schools.*

Federations An arrangement whereby a school or a number of different schools work under the leadership and management of another in order to bring about improvement across the pair or group of schools. A federation of schools or a federated school usually work under a single head teacher and governing body.

Forster's Elementary Education Act (1870) An important Act that set up school boards and built elementary schools to complement the provision of voluntary schools by churches. This effectively established the provision of free state elementary education for all children in England. Cf. *Butler Act 1944, ERA, School Standards and Framework Act 1998 (SSFA), VA schools* and *VC schools.*

Foundation school Many of these were former GM schools and are state schools which have achieved a status which allows them more autonomy than schools which are within an LEA. They employ their own staff and decide their own admission policy; they own their own land and buildings. The first school with foundation status opened in September 2001 and the Government's five-year strategy beyond 2004 is for more to follow.

General Certificate of Secondary Education (GCSE) The central external examination for 16-year olds use in England at the end of KS 4, introduced in 1988, to replace the General Certificate of Education (GCE) and Certificate of Secondary Education (CSE) as the main school-leaving qualification.

Governance Educational governance refers to the control and exercise of authority over education systems and schools. In most countries there is a balance of authority between the national government, the state or the LEA or district, and the individual institution of the school. However, moves since 1988 in England have diminished the role of the LEA and local democracy in favour of national governance with school level accountabilities. Governance of schools in the USA is the responsibility of the 50 individual states, but there are national imperatives and similar patterns to those in England in that the large-scale privatization of schools and education services by a limited number of large corporate bodies has a broad political base of support. Cf. *American education* and *English education.*

Governors   A requirement of all maintained schools is the appointment of a voluntary governing body. The duties of governing bodies have to be set out in an instrument of government as a requirement of the 1944 Education Act and their functions set out in articles of government in relation to headteachers and LEAs. These functions have increased and teachers and parents must have representatives on the governing body following the 1980 Education Act with more responsibilities added by the 1988 Education Reform Act and subsequent legislation. However the governing body requirement for independent state schools are of a different nature and composition and access to becoming a governor is becoming a matter of interest in moves towards privatization. The governors main association is the National Association of Governors and Managers (NAGM). Cf. *Governance.*

Grammar school   A type of school first so named in the fourteenth century to provide free or subsidized education in a particularly locality, usually for boys. By the nineteenth century the Grammar School Act reformed these schools. LEAs, created by the 1902 Education Act, were given power to provide secondary schools on similar lines and the 1944 Education Act stated that the education should be free and compulsory and included grammar schools as part of the tripartite system of secondary schools for differing pupils' abilities; alongside technical and secondary modern schools. Selection for these schools was by way of the 11+ examination. By 1990, grammar schools were only retained by 7 per cent of LEAs, 166 in total, and no new ones have been created since then.

Grant maintained school (GMS)   Schools which chose to opt out of LEA control and become funded directly from the Government. They were established by the Education Reform Act (1988) but replaced from 2001 with foundation schools under the SSFA (1998).

'Great Debate'   On 18 October 1976 the British Prime Minister, James Callaghan, made a speech at Ruskin College, Oxford asking for a public debate on standards in education. A Green Paper, Education in Schools: a Consultative Document, was issued and this began the move in England to centralize education policy over the next decade and which was to continue for 30 years. This was initially around the curriculum and brought the advent of the National Curriculum in 1988 with national testing of pupils at the ages of 7, 11, 14 and 16 bringing increased public accountability, and leading on to a national school inspection service and national strategies for teaching (a decade later) which prescribed the way lessons in literacy and numeracy should be conducted. Cf. *National Curriculum.*

Green Paper   Early proposals for future government policy in the form of a consultative or discussion document. Cf. *White Paper.*

Healthy Schools Award   See *Quality standards.*

Her Majesty's Inspectorate (Inspector) (HMI)   From the 1830s, a few inspectors were appointed to supervise the spending of public money for educating the poor. Following a long tradition, by the 1990s their membership was over 500 and their roles had expanded. HMI were reduced in number and their function in school inspections became mainly to manage the Ofsted established in 1992 privatized programme, as its permanently employed staff. With major changes in 2005 to the school inspection system, with fewer private companies being involved, HMI returns to a more direct role in leading school inspections along with it other functions. Cf. *LEA inspectors* and *Ofsted.*

Higher Level Teaching Assistant (HLTA)   See *TA.*

Inclusion   The continuing process of increasing the presence and participation of more pupils in regular or mainstream schools whilst improving, for all, their quality of life, learning and achievements. It is seen as increasing choice and recognizing diversity and so engaging those groups who, for whatever reason, may be vulnerable or at risk of marginalization or underachievement. It is about extending understanding in order to combat isolation, threat and fear. Many aspects of inclusion policy in England in 2005 are driven by outcomes described in 'Every Child Matters' and in the USA by 'No Child Left Behind'. Cf. *Learning establishment, Individual learning, IEP* and *Personalized learning.*

Inclusion Quality Mark   See *Quality standards.*

Independent learning   See *Individual learning* and *Personalized learning.*

Independent Schools' Inspectorate (ISI)   A title assumed in September 1998 as a successor to the Accreditation Review and Consultancy Service of the ISC and in April 2000 it joined with the Headmasters' and Headmistresses' Conference inspection service.

Individual education plan (IEP)   A plan to meet the identified needs of pupils and especially those with learning difficulties and SEN. The programme sets targets and usually gives parents help and advice on how to be fully involved in the process. Cf. *Individual learning* and *Personalized learning.*

Individual learning   Pupils working on their own in class rather than in a group, maybe by means of a worksheet or a specific element in the programme of study with minimum support from the teacher. This is sometimes known as independent learning. More recently the term includes pupils working at their own pace by using different approaches and learning styles. Cf. *Personalized learning* and *IEP.*

Investor in People   See *Quality standards.*

ISO 9000   See *Quality standards.*

Joined-up working   The situation where large organizations and public services have well coordinated planning and delivery of the different strands of their operations and which complement the aims and objectives of each. The idea is the opposite to what is sometimes known as 'silo' working, where different departments operate in isolation and with little regard for the work of the others. Also, a term used to describe communities that have an infrastructure which gives homes, schools, health centres, libraries and other council services good local electronic communications; sometimes referred to as 'wired-up' communities.

Key stage (KS)   The statutory National Curriculum Programmes of Study (PoS) which pupils are required to follow in state schools are divided into four key stages: KS 1 – ages 5–7; KS 2 – ages 8–11; KS 3 – ages 11–14; KS 4 ages 14–16. Additionally the curriculum for ages 3–5 is called the Foundation Stage and for 16–19 is sometimes referred to as KS 5. The National Literacy and Numeracy Strategies are focused at KS I and 2 whilst for KS 3 they are combined with other subjects and called the KS 3 Strategy.

Leadership   Educational leadership is the action of showing others the way. It incorporates a complexity of skills such as setting strategic direction, sharing a vision, securing commitment and purpose, and providing inspiration and motivation to the pupils, staff, governors, parents and the wider community. It is associated with empowerment and as such is about 'doing the right things' based on values that embrace the highest aspirations of and for the community, and being a step ahead of the current reality. It is about creating new and amended paths and procedures, and may be restrained or liberated by legal parameters. Cf. *Management, Governance* and *Administration.*

League tables   The Government issued a Parents' Charter in 1991 whereby parents would to receive an annual written report informing them of pupils' performance and National Curriculum tests. The report also gives a comparison of pupils of the same age. The DfES publishes league tables of exam results, National Curriculum tests, absence rates, pupils' destinations on leaving school and other performance indicators from all schools; primary schools results were included from 1997. Therefore, 'value-added information' is now also used which takes account of the school's context and characteristics. England is the only UK country to produce league tables of school performance.

LEA inspectors   Employed by LEAs to ensure standards are maintained. Previously known as advisers but changes in their function during the 1980s led to the name change, and their role has been further modified under the LMS which passes to schools the advisory budget so allowing schools to buy in advice locally or from elsewhere. The four-yearly inspections set up by the Education (Schools) Act (1992) under Ofsted changed their role further but LEAs still monitored the implementation of the National Curriculum but did not now inspect unless as part of the privatized Ofsted inspection regime. Cf. *HMI*, *Advisers* and *Ofsted*.

Learning establishment A wide and inclusive social group exercising authority and influence to ensure relevant education across the community and for minorities. Inclusiveness in this context is based on the idea that 'boundaries' around schools and around the communities' workplaces and homes should be transparent to learning processes. It implies the need for a cultural shift based on achieving mutual trust and respect about learning and where those leading education see the centrality of providing effective learning for all in ways that take account of the dynamic needs of the learner and the changes different groups of people in society undergo. Cf. *Personalized learning* and *Individual learning*.

Local Education Authority (LEA) Established under the 1902 Education Act replacing school boards, and being responsible for voluntary schools unlike school boards. Each LEA had to appoint an education committee consisting of elected councillors and co-opted members, the chairman being elected from the political party with a majority at the local election. Education was provided nationally but administered locally giving considerable local democratic power over the detail of provision. The role of LEAs did not change fundamentally throughout the century. More recently, *The Role of the Local Education Authorities in School Education*, was published by the DfEE in 2000 and confirmed the importance of their role in supporting schools to raise standards but increased the delegation of their budget to schools. It also identified where schools should not provide services on their own, such as the supply of school places in the area, planning coordination for SEN and home/school transport and defined a Code of Practice for the relationship between schools and LEAs which promoted autonomy for all but the least successful schools.

Local management of schools (LMS) The delegation of the leadership, management and finances of a school to the governing body and head teacher. This culture and philosophy for the organization and management of schools was brought about as part of the Education Reform Act in 1988. It was part of the general shift in school management to place the control of resources closer to the point of teaching and learning and to give parents more say and influence in their child's education through elected representatives on the school's governing body. It was thought to encourage competitiveness among schools, a sought after characteristic by the Government of the period.

Magnet schools Senior secondary schools (typically 14–18 upper schools) developed in the USA during the 1970s and 1980s with commercial sponsorship. These were schools specializing in vocational or academic subjects, for instance science or the arts, but also providing a broad curriculum. As such they were the forerunners of the CTCs movement in England. Magnet schools were popular in many areas across the USA. Some became highly selective whilst others, which were oversubscribed, conducted random admissions policies in order to attempt to achieve racial integration and social inclusion. Magnet schools met with considerable opposition from school boards and teacher unions because of the take up of places in these schools from families of high-social mobility and the perceived threat of the independence of magnet schools to local democratic influences and controls. Whilst many individual magnet schools were successful, evaluations did not produce any conclusive results that they achieved their wider educational objectives. Cf. *CTC* and *Charter schools.*

Management   Education management is the process of ensuring that the organization is properly directed and that matters are conducted in line with policy, whether applying to people, resources, plant or educational action. It is associated with control and as such is about 'doing things right', following procedures and the established paths but taking initiative where necessary, especially over operational interpretation. Management functions sit at a range of levels, for example, within a private contracting agency or an LEA, and at school level with the governing body, head teacher, bursar, teacher, teaching assistant or site-supervisor, although the duty to discharge overall management responsibility is chiefly with the head teacher. Cf. *Leadership*, *Governance* and *Administration.*

Management Charter Initiative   See *Quality standards.*

Managerialism   A particular style of managing which utilizes a set of principles based on prescribed and measured practices, line command, compliance and quasi-scientific outcomes believed to indicate objective performance and an apparent true basis to information, and therefore competitive advantage. The style is associated with the idea that the control of people's actions, set against a system of detailed specification, brings conformity and an improved standard of consistent service. Cf. *Professionalism.*

National College for School Leadership (NCSL)   Launched in November 2000 as a publicly funded initiative to provide headship training. In April 2001, it took over wider professional development responsibility on behalf the DfES, some programmes being developed jointly with Ofsted and through sizeable contracts with private sector companies, mainly Hay McBer. In 2005, it supports deputy head teachers and a range of school leader roles and bursars.

National Curriculum   The ERA introduced a compulsory National Curriculum for pupils aged 5–16 in schools in England and Wales. This was made up of ten compulsory subjects: English, mathematics, science (known as the core subjects), art and design, geography, history, technology (later to become design and technology and ICT), music and physical education, with a modern foreign languages for secondary-aged pupils. Welsh was added as a foundation subject as a first or second language in Wales. RE, although a compulsory subject, was not classed as part of the National Curriculum but described through a Locally Agreed Syllabus. The National Curriculum has undergone various revisions and amendments. Most notably of these has been the promotion of ICT as part of the extended core subjects, the addition of a range of vocational courses and qualifications for 14–16-year olds as an alternative to the more academic subjects, the general overhaul of 2000 and the addition, in 2002, of citizenship education as a compulsory subject for KS 3 and 4. A National Healthy School Standard supports personal, social and health education (PSHE), an area that includes drug awareness and sex and relationships education. A statement sets out the values, aims and purposes underpinning the curriculum. Sections set out ways in which spiritual, moral, social and cultural development, key skills and thinking skills can be met across the curriculum. Private and independent schools are not required to follow the National Curriculum but many choose to adopt parts of it.

New Public Administration (NPA)   See *NPM*.

New Public Management (NPM)   The term used internationally to describe the change in culture in public services during the 1980s when it was felt that public services should be run like private businesses rather than by local authorities operationally close to the political line of accountability. The term New Public Administration is also used to distinguish from OPA, the state of affairs prior to 1980 characterized by ideas that public and private sectors were best kept at arm's length to avoid blurring the public interest with private and sectional motives.

Office for Standards in Education (Ofsted)   Following the reorganization and reduction in size of HMI a different privatized system of school inspection was introduced in 1992, led by the Chief Inspector of Schools in England and centrally organized by HMI (Ofsted HMI) and other staff. Inspection teams formed to inspect state schools were usually composed of private contracted inspectors (Ofsted contracted inspectors), often self-employed and working for or within a private inspection company. Teams of inspectors were led by a registered inspector and included a lay inspector. Contracts for the inspection of schools were put out to tender and awarded under market competition. From September 2005, the system changed again with greater involvement returning to HMI working directly with fewer private inspection companies as RISPs, and with HMI again leading many inspections themselves, especially of secondary schools.

All schools, primary, secondary private and funded nursery schools, sixth form colleges further education colleges, teacher-training courses and youth work fall to some degree under Ofsted's jurisdiction. Early years childcare and education have been subject to Ofsted inspection since 2001.

From January 1998, LEAs started to be inspected by Ofsted with involvement from the AC. The third cycle of inspections of 150 LEAs was completed by 2005. Cf. *HMI.*

Ofsted/contracted inspectors   A term to distinguish Ofsted inspectors employed independently, by private sector companies or LEA trading units. Cf. *Ofsted/HMI inspectors.*

Ofsted/HMI inspectors   A term to distinguish Ofsted inspectors employed by the public sector of HMI. Cf. *Ofsted/contracted inspectors.*

Old Public Administration (OPA)   See *NPM.*

Opting out   A term referring to a school that had decided to become independent through GM status and therefore no longer under the control of the LEA. This termed followed the Education Reform Act (1988) when schools were encouraged to become autonomous. By 2005, the term is not used to describe the similar movement to foundation status or independent status because the political strategy is for these schools to form the state system and therefore not be an opted-out part of it.

Organisation for Economic Co-operation and Development (OECD)   This organization formed in 1961 aims to promote and formulate economic and social welfare policies by assisting its 24 member governments. Education is one of more than 100 specialized committees and working parties. The CERI carries out much of the work on education. The policies for education from the member countries are published by the OECD and include well-publicized information about the international comparative educational performances of schools, pupils and adults.

Out-of-school activities   A self-explanatory term relating to educational activity usually organized or promoted by a school out-of-normal school time or the school vicinity, often termed extra-curricular activities. Advice on school visits and the supervision of pupils are issued by the DfES. School-governing bodies and LEAs must ensure the health and safety of pupils who are off premises, home or abroad. Actions by teachers and adults that are considered to be reasonable in promoting pupils' welfare and safety precautions in emergency situations, are covered in the Children Act (1989) and associated guidelines. Incidents have raised questions about the risk to pupils' safety and in some aspects a curbing of out-of-school activity has resulted. Cf. *Extended day.*

Parent governors   Parent governors now represent a high proportion of the membership of governing bodies of state schools following the 1980 and 1986 Education Acts when they were given increased representation. They are elected by secret ballot for four years. However, the representation of parents to be on state independent schools and private schools' governing bodies are not protected to the same levels.

Parent Partnership Services (PPS)   These were set up by the Government in England from 1994, usually in an arm's length relationship with LEAs, and evolved with the aim of ensuring parents of children with special needs as well as parents of all children including the very young, have access to information, advice and guidance in relation to the educational needs of their children so they can make appropriate and informed decisions.

Parent power   Giving parents more choice over schools they can select for their children to attend and more power and influence over the way the schools operate has been a popular and political idea since the 1980s. One of the purposes of the 1988 Education Act was to involve parents more in their children's education and was followed by the creation of the Parents Charter in 1991. In a drive to increase the accountability of schools, more information about schools performance was made available, mainly through league tables of examination and test results. In theory this enabled parents to be informed about the choice of school for their children. Parental choice and preference and their rights on school admissions has caused much controversy, is often claimed to be a mere political illusion and remains highly contentious in 2005. Political calls for 'personalized learning' have tones of giving parents the right to expect individual learning plans for their children. Parents are involved with schools through membership of governing bodies, have a direct contact with Ofsted inspection teams and have statutory rights to receive information and attend annual meetings where schools have to account for their actions. Parents participate with LEAs through the parental partnership services and on SOC and LSP. Cf. *School admissions* and *Vouchers.*

Parents' Charter   The Parents' Charter: You and Your Child's Education, Issued July 1991, stated parents' rights and responsibilities in education in the Government's Citizens Charter. The Charter included plans for regular reports on a school's strengths and weaknesses (by independent Ofsted inspectors), publication of school performance in league table rankings in order to compare schools' performances; annual written reports on children's progress and independent assessors on panels to hear appeals by parents who were unable to get a place for their child in the school of their choice. Cf. *Parent power, School admissions, Performance indicators* and *Vouchers.*

Partnership for Schools (PfS)   A joint venture company set up in 2003 by the Government and PUK to develop new and effective methods of procuring school construction and other education service contracts between the public and private sectors.

Performance indicators   Descriptors used to judge the effectiveness of organizations such as schools, LEAs and private education services companies. Performance indicators have financial origins and were applied to cost-effectiveness and value-for-money judgements. They are now fully accepted in the culture of monitoring and evaluating the work of schools and education services. School performance league tables, rates of truancy and National Curriculum tests are regarded as central indicators. The levels of care schools provide, the quality of teaching and learning, shared aims across the schools' leadership and local community are judged in Ofsted reporting. Cf. *CPA* and *Parents' Charter*.

Personalized learning   A politically introduced term in 2004 to describe a focus on individual learning where parents, along with pupils and teachers, become closely involved in the development of learning arrangements which are carefully tailored to the perceived needs of each particular pupil and their preferred learning styles. Personalized learning of this kind, it is argued, is made feasible by the increased and intelligent use of ICT both at home and at school. The term also implies the need to focus on ensuring relevant achievement and progress for each individual pupil, so creating an ethos of achievement for all. Where effective, this develops personal and family pride in success at school and can discourage behaviours which are part of an anti-learning culture reported in some secondary schools characterized by embarrassment over publicly acknowledged achievement, name calling such as 'swot' and 'boffin' and other abuse. Cf. *Individual learning* and *IEP*.

Private Finance Initiative (PFI)   A Government policy that facilitates private sector funding to support publicly funded capital expenditure. In education, this usually takes the form of a partnership between private companies and LEAs where the private company builds, finances and maintains schools or redesigns existing schools. The LEA in return for this investment pays an annual fee (under a long-term contract of about 30 years) and allows the private company to manage, at a profit, the services to the building, its infrastructure and operation, such as cleaning and maintenance, ICT equipment installation and management, school meals and catering and administrative expertise. The Green Paper, Schools: Building on Success (2001) highlighted this initiative as one of the means of transforming secondary education in England through projects such as 'BSF'. There is discussion that PFI credit funding will be available for primary schools to be a part of this project from 2006 to 2010. Cf. *PPP*.

Professionalism   A particular style of managing which seeks to aggregate the contributions of qualified individuals from within a range of accepted perceptions and practices that are constructed through experience, culture and reflective procedures and which in turn build consistent and effective responsiveness to clients' needs. The style is associated with empowering individuals, usually through education and training in performing high-order skills, to bring their best to the management task. Cf. *Managerialism*.

Public Private Partnership (PPP)   A Government initiative to bring joint investment and expertise to public ventures such as the PFI. In education, it is possible for schools and education services to establish new partnerships with public, private and voluntary sector bodies for both the capital building of schools and the delivery of education whereby, for example, LEAs contract out services to private companies under long-term borrowing. Attempts at offering commercial opportunities and at marrying what have been public service education provisions with private practices take a variety of forms and can vary from a private firm acting as consultants to several education authorities on major ventures to more limited aspects of education where strong management support is required. Cf. *PFI*.

QS 9000   See *Quality standards.*

Quality standards   With the expectation on organizations to self-assess and self-evaluate in order to improve their performance continuously and achieve better results, there has been an international proliferation of initiatives which aim to assist in this process and so help 'management' achieve competitive advantage. The concept of these standards gained momentum in the Total Quality Management movement of the 1980s and, through the 1990s, expanded rapidly from manufacturing to service industries. The standards specify requirements throughout the process of the manufacture and sale of products or the delivery of services and usually include elements such as clarity in objectives, self and external assessment, measurement of outcomes against targets and benchmarking. Schools and education services are eligible to gain most of these awards and especially those which are regarded as more relevant to standards in education. These include QS 9000, ISO 9000 (which incorporates the former BS5750), MCI standards, Investors in People and Charter Mark and Schools and organizations are sometimes tempted to collect many such awards or seek an overarching award such as Business Excellence as accreditation of their self-evaluation and accountability. Many government departments and organizations offer variations on these types of award as stimuli to improvement and indications of quality markers in their particular areas of interest and activity, for example, the School Achievement Award, Basic Skills Quality Mark, Sports Mark, Arts Mark, Healthy Schools Award, Inclusion Quality Mark and, in some organizations, even special 'club' memberships. In 2005, quality mark logos abound on letterheads and the walls in schools' reception areas are often adorned with plaques. Tomorrow's Company is a closely related but different approach to organization improvement by advocating inclusive practices focused on stakeholder relationships to create an inspirational business ethos but avoids recognition by measuring and awarding standards.

Regional Inspection Providers (RISPs)   Private sector companies successful in their bids to work in close partnership with HMI to organize and deliver the inspection system from October 2005. The RISPs will operate regionally in the north, midlands and south of England. Cf. *Ofsted*, *Ofsted/HMI* and *Ofsted/contracted inspectors*.

School admissions   The SSFA and the Education Act (2002) govern the procedures for school admissions with the *School Admissions Code of Practice* (2003) giving guidance (which is not enforced by statute) on many of the complicated arrangements within the various regulations. Broadly, LEAs are responsible for securing sufficient school places in their area and are the admission authority for most state schools; but not for independent state schools such as academies, foundation schools and VA schools where the governing bodies are the schools' own admissions authority and operate their own policies. The LEA is also required to establish an admissions forum that has the function of advising the LEA in coordinating admissions and promoting agreement on admission issues. Achieving agreement is easier said than done with increasing numbers of different schools determining policies, applying different admission criteria and following their own interests. Parents have the right to 'express a preference' for the school at which they wish their child to be educated. Procedures are in place for parents to appeal if they are not allocated the school of their choice. Panels and adjudicators deal with appeals that are difficult to settle. About one in ten parents appeal against the allocation of their child's place at a school that was not their preferred choice. The number of appeals is rising. About 90 per cent of pupils secure their first or second choice primary or secondary school. Both in the USA and England, the idea of using a voucher scheme to give parents the power to spend them on the school of their choice, thus allowing the most popular schools to expand, has been considered but have not been found to work successfully in practice. Cf. *Parent power* and *Vouchers*.

School Organization Committee (SOC)   These statutory committees have been set up in LEAs since September 1999. They plan for the provision of school places and consider changes in the opening and closing of schools. Each LEA has to submit an updated five-year rolling plan, the SOP, that sets out its proposals for the provision of SEN pupils and how it will remedy an excess or insufficiency of school places. Membership of the committee has broad constituents and consists of LEA representatives, the Anglican and Roman Catholic Church and members with local minority interests. A representative from either a primary, middle secondary or special school must be in the governors' group. A school adjudicator receives decisions that are not unanimous. Cf. *SOP*.

School Organization Plan (SOP)   The plan drawn up by the SOC. Ensuring sufficient school places to meet present and future needs is the responsibility of LEAs. The SOP is an updated draft five-year rolling programme that sets out proposals for the provision of SEN of pupils and how the LEA will remedy an excess or insufficiency of school places. The plan indicates the need to add or remove places in certain areas, which is a highly contentious business as increasingly individual schools become their own admissions authority. A copy of the plan is then sent to each governing body of all schools in the LEA area. The SOC considers the plan along with any objections. A school adjudicator considers any disagreements. Cf. *SOC*.

School Standards and Framework Act (1998) (SSFA)   An act that brought changes which facilitated the privatization of state schools. It made significant revisions to the basic categories of schools, removed the duty from LEAs to have a curriculum statement, established target-setting mechanisms across education, required LEAs to set up SOCs, altered codes on school admissions and the working relationships between schools and LEAs and strengthened the power of intervention (in failing LEAs) by the Secretary of State. These revisions created openings for new models of LEA organization with greater and accelerated use of the private sector in state education. Cf. *ERA* and *Butler Act 1944*.

Selective school   An independent, private or state school with an admissions policy that limits the entry of pupils to those who meet particular criteria, often those who have reached a certain level of attainment, general ability or show particular aptitude in a specialist subject. Cf. *Grammar schools*.

Single Education Plan (SEP)   A proposal to streamline the planning demands on LEAS (and the private companies that have been brought in to run them) by bringing the various separate strategic planning demands, such as the EDP, the BSP, the EYDCP and the SOP into a single planning format by 2006. However, the proposal is likely to be superseded by a different approach reflecting broader trends and requiring a statutory plan for children.

Specialist schools   Secondary schools developed along the lines of the CTCs, the model originating from magnet schools in the USA being imported to England in 1987 and since 2003 established by the Specialist Schools Trust. Specialist schools are supposed to have particular strengths and have raised standards in their chosen specialism or specialisms. They operate in partnership with private sponsors and they must show continued improvement against a performance agreement. Being a specialist school brings considerable additional government funding. They are expected to share expertise with other schools and their local communities. The range of specialisms includes:

- technology
- arts
- languages
- sports
- business and enterprise
- engineering
- maths
- science

- humanities
- music
- community.

Some of the specialisms have provision for schools to select up to 10 per cent of pupils by aptitude, but fewer than 7 per cent of schools choose to take up the option. Required sponsorship (which is small by comparison with the additional government funding these schools receive) has generally been successfully secured and by 2005 is relatively easy to attract through established networks. Originally only intended to be available for a proportion of schools, they have become central to the government's five-year plan to develop a system of independent specialist schools in place of the traditional comprehensive schools.

Special measures   A category of failing performance in a school judged by Ofsted inspectors to be in need of 'special measures' of support because of low achievement, poor behaviour, less than satisfactory teaching or weak leadership and management, or a combination of these. Following the school's inspection, inspectors make frequent visits to check the progress being made to ensure that the additional resources made available to the school are being used to bring effective and rapid improvements. Other categories of under-performance are 'serious weaknesses' and 'under-achieving' but these are regarded as less serious than 'special measures' and do not trigger the provision of additional resources or follow-up visits.

Sports mark   See *Quality standards*.

Strategic Partnership   The term used to describe the relationship between different sectors, either public or private, operating jointly at the most senior level of leadership and management in operating a service or business. Such partnerships have been one option used in government intervention in LEAs.

Sure start   A government programme providing support for families with children to four years of age, in socially and economically deprived areas, to tackle issues caused by poverty and social exclusion. Parents receive a visit during the first two months of their child's life. It was established by the Department for Education and Skills and includes advice on health services, early learning facilities and advice on nutrition. There were about 400 programmes in 2004 and these are being developed alongside other education and care programmes and Children's Centres. The unit within the DfES with responsibility for Sure Start has adopted that name. Cf. *Educare*, *Extended day*, *Extended schools*, *Out-of-school activities* and *Wrap-around care*.

Teachers' unions and professional associations   Nationally organized groups of those employed in the teaching profession with the purpose of safeguarding the interests, salaries, working conditions and welfare of their members and promoting good educational practice. They promote views on educational issues and consult with national and local government and other organizations. Different bodies represent the teaching profession in England. For schools, there is the NUT, the largest union; the National Association of Schoolmasters/Union of Women Teachers (NAS/UWT); the ATL; and the Professional Association of Teachers (PAT). The NAHT represents Head teachers separately; and the SHA, the NAEIAC represent a large proportion of both private and publicly employed education professionals who have moved on from school-based responsibilities.

Teaching assistants (TA)   Adults who are employed to assist in teaching in the classroom, variously known as LSAs, classroom assistants and special needs assistants. They are often deliberately referred to as teachers' assistants in order to emphasize that it is the teacher they assist rather than replace. The Secretary of State for Education created HLTA in October 2002 and special training for them. In certain circumstances, and to reduce teachers' workload, these advanced TAs could stand in for the teacher, take lessons and mark pupils' work, which is considered by some to be an invasion on the role of fully qualified teachers. As the costs of qualified teachers in state schools are usually in excess of 80 per cent of the schools' budgets, the potential for the deployment of advanced TAs is seen as very significant in the price/profit equation for privately operated schools, many of which already employ unqualified teaching staff.

Three-tier system   Schooling provided by a series of three separate schools organized according to the age range of pupils, often called first, middle and high schools; or lower, junior high, and senior high or upper schools. Ages of transfer are usually around 8, 9 or 10 to middle or junior high school and 12, 13 or 14 to senior high or upper. The system is common in the USA and in many private school systems around the world but less common in state education in England. The decline of the three-tier system in England is due to re-organization in many LEAs from three-tier back to a two-tier system in response to the centralizing trends in education around national frameworks for curriculum, testing and teacher training. Cf. *Two-tier system.*

Tomorrow's company   See *Quality standards.*

Transfer of Undertakings Protection of Employment (TUPE)   The regulations (1981) regarding the rights of employees and the obligations of employers towards the future employment of staff when public services or private companies are taken over by other companies.

Two-tier system   Schooling provided by a primary school (or a collection of schools which constitute the primary school phase such as nursery or kinder garden, infant and junior schools) and then followed by secondary school. The age of transfer is usually at 11. It is the most common system in England around which standardized education policy and practice has been shaped. Cf. *Three-tier system.*

Value-added   The term used to describe the attempt to find a measure of a school's quality based on the actual progress pupils make during their time in a school, rather than from the overall attainment results of the pupils. It attempts to measure the aggregation of progress from when pupils enter a school to when they leave. Conventional published league tables of exam results and National Curriculum tests are unsatisfactory in that they do not give a true picture of the progress made. Tables showing value-added performance (the difference schools have made to pupils' progress in comparison with schools with a similar and different ability levels in the pupil intakes) are now published. However, there are differences of opinion about the basis of how these are calculated and how value-added should be presented. In order for such data to be useful it is necessary to establish the parameters of the extent of pupils' achievement which is to be included. Grammar schools often show well in value-added tables even though they set out with groups of pupils who are already the higher performers.

Vocational education   Education and training designed to prepare people for work and in particular for a range of occupations. Vocational or applied education is very much at the heart of the debate about the future of the curriculum for 14–19-year olds in schools and colleges. The contentious rejection by the Government to adopt proposals put forward by Mike Tomlinson in 2004 (to reshape both the curriculum and examination system for academic and vocational study) illustrates the tension that continues to exist in attitudes about the relationship of the academic and vocational curriculum between the professional and political communities. The national approach to vocational qualifications is through a system of National Vocational Qualifications (NVQs) in which the private sector is seen as having a considerable role to play. Cf. *National Curriculum.*

Voluntary-aided (VA) schools   The SSFA (1998) confirms these as state maintained schools partly funded by the church with about 85 per cent of funding from the Secretary of State for Education (these schools are aided by the LEA). Pupils' admissions and the type of RE taught is usually under the control of the governors. Parents have the right to opt for the 'locally agreed syllabus for RE' as used in other state schools to be taught to their children. Whilst the church meets capital costs the LEAs pay teachers' salaries. About half the schools in this category are Church of England, almost half Roman Catholic, and a minority are of other faiths. Since 1998 many VA schools have become foundation schools. Cf. *Church schools, Dual system, Faith schools, Foundation school* and *VC schools.*

Voluntary-controlled (VC) schools   The SSFA confirms previous legislation that these schools are controlled by the LEA and the LEA is responsible for all the expenditure and maintenance of the buildings. These schools usually maintain a historic relationship with the church. Most of these schools are linked to the Church of England. Cf. *Church schools, Dual system, Faith schools, Foundation school* and *VA schools*.

Vouchers   Schemes in which parents are given payment credits (vouchers) so that they can purchase education for their child at any school of their choice, state or private. In doing this parents would have wide choice and in theory schools would have to be more accountable and responsive to parents who would specify their educational requirements through their choice. Whilst a simple concept, such schemes are difficult in practice and would be very expensive to operate for all. Vouchers would come as a huge financial windfall to wealthier parents who already pay for private education on top of the taxes they pay that contribute to the cost of state education. There have been a number of schemes with vouchers in the USA and more limited attempts in England, the most recent in England being for places at nursery schools in the mid-1990s. Studies and trials in the USA have been small-scale and generally unconvincing, although the possibility of providing vouchers to poorer families as in some experiments in the USA has some parallels with the philosophy of building academies in England at relatively high cost in socially disadvantaged areas. Voucher schemes have lost political appeal due to their impracticalities and general resistance to their use. Cf. *Parent power* and *School admissions*.

White Paper   The name given to an official government discussion document. White Papers are often a prelude to legislation and describe the issues to be contained in the official policy legislation. Cf. *Green Paper*.

Wrap-around care   A term used to describe situations where schools undertake extra responsibility for the care and welfare of pupils beyond the normal expectations of a school day, particularly for younger pupils in primary schools. Providing breakfast and after-school childcare and good liaison with other children's service are typical examples. Cf. *Educare, Extended day, Extended schools* and *Sure start*.

Notes

2 Ancient and modern: aims, history and private and public education systems

1 For both schools and LEAs, statutory and non-statutory planning requirements are numerous and fragmented in their concept. For schools, these plans include school development plans (SDPs), school improvement plans (SIPs), strategic plans (SPs), Raising Achievement Plans (RAPs), plans for gifted and talented pupils and more. Similarly, LEAs are required to have, for example, education development plans (EDPs), behaviour support plans (BSPs), School Organization Plans (SOPs), Early Years Development and Childcare Partnerships (EYDCPs) which are drawn from overarching Local Strategic Partnerships (LSPs) and Best Value Plans (BVPs). These plans must demonstrate how government specifications and targets will be met in the local constituency of schools and LEAs. Linked to these are non-statutory public service agreements (PSAs) which set out the commitment of local authorities to achieving further key targets in education and other areas of public service. Corresponding comprehensive performance assessments (CPAs) are used to audit the proportional corporate performance and capacity of the authority against the PSAs which, if achieved, may lead to rewards and increased freedoms for the local authority. Even with rationalization to a single statutory plan for children, the bureaucratic cycle of planning implementation, evaluation, audit and inspection is costly and one that is seen as overburdensome. The view often expressed is that with the expansion of the number of independent education providers market forces would reduce this corporate planning requirement and bring associated savings to the taxpayer.

7 Parents, choice and information

1 From the mid-1990s parents' presence has, not before time, increased into many areas of schooling. Parents are usually included, with other stakeholders, on SOCs which are the bodies set up by LEAs to consider plans (set out in the SOP) for the establishment of new schools and the alteration or closure of existing maintained schools in their LEA and beyond it, and to amend and approve those plans. With the introduction of state independent schools, such as academies, the Secretary of State must consult with the LEA about proposals to establish such a school in that authority's area. Indeed for LEAs to qualify for new funding streams (e.g. within PFIs, such as BSF), they need to demonstrate that academies feature in the possible scenario of provision. New arrangements are complicated and have changed the primacy of the LEAs' role in establishing new schools, but parents usually have some representation via the SOC.

From before their children start school, parents have been encouraged by government to become increasingly involved with their children's education. They are involved in the Baseline Assessment of their children on entry to school, and schools, since 1998, have been required to publish and report to parents, the results. Schools have been required to have home–school agreements, since 1999. The provision of family literacy and numeracy schemes in many schools and parental involvement in devising and submitting Sure Start bids (an initiative to improve the health and well being of over 400,000 young children and their families in the most deprived areas of England) has been widespread. Chapter 4 describes the contribution parents are invited to make, during Ofsted school inspections. The DfES has actively promoted the idea of parents as partners in education through their websites and in a range of publications, for example, *Help your Children to Learn* (DfES 2001a), a series written for parents by a parent support group. The requirement for parents to be included as members of EYDCPs and the intention for them to be involved in Children and Young People's Plans (CYPPs) is evidence of this continuing commitment.

Government commitment has been particularly visible in its encouragement of partnership between parents, LEAs, schools and voluntary bodies in the work of identifying, assessing and arranging provision for pupils with SEN.

Bibliography

Abbott, J. (2002) 'So what's the story?', unpublished script of speech to Society of Education Officers (SEO) ConfEd summer conference, London, 12 July.

Aitkin, J. (2000) 'Where are the heroes? Educational leadership in recent times', in K. Ballard (ed.) 'Including ourselves', in J. Allan (ed.) (2003) *Inclusion, Participation and Democracy: What is the Purpose?* Dordrecht: Kluwer Academic.

Allan, J. (2003) *Inclusion, Participation and Democracy: What is the Purpose?* Dordrecht: Kluwer Academic.

Allen, L. (2003) *Schools beyond the Classroom, Managing Collaboration for Social Inclusion.* London: New Local Government Network (NLGN).

Audit Commission (1996) *Trading Places: The Supply and Allocation of School Places.* London: Audit Commission.

Audit Commission (2001) *Change Here! Managing Change to Improve Local Services.* London: Audit Commission.

Audit Commission (2002) *A Force for Change.* London: Audit Commission.

Bagley, C., Woods, P. A. and Glatter, R. (2000) *Rejecting Schools: Towards a Fuller Understanding of the Process of Parental Choice.* Robinson College, Cambridge: British Educational Management and Administration Society (BEMAS).

Bagley, C., Woods, P. A. and Woods, G. (2001) 'Implementation of school choice policy: interpretation and response by parents of students with special educational needs', *British Educational Research Journal*, 27(3): 287–307.

Baldock, S. (2003) 'St Paul's School: a personal perspective', in *The Mercers' Company Review.* London: The Mercers' Company.

Ball, S. J. (2003) *Class Strategies and the Education Market: The Middle Classes and Social Advantage.* London and New York: RoutledgeFalmer.

Ballard, K. (2003) 'Including ourselves', in J. Allan (ed.), *Inclusion, Participation and Democracy: What is the Purpose?* Dordrecht: Kluwer Academic.

Balls, E., Healy, J. and Koester, C. (2004) *Starting them Young: A Culture of Enterprise for All.* London: Academy of Enterprise and The Smith Institute.

Bangs, J. (2003) 'Firm asks sponsored school to "brand" letterheads', in *Times Educational Supplement* 17 October 2003. Available: http://www.tes.co.uk (24 October 2003).

Bannock Consulting (2003) *Evaluation of New Ways of Working in LEAs.* Available: http://www.indepen/co.uk panda/docs/DfES_Report (31 March 2004).

Barber, M. (2000) 'High expectations and standards for all no matter what: creating a world class education service in England', unpublished revision of paper presented to International Congress for School Effectiveness and Improvement (ICSEI) conference, Hong Kong, January.

Bell, D. (2004a) 'Viewpoint', in *Times Educational Supplement* 30 April 2004. Available: http://www.tes.co.uk (7 May 2004).

Bell, D. (2004b) Letter to all inspectors: 'Improving Ofsted and the Future of Inspection' (October 2004). London: Ofsted.

Bell, D. (2004c) 'Results gap is still too wide' quoted by J. Slater in *Times Educational Supplement* 8 October 2004. Available: http://www.tes.co.uk (10 December 2004).

Blair, T. (2003) 'Schools to be built in failing boroughs', in *The Independent* 14 November.

Bourdieu, P. and Boltanski, L. (2000) 'Changes in the social structure and changes in the demand for education', in S. J. Ball (ed.), *Sociology of Education: Major Themes*. Vol. 2. London: RoutledgeFalmer.

Boyd, R. (2001) *Independent Schools, Law Custom and Practice*. Bristol: Jordans.

Brighouse, T. (2004) quoted by W. Stewart in 'Tsar calls for non-selective London – wide admissions', in *Times Educational Supplement* 8 October 2004. Available: http://www.tes.co.uk (10 October 2004).

Brighouse, T. and Moon, B. (1995) *School Inspection*. London: Pitman.

Brown, G. (2004) 'Introduction', in E. Balls, J. Healy and C. Koester (eds), *Starting them Young: A Culture of Enterprise for All*. London: Academy of Enterprise and The Smith Institute.

Browne, S. (2003) 'Practice of inspection', in *Inspecting Schools. Handbook for Inspecting Secondary Schools*. London: Ofsted.

Bush, T. and West-Burnham, J. (1994) *The Principles of Educational Management*. England: Longmans.

CABE and RIBA (2004) *21st Century Schools Learning Environments of the Future*. London: Building Futures CABE/RIBA.

Carnoy, M. (2000) 'School choice? or is it privatisation?', *Educational Researcher*, 29(7): 15–20.

Carpenter, B. (2000) 'Sustaining the family: meeting the needs of families of children with disabilities', *British Journal of Special Education*, 27(3): 135–45.

Crouch, C. (2003) *Commercialization of Citizenship: Education Policy and the Future of Public Services*. London: Fabian Society.

Crowne, S. (2000) DfEE letter to C. B. Green, 13 December 2000.

Crowther, J. (1959) *Fifteen to Eighteen*. (Crowther) report of the Central Advisory Council for Education (England). London: HMSO.

Darvill, P. (2000) *Sir Alec Clegg: A Biographical Study*. Hertfordshire: UK Able Publishing.

Dehli, K. (2000) 'Traveling tales: education reform and parental choice in postmodern times', in S. J. Ball (ed.), *Sociology of Education: Major Themes*. Vol. 4. London: RoutledgeFalmer.

Department for Education and Employment (DfEE) (1996) *Self-government for Schools* (Cm 3315). London: The Stationary Office.

Department for Education and Employment (DfEE) (2000) *The Role of the Local Education Authority in School Education* (0199). Nottingham: DfEE Publications.

Department for Education and Science (DES) (1979) *Local Education Authority Arrangements for the School Curriculum Report on the Circular 14/77 Review*. London: HMSO.

Department for Education and Science (DES) (1981) *The School Curriculum*. London: HMSO.

Department for Education and Skills (DfES) (2001a) *Help your Children to Learn*. Strikers, London: Prolog.

Department for Education and Skills (DfES) (2001b) *The Special Educational Needs and Disability Act*. London: DfES.

Department for Education and Skills (DfES) (2002) Action to be taken to improve Walsall's Education Service following highly critical Ofsted re-inspection report. Press release 10 April 2002.

Department for Education and Skills (DfES) (2003a) *Classrooms of the Future: Innovative Designs for Schools*. London: DfES.

Department for Education and Skills (DfES) (2003b) *A New Specialist Schools System: Transforming Secondary Education*. London: DfES.

Department for Education and Skills (DfES) (2004a) *Five Year Strategy for Children and Learners: Putting People at the Heart of Public Services*. London: DfES.

Department for Education and Skills (DfES) (2004b) *Every Child Matters: Change for Children*. London: DfES.

Department of Transport, Local Government and the Regions (DTLR) (2001) *Strong Local Leadership-Quality Public Services*, quoted in Audit Commission (2002) *A Force for Change*. London: Audit Commission.

Drucker, P. (1992) *Managing for the Future*. Oxford: Butterworth-Heinemann.

Dunford, J. (2004) 'Heads roll at flagship academies', in *Times Educational Supplement* 30 July. Available: http://www.tes.co.uk (8 August 2004).

DuQuesnay, H. (1995) 'The LEA of the future: school accountability, inspection and support', in T. Brighouse and B. Moon (eds), *School Inspection*. London: Pitman.

Erasmus, D. (1519) 'Extract of letter to Jonas Jodocus', in *The Mercers' Company Review 2003*. London: The Mercers' Company.

Evans, G. (2004) 'Cash-back for sponsors', in *Times Educational Supplement* 13 August. Available: http://www.tes.co.uk (20 August 2004).

Farrell, M. (2003) 'Cracks in private cash deals', in *Times Educational Supplement* 26 September. Available: http://www.tes.co.uk (10 October 2003).

Ferguson, N., Earley, P., Fidler, B. and Ouston, J. (2000) *Improving Schools and Inspection: The Self Inspecting School*. London: Paul Chapman Publishing.

Fleming, D. P. (1944) *The Public Schools and the General Educational System*. Board of Education Report of the (Fleming) Committee on Public Schools. London: HMSO.

Flintham, A. (2004) *When Reservoirs Run Dry: Why Some Headteachers Leave Headship Early*. Available: http://www.ncsl.org.uk/research (30 December 2004).

Forsyth, C. (2004) 'That's it for Mick', in *Northampton Herald and Post* 2 December.

Foster, A. (2002) 'Walsall must tackle its weaknesses', press release 16 January.

Friedmann, M. (1995) 'Letter in Washington Post', in C. Woodhead (ed.) (2002: v), *Class War: The State of British Education*. London: Time Warner.

Gewirtz, S. (2002) *The Managerial School: Post-welfarism and Social Justice in Education*. London: Routledge.

Graham, J. (2004) 'Ofsted says sorry for report errors', in *Times Educational Supplement* 18 June. Available: http://www.tes.co.uk (20 June 2004).

Green, C. B. (2000a) Letter to DfEE, 13 December 2000.

Green, C. B. (2000b) Letter to headteachers of all schools in Walsall, 28 December.

Green, C. B. (2001a) 'Walsall shapes up', in Williams, J. (ed.) (2001) *Parliamentary Brief: Winning on Education*? London: The Independent Commentary on British Political Affairs.

Green, C. B. (2001b) 'Chief education officer's statement', unpublished, Walsall Education, October 2001.

The Guardian newspaper (2004) 'Second fiddle', in *The Guardian* 16 March.

Housing Today (2004) 'No stars for housing service', in *Housing Today 376*, 2 April 2004, published by The National Housing Federation and the Builder Group.

HRH The Princess Anne (1997) 'Letter of foreword', in *The Livery Companies of the City of London*. London: Pentland.

Jones, G. (2001) 'The public sector ethos under attack', in Hilary Kitchin (ed.), *A Democratic Future*. London: Local Government Information Unit.

Kay, J. and Bishop, M. R. (1988) *Does Privatisation Work? Lessons from the UK*. London: Centre for Business Strategy, London Business School.

Lauder, H., Hughes, D., Watson, S., Waslander, S., Thrupp R., Strathdee, I., Simiyu, A., Dupuis, J., McGlinn, J. and Hamlin, J. (1999) *Trading in Futures: Why Markets in Education Don't Work*. Buckingham: Open University Press.

Le Grand, J. and Bartlett W. (1993) *Quasi Markets and Social Policy*. Basingstoke: Macmillan.

Leming, E. (2002) 'Parent partnership and school improvement', in S. Wolfendale (ed.), *Partnership Services for Special Educational Needs*. London: David Fulton.

Local Government Chronicle (LGC) (2001) *Market Report: Education Partnerships*. London: LGC Public Sector Market.

McCaig, C. (2001) 'New labour and education, education, education', in S. Ludlam, and M. J. Smith (eds), *New Labour in Government*. Basingstoke: Macmillan.

Mansell, W. and Stewart, W. (2004) 'Academies going cheap?', in *Times Educational Supplement* 13 August. Available: http://www.tes.co.uk (15 August 2004).

Marsh, L. (1986) *Teaching Today for Tomorrow, The Christian Schiller Memorial Lecture, 1986*. York: Schiller Fellowship Spooner.

Matthews, P. and Sammons, P. (2004) *Improvement through Inspection: An Evaluation of Ofsted's Work*. London: Institute of Education, London University and Ofsted.

National Association of Educational Inspectors Advisers and Consultants (NAEIAC) (2004) Ofsted Inspectors' Fees, unpublished NAEIAC Survey 2004.

National College for School Leadership (NCSL) (2003) *Strategic Direction and Development of the School*. London: National Professional Qualification for Headship, NCSL.

National Union of Teachers (NUT) (2004) 'Bringing down the barriers', in *The Teacher*. Available: http://www.teachers.org.uk (3 December 2004).

Newsom, J. H. (1963) *Half our Future*. (Newsom) report of the Central Advisory Council for Education (England). Ministry of Education. London: HMSO.

Northamptonshire County Council (NCC) (1984) *The School Curriculum: A Framework of Principles*. Northampton: NCC.

Office for Standards in Education (Ofsted) (1995) *Inspection Quality 1994/95*. London: Keele University and Touche Ross with Ofsted.

Office for Standards in Education (Ofsted) (1999) *Inspection of Walsall Local Education Authority. December 1999*. London: Ofsted in conjunction with the Audit Commission.

Office for Standards in Education (Ofsted) (2001) *Specialist Schools: An Evaluation of Progress*. London: Ofsted.

Office for Standards in Education (Ofsted) (2002a) *Inspection of Walsall Local Education Authority Draft Report* (26 February), unpublished draft by Ofsted in conjunction with the Audit Commission.

Office for Standards in Education (Ofsted) (2002b) *Inspection of Walsall Local Education Authority* (April). London: Ofsted in conjunction with the Audit Commission.

Office for Standards in Education (Ofsted) (2002c) *Framework for the Inspection of Local Education Authorities* (January). London: Ofsted in conjunction with the Audit Commission.

Office for Standards in Education (Ofsted) (2002/03) *LEAs at a Glance.* London: Ofsted.

Office for Standards in Education (Ofsted) (2003a) *School Place Planning.* London: Ofsted.

Office for Standards in Education (Ofsted) (2003b) *Excellence in Cities and Education Action Zones: Management and Impact*, HMI 1399. London: Ofsted.

Office for Standards in Education (Ofsted) (2004a) *Independent Schools Council Inspections HMI 2075* (February). London: Ofsted.

Office for Standards in Education (Ofsted) (2004b) *Annual Report of HMCI of Schools.* London: Ofsted.

Office for Standards in Education (Ofsted) (2004c) *Strategic Planning in LEAs* (October). London: Ofsted.

Office for Standards in Education (Ofsted) (2004d) *A New Relationship with Schools.* London: Ofsted.

Office of Public Services Reform (2002) *Reforming our Public Services Principles into Practice.* London: Office of Public Services Reform.

Olins, W. (2001) 'Back cover', in K. Robinson (ed.), *Out of our Minds, Learning to be Creative.* Oxford: Capstone.

Open University (OU) (2000) 'Reframing educational government at local level', unpublished research outline. Milton Keynes: OU.

Pakulski, J. and Waters, M. (1996) *The Death of Class.* London: Sage.

Partnership4schools (2004) *Local Education Partnerships.* Available: http://www.info@p4s.org.uk (23 June 2004).

Pearson, S. (2004) 'The history of Goldings Middle School 1973 to 2004', unpublished report by Goldings Middle School, Northampton.

Plowden, B. (1965) *Children and their Primary Schools.* (Plowden) report of the Central Advisory Council for Education (England). DES. London: HMSO.

Posner, R. (2003) *Law, Pragmatism and Democracy.* Cambridge, MA: Harvard University Press.

PricewaterhouseCoopers (2000) 'Walsall Metropolitan Borough Council/DfEE LEA support project-final Report', unpublished report by PricewaterhouseCoopers.

Robinson, K. (2001) *Out of our Minds, Learning to be Creative.* Oxford: Capstone.

Robinson, S. L. (1996) 'Teachers' work restructuring and postfordism: constructing the new "professionalism" ', in I. Goodson and A. Hargreaves (eds), *Teachers' Professional Lives.* London: Falmer Press.

Rotherham, A. (2003) 'United by a challenge for change', in *Times Educational Supplement* 11 June. Available: http://www.tes.co.uk (17 July 2004).

SercoQAA (Undated) 'Information for Walsall stakeholders', unpublished information sheet in use 2001.

Shipman, M. (1990) *In Search of Learning.* Oxford: Blackwell.

Sinnott, S. (2004) quoted by W. Stewart in 'Tsar calls for non-selective London – wide admissions', in *Times Educational Supplement* 8 October. Available: http://www.tes.co.uk (10 October 2004).

Smith, A. (1937) *The Wealth of Nations*. New York: Random House.

Steele, J. and Corrigan, P. (2001) *What Makes a Service Public?* Public Management Foundation (May), quoted in Audit Commission (2002), *A Force for Change*. London: Audit Commission.

Stewart, W. (2004a) 'Woodhead buys his own school', in *Times Educational Supplement* 3 December. Available: http://www.tes.co.uk (10 December 2004).

Stewart, W. (2004b) 'Tsar calls for non-selective London – wide admissions', in *Times Educational Supplement* 8 October. Available: http://www.tes.co.uk (10 October 2004).

Taylor, C. and Ryan, C. (2005) *Excellence in Education: The Making of Great Schools*. London: David Fulton.

Taylor, P. (2004) 'The iniquity of Ofsted', in *Times Educational Supplement* 14 May. Available: http://www.tes.co.uk (10 July 2004).

Times (The Times newspaper) (2004) 'Hit squads to take over worst councils', 12 December 2002.

Times Educational Supplement (TES) (2003) 'National Audit Office Report' 28 November. Available: http://www.tes.co.uk (10 December 2003).

Times Educational Supplement (TES) (2004) 'Tobacco firm to help fund private schools', 20 August 2004.

Tooley, J. (1999) *The Global Education Industry*. London: Institute of Economic Affairs.

Tulloch, M. (2004) Letter, in *The Observer* 24 October 2004.

Weekly Telegraph (The) (2004) Number 672, 9 June 2004.

West-Burnham, J. (1994) 'Objections to industrial models of management in education', under 'Management in educational organizations', in T. Bush and J. West-Burnham (eds), *The Principles of Educational Management*. England: Longmans.

Whitbourn, S., Morris, R., Parker, A., McDonogh, K., Fowler, J., Mitchell, K. and Poole, K. (2004) *What is an LEA for?* 2nd edition. Berkshire: National Foundation for Educational Research (NFER).

Whitburn, R. (2004) 'Meet the real inspectors', in *Times Educational Supplement* 11 June. Available: http://www.tes.co.uk (12 June 2004).

Wilkins, R. (2004) 'Building bridges between contradictory policies: school improvement in England', unpublished paper presented at the International Congress for School Effectiveness and Improvement (ICSEI) January. Rotterdam: ICSEI.

Williams, J. (2001) 'Walsall shapes up', in *Parliamentary Brief: Winning on Education?* London: The Independent Commentary on British Political Affairs.

Williams, P. (2002) DfES letter to Walsall Education, 6 February 2002.

Wilson, D. (2001) *Communities and Government – Potential for Partnership*. Wellington, New Zealand: Ministry of Social Policy.

Wolfendale, S. (2002) *Parent Partnership Services for Special Educational Needs*. London: David Fulton.

Woodhead, C. (2002) *Class War: The State of British Education*. London: Time Warner.

Woods, G. J. and Woods, P. A. (2002) 'Creativity in education policy: sociological and spiritual perspectives', unpublished paper presented at Creativity Research Group, Open University, January 2002.

Wragg, T. (2003) 'Inspect the uninspected', in *Times Educational Supplement* 11 June. Available: http://www.tes.fefocus.co.uk (11 June 2003).

Index

Note: Page numbers in italics refers to tables.

The Privatization of State Education

Overcoming barriers to learning and raising standards of achievement are central efforts in education. In the UK, the government has made education its leading domestic priority and the centre of its drive to improve public services by using the private sector to bring about improvements and to break the status quo. Likewise, throughout the world private interests are now impinging heavily upon how state education is perceived; the 'educational apartheid' between state and private is diminishing across schools and local authorities. This book provides an incisive commentary on this rapidly changing phenomenon. It clarifies and evaluates a variety of policy initiatives and implementation issues in England and parallel developments elsewhere in the world.

The ways in which change is being forced along in a range of guises from public partnerships to private company deals are illustrated with many real and contentious examples. Partnership arrangements, sponsorships, new categories of state independent schools and private sector take-overs of schools and education authorities form the patchwork of how state education is becoming privatized. Will these changes bring more choice and improved standards? How valuable to parents is the information presented in league tables and inspection reports? How will this impact on the future of education? This provocative and critical book moves forward this highly topical debate by providing a direct, in-depth and jargon free commentary on what is happening under the banner of privatization.

In this book **Chris Green** calls upon his many years in education as a teacher, head teacher, local authority senior education inspector, Ofsted registered inspector, assistant director of education and chief education officer. His experience is drawn from English and international settings across both primary and secondary schools in private and state schools and education services. As one of the few chief education officers to have achieved successful public sector outsourcing to the private sector, he is ideally suited to write this authoritative appraisal of the privatization of education.